CHARLES PEIRCE
AND SCHOLASTIC
REALISM

A Study of Peirce's Relation
to John Duns Scotus

By

JOHN F. BOLER

University of Washington Press
Seattle

1963

This book is published with the assistance
of a Ford Foundation grant.

27042

TO MY PARENTS

Preface

IN 1903, commenting on an article he had written more than thirty years before, Charles Peirce said that he had changed his mind on many issues at least a half-dozen times but had "never been able to think differently on that question of nominalism and realism" (1.20). For anyone acquainted with Peirce's writings, this remark alone could justify a study of "that question."

The present monograph began as a doctoral dissertation. It has not substantially transcended those humble origins, and this deserves a word of comment. In the first place, the barrage of references is not meant to overwhelm the reader with "scholarship." On the contrary, I hope the references will stimulate the reader to a renewed examination of certain passages in Peirce and, more important, to a comparison of passages he may not formerly have recognized as related. In some cases, notably my discussion of Peirce's logic in Chapter III, I deliberately overreferenced simply because I found that secondary sources have sometimes neglected these areas. As a result, I hope the present book will be of service to students of Peirce who are working on problems outside the limited area of his realism.

Second, it should be obvious that I have not attempted to write anything like "an introduction to Peirce." I presume an acquaintance not only with Peirce's own writings but with some of the commentary already available in book form. More important, I have not tried to expand my earlier research into a general study of Peirce's thought. This is not because I think the various aspects of Peirce's philosophy can be treated in isolation from one another; rather, I feel that the greatest need in Peirce scholarship at present is for careful analyses of specific problems. To be sure, such an approach creates some special difficulties. But I have tried as far as possible to confine within the Introduction the unavoidable vagueness and confusion that result from dealing, in a relatively short space, with the whole of Peirce's thought while going into considerable detail about only a part of it.

My indebtedness to both faculty and fellow students at Harvard is a pleasure to acknowledge but too extensive to describe. I owe special thanks to D. C. Williams and Morton White, whose encouragement and helpful criticisms were largely responsible for the completion of the project. John E. Murdoch, now at Princeton University, read an early draft of Chapter II. Dagfinn Follesdal and Peter Fuss read the entire manuscript in draft; the latter especially has cheerfully borne the burden of listening to Peirce's realism for some time now.

Arthur Smullyan, chairman of the department of philosophy at the University of Washington, was particularly helpful in seeing the manuscript through to publication. I also wish to thank the department for providing secretarial assistance in its preparation.

The Harvard philosophy department has kindly allowed me to consult and make quotations from the Peirce manuscripts on deposit at the Harvard Library. I am similarly indebted to the Johns Hopkins University Library for allowing me to examine the special collection of Peirce's books maintained there. The efficiency and helpfulness of the staffs at both libraries are particularly appreciated. I am also grateful to the Harvard University Press, for permission to quote from the *Collected Papers of Charles Sanders Peirce*.

Finally, I wish to thank the Agnes H. Anderson Research Fund for their help in defraying publication costs.

J. F. B.

Abbreviations Used in References

CHARLES SANDERS PEIRCE

1. Wherever possible, reference to Peirce's writings is by volume and paragraph number alone of the *Collected Papers of Charles Sanders Peirce*, edited by Arthur Burks, Charles Hartshorne, and Paul Weiss (8 vols.; Cambridge: Harvard University Press, 1931–58). For example, "1.20" indicates that the passage is in paragraph 20 of Volume I of the *Collected Papers*. Unless otherwise indicated, the dating is that given by Burks; see *Collected Papers*, VIII, 325–30.

2. Reference to Peirce manuscripts in the Archives of Widener Library at Harvard University is made according to the Catalogue of C. S. Peirce Manuscripts, prepared in 1941 by Knight W. McMahon and maintained in the Archives. This system is described briefly in the bibliography prepared by Burks and appended to Volume VIII of the *Collected Papers* (cf. pp. 253–54). In keeping with Burks's usage, manuscript references are identified as, for example, "Widener I A 2," following McMahon's classification. The Peirce manuscripts have been reorganized within the past year, and a descriptive catalogue is being prepared. Since the new reference numbers are not yet available, the old ones have been used here. The new catalogue, when ready, will contain a cross-reference key.

3. Reference to entries in the bibliography itself are made according to Burks's own scheme. Thus, "CP-Bibl. G-1871-1" indicates entry 1 under "1871" in Section 1 (General) of the bibliography in the *Collected Papers* (Vol. VIII).

JOHN DUNS SCOTUS

References to the works of Scotus are from *Joannis Duns Scoti Opera Omnia* (26 vols.; Paris: Vives, 1891–95). To facilitate the location of passages, I have given the volume and page number of this edition in each reference. The following are examples of commonly used abbreviations:

1. *Oxon.*, II, d. 3, q. 1, n. 8 (XII, 54b) = *Opus Oxoniense*, Book II, distinction 3, question 1, marginal number 8; (Vives) Volume XII, page 54 (right column).

2. *Rep. Par.*, II, d. 34, q. *unica*, n. 3 (XXIII, 170 a/b) = *Reportata Parisiensia*, Book II, distinction 34, the only question, marginal number 3; (Vives) Volume XXIII, page 170 (both columns).

3. *In Metaph.*, VII, q. 18, n. 4 (VII, 454a) = *Quaestiones subtilissimae super libros Metaphysicorum Aristotelis*, Book VII, question 18, marginal number 4; (Vives) Volume VII, page 454 (left column). (My abbreviation, *In Metaph.*, should not be interpreted as indicating that this work is a commentary in the strict sense.)

Contents

	Introduction	3
I.	*The Problem of Realism*	19
II.	*The Realism of John Duns Scotus*	37
III.	*Realism and Logic*	67
IV.	*Realism and Pragmatism*	94
V.	*Realism and Idealism*	117
VI.	*Peirce and the Problem of Universals*	145
	Bibliography	167
	Index	173

Charles Peirce and Scholastic Realism

A Study of Peirce's Relation to John Duns Scotus

Introduction

THE question answered by realism as it is opposed to nominalism—
and it is the structure of that realism which I propose to examine—
is stated by Peirce as follows: "whether *laws* and general *types* are
figments of the mind or are real" (1.16).[1] If this question were as
straightforward as it might seem, we would expect that Peirce
could be equally straightforward about the answer. But while no
one has ever denied that Peirce *said* he was a realist or that he *said*
that his realism was an important aspect of his philosophy, it has been
maintained, and with some justice, that it is impossible to find a
clear statement of that realism in his writings.[2]

My own interest in the topic was whetted particularly by Peirce's
calling himself a Scotistic realist (as in 4.50). It seemed a strange label
for a man who has been generally presented as part idealist but

---

[1] Besides the normal, though extensive, use of quotations from Peirce's writings, I have been rather liberal about the number of words and phrases I put in double quotes. Some of these are my own "scare-quotes"; but most of them indicate technical, or simply odd, usage by Peirce and Scotus. Frequently, however, both Peirce's and my own arguments are *about* words and concepts. Since Peirce himself is neither constant nor consistent in the way he shows the distinction of use and mention, I have adopted single quotes for words, terms, and propositions, and italics for concepts and definienda. This is arbitrary both for what it groups together and what it distinguishes; but I am not trying to make a *philosophical* point.

When I have quoted from Peirce, I have not changed his punctuation; unless otherwise indicated, italics are in the original.

[2] Justus Buchler, *Charles Peirce's Empiricism* (New York: Harcourt, Brace and Co., 1939), p. 123.

3

mostly pragmatist. When it turned out that Peirce was compara-
tively well read in medieval logic, it occurred to me that he might
have a specific reason for selecting Duns Scotus out of all the
scholastic realists. The more I pursued this line of thought, the more
it seemed that Peirce's realism had its own peculiar structure, which
might account not only for his calling it Scotistic, but even for how he
could call himself a pragmatist and an idealist as well.

Unfortunately, to say that the structure of Peirce's realism is
"peculiar" and to imply, as I do, that his idealism and pragmatism
are also distinctive raise a problem at the outset. Partly, it is the
problem I suspect anyone encounters when he attempts a close examination of "isms": after distinguishing, analyzing, and refining, one
comes to doubt the usefulness of talking in such terms in the first
place. For my own part, I would gladly abandon the terms; but it is
Peirce himself who talks of realism, pragmatism, and idealism, and
so it is necessary not only to retain the terms but to be as clear as
possible about what Peirce means when he uses them. Manley
Thompson has suggested that any analysis of Peirce would do well to
take its "crucial points of departure from statements that Peirce
made about Peirce." [3] On the basis of my own studies, I have come to
feel that it is in Peirce's statements about his realism, pragmatism,
and idealism that we find some of the most fruitful clues to the general structure of Peirce's philosophy.

As the reader is no doubt aware, commentators have not always
agreed on the proper interpretation of Peirce's thought.[4] It is probably for his pragmatism that Peirce is generally known; but it must
be pointed out that a number of readers have been equally impressed
by his idealistic metaphysics. While the attempt to base a synthesis of
Peirce's philosophy on his idealism is undoubtedly to grab the muddy
end of the stick, one has to admit, I think, that the writers who have
taken this approach have come the closest to finding anything at all

---

[3] Manley Thompson, *The Pragmatic Philosophy of C. S. Peirce* (Chicago:
University of Chicago Press, 1953), p. xii.
[4] For a brief discussion of the controversy, see Thompson, *ibid.*, pp. xi ff.

like an integrated system in Peirce's writings.[5] To be sure, those commentators who have rallied behind the banner of an empirically oriented pragmatism have the decided advantage of a position which in itself is neater and more easily described.[6] But as more and more of Peirce's own conceptions fall before a strict pragmatic maxim, it begins to seem that cleanliness may not be an adequate criterion.[7]

T. A. Goudge has simply made a dualism of what he calls the naturalist and transcendentalist sides of Peirce, and used this as the basis of his interpretation.[8] Goudge's book is valuable for just the reason he gives: he does not have to ignore half of Peirce's writings; [9] but still one hopes there is some further resolution to such a polarity.

It is at this point, I think, that some commentators have turned their attention to the question of what Peirce might mean by his "scholastic" realism.[10] They hoped to find in Peirce's realism a position that would explain why his pragmatism seems to place a nominalistic emphasis on individual experiments and reactions, and, *at the*

[5] *Ibid.*, p. xii. The best example of this among books on Peirce is probably James K. Feibleman, *An Introduction to Peirce's Philosophy* (New York: Harper and Bros., 1946). Both C. Hartshorne and P. Weiss, the editors of the first six volumes of the *Collected Papers*, seem to have favored this line of interpretation (see the Bibliography for their articles). Such an interpretation also suggests affinities between Peirce and A. N. Whitehead (Thompson, *Pragmatic Philosophy of Peirce*, p. xii); see William Reese, "Philosophical Realism: A Study in the Modality of Being in Peirce and Whitehead," in *Studies in the Philosophy of Charles Sanders Peirce*, ed. Philip Wiener and Frederic Young (Cambridge, Mass.: Harvard University Press, 1952).

[6] A very good case for holding pragmatism as the essential theme of Peirce's philosophy is made by Thompson, p. xii. He is aware, of course, of the danger in too narrow an interpretation of the pragmatic maxim, as well as of the need for criticism of Peirce's pragmatism itself (pp. 248 *ad fin*).

[7] See E. C. Moore, Metaphysics and Pragmatism in the Philosophy of C. S. Peirce (unpublished dissertation, University of Michigan, 1950). Among those who paved the way for Moore was Arthur Burks (see articles in the bibliography). A brief statement of Burks's approach can be found in *Classic American Philosophers*, ed. Max Fisch (New York: Appleton-Century-Crofts, Inc., 1951), pp. 41–53.

[8] T. A. Goudge, *The Thought of C. S. Peirce* (Toronto: University of Toronto Press, 1950), pp. 5–7.

[9] *Ibid.*, p. 4, and note 4, where he criticizes Feibleman.

[10] As in 5.77n. See E. C. Moore, "The Scholastic Realism of C. S. Peirce," *Philosophy and Phenomenological Research*, Vol. XII, No. 3 (March 1952), pp. 406–17.

same time, why his idealism tends to give ideas and laws an independent life of their own. And it is true that scholastic manuals, especially of a more recent vintage, sometimes present their "moderate" realism as a mean between nominalism and idealism.[11]

A closer look, however, shows that moderate realism is not the sort of mean that would bring idealism and nominalism closer together, for it is hostile to both, as extremes. While the interpretation of Peirce as a moderate realist helps to explain why he should have so much to say against nominalism, it makes it even harder to understand why he had so much to say *for* idealism. Actually, Goudge had already seen that a moderate realism fits in with the naturalist side of Peirce's thought; consequently he separated Peirce's statements of a more extreme realism and placed those on the transcendental side.[12] In short, treating Peirce as a moderate realist does not really help to integrate his general system, and actually tends to create an analogous problem within his realism.

Despite the valuable information they have developed concerning Peirce's realism, previous studies seem to me to have missed, or generally obscured, two very important points. Actually, these two points are important for the general orientation of Peirce's thought as well as for the special problem of his realism.

In the first place, many of the commentators on Peirce seem to see "the scholastics" just about as they do polar bears: if you've seen one, you've seen them all.[13] Peirce's own research in the history of logic had brought him into contact with medieval thinkers (1.3), and he could appreciate the distinctiveness of their positions. When he ex-

---

[11] For example, J. Maritain, *An Introduction to Philosophy* (New York: Sheed and Ward, Inc., 1937), pp. 159–62, and esp. p. 160, n. 1. This seems to be the tack that Moore follows in his article.

[12] Goudge, *Thought of Peirce,* pp. 6, 95–103, 258.

[13] Few Peirce commentators have gone beyond a rather uncritical reading of secondary sources on Scotus; the value of Moore's otherwise excellent thesis is somewhat diminished by this (see n. 77, chap. ii, below). Feibleman seems to have some appreciation of the distinctiveness of Scotus' position (*Introduction to Peirce's Philosophy,* p. 59). The major exception is Charles K. McKeon: "Peirce's Scotistic Realism" (in Wiener and Young, *Studies in the Philosophy of Peirce,* pp. 238–50), but his presentation is, unfortunately, sketchy.

For the trouble one can get into by handling polar bears this way, see James Thurber's "Death in the Zoo."

presses a specific preference for Duns Scotus (as in 1.6), Peirce can reasonably be assumed to have adopted a position that cannot adequately be handled under the more general aspects of scholastic realism.[14] As I hope to show, when the distinctive character of Scotus' treatment of the problem of universals is taken into account, revealing connections develop between Peirce's realism and idealism.[15]

The second neglected issue bears more directly upon the orientation of Peirce's thought. In a letter to the Italian pragmatist Calderoni, Peirce explains that he has found it necessary to champion an even more extreme realism than that of Scotus (8.208).[16] Given some of Peirce's statements about the reality of laws and ideas, this is not exactly a surprise.[17] It was a surprise to me, however, when Peirce gave as a reason for his extreme realism the fact that he was a pragmatist.

If Peirce is accurately describing his own motives here, there may be good reason to reconsider the problem of finding a system in his writings. Earlier hopes for a synthesis were based on the possibility that his realism would serve to bring his pragmatic and idealistic statements together in a somewhat more moderate position. But from Peirce's own remarks it seems that pragmatism is to provide the clue to the unity of his thought *and* that it will function by making his realism more extreme.

The significance of these two neglected issues should become clearer as I go on. However, I would like to return for a moment to the problem of "ism" words in Peirce. Frankly, I do not intend to put

---

[14] In a review of William Turner's *History of Philosophy*, Peirce says that the treatment of Scotus is better than might be expected of a Thomist, but that it fails to explain the distinctive reasons that led Scotus to his position. *The Nation*, Vol. 79 (7 July 1904), pp. 15–16.

[15] That Peirce's realism and idealism are connected is hardly a new idea. See, for example, Morris Cohen's Introduction to *Chance, Love and Logic*, ed. Cohen (New York: Harcourt, Brace and Co., 1923), p. xxx.

[16] Until the publication of vol. VIII of the *Collected Papers*, the extent of Peirce's disagreement with Scotus was not really clear: see 1.6, 1.560, 5.77n1, 5.470, 6.175.

[17] For example, Peirce says that general ideas "have a power of finding and creating their vehicles and conferring upon them the ability to transform the earth" (1.217); and that they have "the unified living feeling of a person" (6.270).

much emphasis on the question of whether Peirce is *really* a realist. Rather than try to establish fixed points of reference outside Peirce's system, I want to examine as far as possible what he means by his realism.[18]

More is at stake here than simply letting Peirce define his own terms. Considering his propensity for making up new words, it is clear enough that he intended to associate himself with some tradition (or other) in keeping 'realism' and 'idealism.'[19] This fact must be accounted for as well. Indeed, it is one of my major contentions that a closer analysis of Scotus' realism will help to clarify Peirce's own position. What I want to emphasize, however, is the need to treat Peirce's realism, pragmatism, and idealism as related to one another. In the effort to examine some one aspect of Peirce's philosophy, there should be no rush to establish a clear-cut "definition"—for example, of his realism—especially if such a definition militates against other aspects of his philosophy.

It is of course possible, even on his own use of terms, that Peirce has misdescribed his own work; and it would surely be nothing new if a philosopher were mistaken about the value of his own contribution. In general, there should be no objection to a critic's selecting what is "good" in Peirce from what is "bad." Before this is done, however, one should decide what is Peirce; and it is false kindness to do that by selecting only what is "good." Since Peirce is involved in an effort to construct a complete system (1.1), the issue passes from the area of charity into that of accuracy.[20] What he is saying often enough

---

[18] 'Realism,' 'pragmatism,' and 'idealism' have already been used in too many ways to have much definite meaning of their own. One could, perhaps, shore them up with definitions; or one might attempt the odious task of classifying, for example, "all possible" realisms. Either approach would be all right for a critic imposing a form, for then the words are his. In the case at hand, the problem is precisely that the words belong to Peirce. However, I shall presently suggest a rough characterization of the three "isms" as they appear in Peirce, and I shall have some remarks to make later about the justice of Peirce's calling himself a scholastic realist.

[19] Peirce should have been clearer about it, however, since his own "first rule of good taste in writing" is: "If a reader does not know the meaning of the words, it is infinitely better that he should know that he does not know it" (2.223).

[20] Cf. Thompson, *Pragmatic Philosophy of Peirce*, pp. xii–xiii.

derives its meaning from its place within that system, and any attempt to take Peirce's words "at their face value" [21] runs the risk of quoting out of context.

It would seem that Peirce himself was aware of the problem. At one point he has a mythical "questioner" object that, among other things, Peirce's pragmatism does not make action the be-all and end-all of life, that it makes meaning to be general, and that it treats the general as of the nature of a sign. Peirce admits that this is a pretty accurate characterization, and then he adds: "But when those admissions have been unreservedly made, you find the pragmaticist still constrained most earnestly to deny the force of your objection, you ought to infer that there is some consideration that has escaped you" (5.429).

The thought that something has probably escaped him comes all too frequently to the reader of Peirce. To some extent, the trouble seems to be that Peirce was thinking in terms of a grand system but managing to get only fragments of this system on paper.[22] While I make no claim to have solved the problem of reconstructing the system behind Peirce's thought, I have made every attempt to place his realism within the general context of what I can comprehend of that system. To give the reader a glimpse of my own interpretation, I want next to consider, in a general way, some peculiarities in Peirce's attempt at a synthesis of realism, pragmatism, and idealism. For a start, I will try to delineate roughly his use of these three terms.

The relatively well-established distinction between epistemological and metaphysical realism provides a convenient place to stand.[23] Epistemological realism maintains that things are pretty much the way we know them to be. This implies, generally, that things are capable of being known—are intelligible—and that our ideas or thoughts, when true, conform to these real things as their objects. The position

[21] As in Goudge (see esp. *Thought of Peirce*, p. vii). Goudge sees well enough the risks involved in selection, but he seems to discourage the attempt to fit pieces together.

[22] This suggestion is not new either. See Arthur Burks's "Peirce's Theory of Abduction," *Philosophy of Science*, Vol. XIII, No. 4 (October 1946), p. 301.

[23] See *The Dictionary of Philosophy*, ed. Dagobert Runes (New York: Philosophical Library, 1942), p. 264. Peirce himself does not explicitly mention the distinction.

need not be anything more than a common-sense opinion which stresses, first, that we cannot think whatever we want: something forces our opinions and is, at least to that extent, independent of our minds; and second, that we can attain a tolerably accurate knowledge of that something.

Peirce does not often use 'realism' in this connection.[24] In his criticisms of Royce for failing to understand the "realist position" (as in 8.128 ff), it does seem that epistemological realism is the issue. But Peirce's more extended and more detailed treatment of that question is usually presented in terms of his "critical commonsensism," for which he tells us he is indebted to the Scottish realists (5.439). There are, however, a number of other passages in which, although realism is not mentioned, the main features of epistemological realism (at least so vaguely defined) are evident.[25]

Metaphysical realism can be given an even briefer characterization at this point, since we will be going into some detail in the following chapters. Roughly, it holds that universals or generals are more than a convenience for referring to individuals (4.1, 1.16). As Peirce says:

Anybody may happen to opine that "the" is a real English word; but that will not constitute him a realist. But if he thinks that, whether the word "hard" itself be real or not, the property, the character, the predicate, *hardness* is not invented by men, as the word is, but is really and truly in the hard things and is one in them all, as a description of habit, disposition, or behaviour, *then* he *is* a realist [1.27n1].

'Idealism' occurs perhaps less frequently among Peirce's self-characterizations but is no less essential.[26] Here, too, I should like to

---

[24] ". . . when Hamilton, with the term 'perceptual dualism' at hand, chose to call *that* 'realism,' in my opinion he filched a term he had no right to"; Widener I B 2, "Detached Ideas on Vitally Important Topics," Lecture II.

[25] "It appears that there are certain mummified pedants who have never waked to the truth that the act of knowing a real object alters it. They are curious specimens of humanity, and as I am one of them, it may be amusing to see how I think" (5.555). Peirce says on a number of occasions that we do know things themselves (e.g., 5.312, 6.95), and at least once he directly associates this with realism (8.16).

[26] "The one intelligible theory of the universe is that of objective idealism" (6.25). Peirce's remark that Royce's *World and the Individual* is "valid in the main" (5.358n) also deserves mention. In a review of that work, Pierce suggests that idealism will be the scientific metaphysics of the future (8.118).

distinguish an epistemological and metaphysical use of the term.[27] Peirce maintains, for example, that since an idea can resemble or represent only another idea, reality itself must be "thoughtlike" or of the nature of an idea (6.158, 5.310, 8.151). Epistemological idealism is not what I would call a common-sense opinion; but, at least on Peirce's description, it is only an extension of the principle that we can know things. If our knowledge of the real is accurate, it must be like the real (6.339).

It might be suggested that the object of knowledge and the real thing are not identical, so that the former could be thoughtlike while the latter need not be.[28] Peirce's objection to this is simply that it pushes the same problem back one step; in the final analysis the real itself is unknowable. Thus he says that every "unidealistic philosophy" must believe in "some absolutely inexplicable, unanalyzable ultimate" (5.265). At the same time, Peirce makes it clear that his idealism is objectively oriented: he denies quite strenuously that we can *know* only our own thoughts (5.85, 5.311, 6.95, 6.339, 7.339). Actually, his idealism seems to be based on a denial of Cartesian dualism,[29] and Peirce remarks that it might have been called "materialism" except for the stress upon peculiarly psychic activity (6.277).[30]

---

[27] The names appear in Runes, *Dictionary of Philosophy*, p. 637, but the distinguishing characters of the definitions as I am using them are derived from Peirce.

[28] It must be pointed out that Peirce's own noetic is, shall we say, somewhat subtle. The "immediate thought object" is a sign of the "dynamical [existent] object" (5.473); and it turns out that an infinite number of possible signs between these two. The rather obvious objection that we can then never attain knowledge of the existent object is one of the things, I think, which led to Peirce's preoccupation with the paradox of Achilles and the tortoise. The paradox, he says, lies in the difficulty of describing what Achilles does with consummate ease (6.178; see also 2.27, 2.666, 5.181, 5.250). If one could straighten this out, it might help us understand Peirce's theory of the community of interpretation.

'Object,' however, is a difficult word in nearly every theory of knowledge.

[29] This has been obscured, I think, by an ambiguity in the punctuation of 5.353. The passage occurs in an article entitled, "Further Consequences of Four Incapacities," which is a continuation of Peirce's criticism of the Cartesian philosophy (cf. CP-Bibl. G-1868-2). 5.353 is clearly a form of *reductio ad absurdum* in which the idealist theory is assumed false. When this supposition proves untenable, the *reductio* "affords a most important argument in favor of that theory of reality . . ." [viz., the idealistic theory]. See also 6.24 ff.

[30] "But if materialism without idealism is blind, idealism without materialism

---

This brings us to metaphysical idealism, which is most simply expressed in Peirce's avowed panpsychism (2.264). Peirce considers physical laws inadequate for explaining psychical activity,[31] whereas he thinks that physical activity can be subsumed under psychical laws (6.25). Although he sometimes speaks as if this hypothesis were justifiable solely on the basis of its simplicity (6.24), there is definitely a more positive side to it. He writes to James, for example:

[Some people] think that the proposition that truth and justice are the greatest powers in this world is metaphorical. Well I, for my part, hold it to be true. No doubt truth has to have its defenders to uphold it. But truth creates its defenders and gives them strength.[32]

This is neither an isolated statement in Peirce nor a mere aside. He says in other places that ideas are real and efficient (5.431), that they have the unity of feeling of living persons (6.270), and that they get themselves realized (1.217).

Pragmatism is not so neatly separable into two positions; at least a discussion of whether it is epistemological or metaphysical (or either) would carry us somewhat far afield. But Peirce himself makes a useful distinction between a broad or general pragmatism and a special or technical theory (5.413–14). In its general form, pragmatism would seem to be an antirationalism which insists that all conceptions must be referred to some empirical test. As such, it is reflected in ordinary experiences like squeezing fruit to see whether it is ripe or shaking presents to see if they are liquid. Thus Peirce can say of his pragmatism that it is merely the thoroughgoing application of the maxim: "By their fruits you shall know them" (5.465, 5.402n2).

In its technical form in Peirce,[33] pragmatism holds that the meaning of a statement consists in the truth of a conditional proposition

---

is void." *Values in a Universe of Chance*, ed. P. Wiener (Stanford: Stanford University Press, 1958), p. 11.

[31] For an example of Peirce's objection to the "materialistic" or "mechanistic" explanation, see 6.68 ff. and 6.274.

[32] R. B. Perry, *The Thought and Character of William James* (2 vols.; Boston: Little, Brown and Co., 1935), II, 424; see also 5.431.

[33] Although Peirce has expounded a technical form of pragmatism by which he distinguishes himself from the broader form of pragmatism that he shared with writers like James and Schiller, we should not be led to assume that these other writers did not hold to technical forms of pragmatism of their own—forms that have their own special merits.

stating what would happen as a result of certain tests. Two points are of special import here: that apparently simple conceptions like *hardness* are at bottom conditional in form (1.615); and that such conceptions relate not so much to what does happen in any one test, but to what *would* happen in response to a certain type of test (5.467).[34] As I hope to show, this special form of pragmatism has some impact on the structure of other philosophical theories that a pragmatist may hold.

With these brief characterizations behind us, we can now examine two notions that appear frequently in his writings, and which bear upon the final form realism takes for Peirce. They may also help to show why it is necessary to bring idealism and pragmatism into the picture as well.

The first of these notions, the peculiar definition of *reality*, may be viewed as growing out of the tension between epistemological realism and idealism. There is actually no contradiction between the two positions as stated, for realism stresses the objectivity of our knowledge while idealism lays emphasis on the similarity of object and mind.[35] Since each theory maintains that the real, as the object of knowledge, is intelligible, they would both be hostile to the doctrine of an unknowable thing-in-itself. On the other hand, the basic point of reference for realism is the object, so that to obtain truth the mind must conform to the object; idealism, with its point of reference as the mind, insists that if we can have knowledge, the object of that knowledge must be like the mind (6.339).

The point of particular interest in Peirce is the way pragmatism serves to prevent each position from gravitating to its extreme. In emphasizing the objectivity of knowledge, realism might tend to leave the knower too passive in the knowing process and thus slight

---

[34] Peirce's emphasis on the "would-be" is discussed in more detail in chap. iv. It is predominantly an aspect of Peirce's later writings, and seems to be one of the major reasons why he changed the name of his doctrine to 'pragmaticism' (5.414). See esp. 8.380–82.

[35] "Even the idealists, if their doctrines are rightly understood, have not usually denied the existence of real external things" (7.335). See also 7.561–64 and notes, where idealism is related to "Common Sense" and the "doctrine of immediate perception."

the contribution of the knowing mind. But pragmatism points out that the knower must ask questions of reality. Knowledge, then, will consist in answers, and therefore be dependent upon the way in which the questions are asked. Idealism, on the other hand, in laying stress upon the unity of knower and object, might tend to neglect the need for experience altogether, making the whole knowledge process a product of the activity of the knower. Here pragmatism warns that although we can dictate the questions, we cannot dictate the answers.

Yet pragmatism itself seems to need something like the principle of intelligibility, which is behind epistemological realism and idealism. There would be no sense in asking questions of the real world if it were so far away that it could neither hear our questions nor make us hear its reply.[36]

In his review of Fraser's *Works of Berkeley* [37] Peirce seems to be working at a synthesis of epistemological realism and idealism, and he tells us there that it is his conception of reality which coordinates them (8.12 ff).[38] We find, says Peirce, that our opinions are constrained; there is, therefore, something that "influences our thoughts and is not created by them": this is "the real," the thing "independent of how we think it" (8.12). But problems arise if we hold that the real is that which influences our sensations, which in turn influence our thoughts; in general, such an attitude implies that in working harder to understand the world, the mind is really only placing more impediments between the real and the idea eventually produced. Such problems disappear, according to Peirce, if reality is taken not as the

---

[36] "Experimentation is strictly appeal to Reason. Chemist sets up retort, introduces ingredients, lights fire, and awaits results. Why so confident?" (6.568) "Philosophy tries to understand. In doing so, it is committed to the assumption that things are intelligible, that the process of nature and the process of reason are one" (6.581; see esp. 5.384). See John Dewey, "The Pragmatism of Peirce," in Cohen, *Chance, Love and Logic*, p. 308.

[37] See 8.7–38, where the review is published in its entirety. The date of the review was October 1871.

[38] An editorial comment on Peirce's review appeared in *The Nation*, commending Peirce for his exposition of the scholastics. Peirce felt it necessary to point out that what this notice had apparently missed was the crucial importance of the difference in the conceptions of reality. *The Nation*, Vol. 13 (14 December 1871), p. 386. See CP-Bibl. N-1871-1.

source or stimulus of the knowledge process, but as its goal or completion (8.12).

If on the face of it Peirce's conception of reality seems a little odd, we might consider an oversimplified application in scientific inquiry. It may be, for example, that Copernicus got the idea for his hypothesis when he was looking at things from a moving platform. But the "objectivity" of his theory is not validated by tracing it to some such suggestion; it is validated by checking the results of, among other things, its predictions. In general, a scientific hypothesis is not accepted because of where it came from but because of where it leads.[39] The alert reader may sense already the suggestion of a relation to pragmatism. Peirce says:

. . . to assert that there are external things which can be known only as exerting a power on our sense is nothing different from asserting that there is a general *drift* in the history of human thought which will lead it to one general agreement, one catholic consent [8.12].

Peirce eventually comes to define *reality* as what will be thought in the ultimate opinion of the community (as in 5.311 and 5.430). We shall see more of the importance of pragmatism in this connection,[40] and also examine the reasons behind Peirce's rather remarkable (but little remarked) statement that he is indebted to Scotus for his technical use of the term 'reality' (4.28, 6.495, 8.319). For the moment, it is enough to point out that in this definition of *reality* Peirce's epistemological realism is present in the insistence that an individual's thinking must comply with something other than itself; his epistemological idealism is likewise maintained in the notion that the "other" is the ultimate *thought* of the community (7.336, 5.316, 5.408).[41]

---

[39] Of the contention that "no scientific discovery is worth confidence unless the method of finding things out is sound," Peirce says that it sounds like judging the fruit not by its taste but by the character of the tree (Widener I C 1a, b, an untitled MS beginning, "I underwent a surgical operation . . . ," pp. 2–3).

[40] Peirce calls this view of reality his "conditional idealism," and says it is a "corollary of pragmatism" (5.494).

[41] Since so much depends on it, it is rather unfortunate that Peirce is not clear about the ultimate status of the community of interpretation. Sometimes it seems that the community's thought constitutes reality, while at other times it seems

The special conception of reality is significant for Peirce's metaphysical realism simply because it allows him to maintain that a universal or general can be thoughtlike and still real. Nominalists sometimes contend that a general is just a "word," a fiction created by the mind as a convenience for talking about the world (4.1). Peirce is ready to grant that a general is of the nature of a word,[42] but he points out that on his definition of *reality* this does not in any way prevent a general from being real (1.26). As a matter of fact, he feels that the nominalist betrays a misunderstanding of the make-up of the world when he speaks of a "*mere* word" (8.191). Peirce sums up his position as follows:

The nominalists say it is a mere [word]. Strike out "mere," and this opinion is approximately true. The realists say it *is* real. Substitute for "is" *may be*, that is, *is* provided experience and reason shall, as their final upshot, uphold the truth of the particular predicate, and the natural existence of the law it expresses, and this is likewise true [3.460].[43]

Can metaphysical idealism be far away? Well,

[the great realists] showed that the general is not capable of full actualization in the world of action and reaction but is of the nature of what is thought, but that our thinking only apprehends and does not create thought, and that that thought may and does as much govern outward things as it does our thinking [1.27].

That an extreme metaphysical realism could find some common ground with objective idealism is probably not too strange. Peirce

---

that only the community can attain a true knowledge of reality. (Cf. 2.654, 5.311, 5.407, 8.26, 8.113; see also the discussion of truth: 5.375n2, 5.565 ff.) On the basis of Peirce's corrections in 5.384, we might distinguish "the real" as the true thing and "reality" as the true conception (see also 1.515). But I have been unable to juggle the other passages to fit the interpretation.

[42] "Now it is proper to say that a general principle that is operative in the real world is of the essential nature of a Representation and of a Symbol because its *modus operandi* is the same as that by which *words* produce physical effects" (5.105). When Peirce uses 'word' in this context, he is not talking about an inscription or sound; he means something closer to a "concept" or "idea." In turn, an idea is not an event in someone's mental biography; although it has its own peculiar mode of being, "it is not a lifeless thing" (3.460). See below, pp. 71–73; pp. 135 ff.

[43] Peirce sometimes speaks as if realism and nominalism were reconcilable half-truths (see 7.336–39). What it amounts to, however, is that some people who call themselves nominalists do make some true statements.

tells us that one of the pillars of his idealist cosmology, the theory he calls "synechism" (see 6.169 ff.), is closely connected with his realism:

Almost everybody will now agree that the ultimate good lies in the evolutionary process in some way. If so, it is not in individual reactions in their segregation, but in something general and continuous. Synechism is founded on the notion that the coalescence, the becoming continuous, the becoming governed by laws, the becoming instinct with general ideas, are but phases of one and the same process of the growth of reasonableness [5.4].

But we must not miss the last sentence of this same paragraph: "It is not opposed to pragmatism in the manner in which C. S. Peirce applied it, but includes that procedure as a step" (5.4).

How did pragmatism manage to get itself involved in this sort of thing? [44] The clue to that lies with Peirce's notion of the "would-be," which makes of the pragmatist a realist of an extreme sort (8.208). A character—hardness, say—does not consist in the actual responses to actual tests; as we shall see, Peirce criticizes his own early formulations of the pragmatic maxim for suggestion that it does (5.453). Hardness is something general, involving the relation of a type of test to a type of response. What is more, Peirce is not just denying that the would-be is the same as a totality of actualities; the very fact that a character is a *would*-be indicates that it has a different mode of being from that of actual events. The theory also involves the notion of really active (general) principles (5.100–1), which govern actual events and operate after the manner of a word or idea (5.105–6).

Precisely what this involves—what it means for a general to be real and "like a word," and how it "governs" events—I shall be examining in the following chapters. But I wanted to suggest here at the beginning the significance of the order I am following. For, as I hope will become clearer, it is necessary to see the impact of pragmatism on realism to understand the character of Peirce's extreme realism

[44] The reader who is scandalized that pragmatism should be mixed up with metaphysical questions might look at 5.436 and 5.453, where pragmatism is said to be "closely associated with Hegelian absolute idealism" and with scholastic realism. (It might also be noted that these two passages tend to strengthen the interpretation of pragmatism as the clue to the relation of realism and idealism in Peirce.) See also John Dewey's remarks on pragmatism and metaphysics in Peirce: Cohen, *Chance, Love and Logic*, p. 305.

and its affinities to his idealism. Perhaps even more important, I wanted to bring out into the open the idealistic elements in Peirce's thought. My special concern in this study is with Peirce's realism, but that is not an isolated topic. The definition of *reality* and the related notion of a real general as an objective thought are essential to Peirce's realism, and they land him right in the lap of idealism—or so it seems to me.[45] I am not concerned here with whether this is good or bad; it is just that before he enters into the labyrinth of Peirce's arguments (and mine), the reader should have some idea of where he is going.[46]

[45] In fact, I do not think Peirce was driven to idealism, but that it was a position he held all the time. See below, chap. vi, pp. 151–53.

[46] For the reader who hates detective stories and is already acquainted with Peircean terminology and argumentation, it may be helpful to begin with the summary presented in chap. vi. He can catch up to the rest of us easily enough, for we will be moving rather slowly.

I

The Problem of Realism

As a first step toward understanding the position that Peirce calls his realism,[1] it is necessary to be as clear as possible about the problem that gives rise to it. The very fact that Peirce calls himself a scholastic realist should suggest this. The so-called "problem of universals," although not the only one that occupied the scholastics, took on an increasing significance in the course of the controversy that raged around it. To the later scholastics the problem had become a sort of touchstone for philosophical systems; and realism, as a solution to the problem, is meant to provide a basic framework for theories about the make-up, and our knowledge, of the world.

Peirce's own statements indicate that he does consider his own realism to be an important theory about a very real issue:

In calling himself a Scotist, the writer does not mean that he is going back to the general views of 600 years back; he merely means that the point of metaphysics upon which Scotus chiefly insisted and which has passed out of mind, is a very important point, inseparably bound up with the *most* important point to be insisted upon today [4.50; see also 1.6, 4.1].

And again: "But though the question of realism and nominalism has its roots in the technicalities of logic, its branches reach about our life" (8.38).

If Peirce is going to defend realism as a necessary element in any complete philosophy, he owes some explanation of why modern

[1] From this point on, unless otherwise specified, it is always Peirce's *metaphysical* realism that is being talked about.

philosophy should have been swept by a "tidal wave of nominalism" (1.19, 2.12, 8.208). That so many philosophers whom Peirce admires for other reasons should be mistaken on this issue certainly requires a reason. The reason Peirce gives is that the significance of the problem was lost, and modern philosophy developed unaware of it while concentrating on other issues; in short, the rise of nominalism was an historical accident (2.166, 6.348). In the struggle for control of the universities, the humanists sided with the followers of Ockham in an attempt to overthrow the Dunces,[2] who were then in power. As a political favor, but with little concern for or understanding of the real issues involved, the humanists championed nominalism.[3]

But if nominalism was misbegotten, realism on its own side was badly defended. The narrow, rationalistic anti-empiricism of the Dunces made the position unpalatable to those occupied with the growth of the new sciences (6.361, 7.666). The historical accuracy of Peirce's account is not the question here. What is important is that in order to make the problem alive again, Peirce will have to correct misinterpretations of the earlier controversy and expose the phenomenon of real generality in a way significant to the modern mind.[4] It may even be necessary to restate the issues: for the question of nominalism and realism is a broad one, and ". . . it is proper to look beyond the letter [of scholastic formulations] to the spirit of it" (4.1).

The most common and striking argument that the scholastic realists advanced for their position was the necessity of justifying scientific knowledge.[5] Science, as Aristotle had said, deals with generals; and if science is true of the real world, the objects of scientific conceptions must be somehow real. In an early attempt to present his

---

[2] A Scotist was sometimes called a "Duns." See 1.17 for Peirce's account of the development of this word. See also *Charles S. Peirce's Letters to Lady Welby*, ed. Irwin C. Lieb (New Haven: Whitlock's, Inc., 1953), p. 38.

[3] Peirce takes this up in quite a few places: 1.16 ff., 2.166–68, 5.312, 6.361, 7.666. For a late and readable account, see *Letters to Lady Welby*, pp. 37–39.

[4] "The nominalistic *Weltanschauung* has become incorporated into what I will venture to call the very flesh and blood of the average modern mind" (5.61).

[5] See Scotus *In Metaph.*, VII, q. 18, n. 3 (VII, 454a). Although it would be anachronistic to identify our current notion of experimental science with the scholastic *scientia*, it would be historically naïve to deny any pertinent connection. See 6.361.

realism, Peirce took up the cudgels against nominalistic trends in both modern philosophy and modern science.[6] But after reading F. E. Abbot's *Scientific Theism*,[7] published in 1885, Peirce saw his earlier criticism of nominalism in science as superficial and of minor importance (1.20). Now he could state his position even more strongly. Science itself is realistic in outlook, and it is the philosophers who have muddied the waters (1.20, 1.6, 1.32–34, 2.166).

The Harvard Experiment

In 1903 Peirce was invited to give a series of lectures at Harvard on pragmatism.[8] These lectures, and the series of articles for the *Monist* that grew out of them,[9] show a considerable preoccupation with the problem of real generality.[10] This is not surprising, since the lectures were evidently engineered by James and Royce, and were probably attended by persons whose interest in pragmatism had been stimulated by these men.[11] Nor is it surprising that Peirce concentrated on the issues that distinguished his pragmatism from what he suspected had been taught to his audience. In fact, the lectures provide one of the simplest and most direct presentations of the reasons behind Peirce's realism.

Peirce proposes to "attack the question experimentally" (5.93). He takes a stone and holds it where there will be no obstacle between it and the floor, and then he predicts that when he releases the stone it will fall to the floor. Of course his audience knows that he can predict what will happen in this case, but he asks, *"How can I know what is going to happen?"* (5.94) [12] It is not clairvoyance, for Peirce

---

[6] This was in the review of Fraser's *Berkeley* in 1871 (8.7–38).

[7] F. E. Abbot, *Scientific Theism* (Boston: Little, Brown and Co., 1885). Peirce was interested mainly in the Introduction. See also 4.1, 4.50, 5.423.

[8] Most of this material is in the *Collected Papers*, Vol. V, Book 1. See CP-Bibl. G-1903-1, for a more detailed listing.

[9] Not all of these were published or even completed. See CP-Bibl. G-1905-1.

[10] The issue is actually a little broader. Peirce is interested in presenting his "categories," especially thirdness, which includes his realism. See below, chap. v, pp. 120–27.

[11] See Perry, *Thought and Character of James*, p. 426.

[12] "How magical it is that by examining a part of a class we can know what is true of the whole class, and by study of the past can know the future; in short, that we can know what we have not experienced!" (5.341)

has no experience of the future event. "Still," he says, "it remains true that I *do know* that the stone will drop, as a *fact*, as soon as I let go my hold. If I *truly know* anything, that which I know must be *real*" (5.94).[13]

Peirce then explains that he can make such a prediction because he knows what *kind* of thing he is dealing with:

> I know that this stone will fall if it is let go because experience has convinced me that objects of this kind always do fall; and if anyone present has any doubt on the subject, I should be happy to try the experiment, and I will bet him a hundred to one on the result [5.95].

The only "sane hypothesis" to account for such predictable uniformity is that there is some "active general principle" (5.100):

> If anybody could doubt [this hypothesis] in the case of the stone—which he can't—and I may as well drop the stone once for all—I told you so!—if anybody doubts this still, a thousand other such inductive predictions are getting verified every day, and he will have to suppose every one of them to be merely fortuitous in order reasonably to escape the conclusion that general principles are really operative in nature. That is the doctrine of scholastic realism [5.101].

By augmenting this brief presentation with selections from other places in Peirce's writings, it should be possible to get a tolerably accurate picture of the problem.

The stone that Peirce was holding was, of course, an individual stone; and the uniformity he had observed in the past involved a number of individual things. What interests him, however, is how this uniformity is different from that, say, of a run of sixes with honest dice. In the latter case we are not willing to predict that the next throw will turn up six; in the former case, however, there is a general rule to which the actions of the stone conform, and which constitutes the basis of the prediction (1.26, 2.684, 5.99, 6.99).

The Objective and the Subjective

Let us take one of Peirce's more general statements and work back. The issue between nominalism and realism, as Peirce sees it, is

---

[13] "That which any true proposition asserts is *real*, in the sense of being as it is regardless of what you or I may think about it. Let this proposition be a general conditional proposition as to the future, and it is a real general such as is calculated really to influence human conduct; and such the pragmaticist holds to be the

"whether *laws* or general *types* are figments of the mind or real."
This, he says, is a metaphysical question; but

... as a first step towards its solution, it is proper to ask whether, granting our common-sense beliefs are true, the analysis of the meaning of those beliefs shows that, according to those beliefs, laws and types are objective or subjective [1.16].

The significance of Peirce's contrast of the objective with the subjective is an important one; it comes through somewhat more clearly in the analogous discussion of real modality.[14]

Suppose, for example, that I am asked for someone's house number, which I have forgotten. I might say, "I think it's number 50, or possibly 30." I do not mean that the person has a possible house number: evidently he has some definite and actual number. The use of 'possibly,' then, is not meant to refer to an "objective possibility," for the number is not just a possible one. Indeed, if I knew the number, I would not speak of possibility at all. Here the possibility is "subjective," reflecting only the speaker's lack of knowledge. But if I were to say, "I may possibly go to the beach tomorrow," then, as Peirce has it, I would be referring to a real lack of determination, which is not just my ignorance of the future but an "objective possibility." [15]

Now we can try to formulate the problem of objective generality in the light of this distinction. The question Peirce is asking is: Are laws and general types only factors of our own modes of representing individual things, or have they some kind of objective correlate? The nominalist, says Peirce, makes generals a mere convenience whose only value is that they are compendious. The realist demurs more or less strongly (4.1).[16]

---

rational purport of every concept" (5.432; see also 5.312, 6.493). Of course, the problem still remains as to "what it is" that a proposition asserts in such cases.

[14] As we shall see later, Peirce uses the issue of "real possibility" as an essential part of his realism, and to indicate a connection between realism and pragmatism (5.453). Here I am using it only to explicate his use of 'subjective' and 'objective.' The example in the following paragraph is Peirce's (5.454–55).

[15] Peirce calls nominalistic the definition of the possible as "that which is not known in a real or assumed state of information." On the contrary, he says, such a thing is not known to be true *because* it is possible (6.367).

[16] At one point Peirce writes to James: "You can't find a place where I distinguish the objective and subjective sides of things" (8.261). But this does not prevent him from holding that reality and figment are the "heaven and hell idea in the domain of thought" (2.650; see also 5.311, 5.554). So far as his

Peirce feels that the alternative is a real one; the conceptualist attempt to hold the middle ground results, at the very best, in a "truism about thinking" (1.27). After all, one need only see that every proposition contains a predicate in order to realize that our thinking is characterized by the use of generals; but that does not yet touch the issue dividing the nominalist and realist: whether the *object* of that thinking involves real generality (1.27).[17]

The Scientific Object

We might ask here why a realist is even tempted to say that there is some "object" that is general and real. Peirce turns to science for examples. In any experiment a chemist must handle this piece of gold or that beaker of acid. But

> . . . after the experiment is made, the particular sample he operated upon could very well be thrown away, as having no further interest. For it was not the particular sample that the chemist was investigating, it was the molecular structure . . . which in all his samples has as complete an identity as it is in the nature of Molecular Structure ever to possess [4.530].[18]

It was the same with Peirce's own little experiment: any stone would do. It is the indifference of science to individual samples that the realist finds important. If the scientist throws away his sample, what was it he was looking for?

Peirce brings up the same point in a more homely example. If a cook wants to make an apple pie, she follows a collection of rules in her recipe book. "She has no particular apple pie she particularly prefers to serve; but she does intend to serve an apple pie to a particular

realism is concerned, the insistence on objective generality seems to involve mainly the notion that generality is not solely a feature of the way we represent the world. See chap. iii, pp. 71–73.

[17] Here again we are faced with the crucial use of 'object,' which I shall try to say something about in the next section. For my present purposes it might be enough to rephrase 'whether the object of that thinking etc.,' to read 'whether real generality is objective.'

[18] "When an experimentalist speaks of a *phenomenon*, such as 'Hall's phenomenon,' 'Zeeman's phenomenon,' and its modification 'Michelson's phenomenon,' or 'the chess-board phenomenon,' he does not mean any particular event that did happen to somebody in the dead past, but what *surely will* happen to everybody in the living future who shall fulfill certain conditions" (5.425). For the relation of this to pragmatism, see 5.426.

person" (1.341). It is the same with her actions in making the pie. Although the cook must handle particular apples, her indifference to individual apples indicates that what she wants is an *apple* and not a *this*. When she selects apples, ". . . what she desires is something of a given quality; what she has to take is this or that particular apple" (1.341). As Peirce says elsewhere:

> The great argument for nominalism is that there is no man unless there is some particular man. That, however, does not affect the realism of Scotus. . . . There is a real difference between man irrespective of what the other determinations may be, and man with this or that particular series of determinations . . . [5.312].[19]

The rather obvious question at this point is: What is this real difference? If there were an equally obvious answer, we might end our inquiry right here. Instead—for I hope the reader has not abandoned me at the last sentence—we must approach the answer by reformulating the question. What reasons, then, might a philosopher have for taking something general to be real? We can begin with the negative side: Peirce does not think that you can find generals in the sense that an archeologist finds vases.

As a matter of fact, Peirce feels that the realist position has been misunderstood because of a nominalistic prejudice that whatever is real must have the same mode of reality as all other real things (1.21, 2.115–16).[20] Convinced of the reality of laws and types, but considering them to be existent singulars, some philosophers have produced a "nominalistic Platonism" that has been a "stumbling block to historians of philosophy" (8.10, 5.470, 5.503). Actually, says Peirce, the real contribution of nominalism lies in its insistence that a law or gen-

---

[19] I should not want to be accused of suppressing evidence, so I shall quote the remainder of this paragraph: ". . . although undoubtedly this difference is only relative to the mind and not *in re*. Such is the position of Scotus. [Ockham's] great objection is, there can be no real distinction which is not *in re*, in the thing-in-itself; but this begs the question for it is itself based on the notion that reality is something independent of representative relation" (5.312). This is not as straightforward as it seems, as I hope will be clear by the end of chap. ii; see esp. n. 76, chap. ii, below.

[20] We shall see more of Peirce's attitude toward "modes of being" in chap. v. It must be granted Peirce, I think, that "only what is individual can be real" is not a self-evident truth on every definition of *individual*.

eral type is of the nature of thought; the unfortunate blindness of nominalism is that it concludes from this that generals cannot be real.[21]

Peirce insists that no great realist of the thirteenth or fourteenth century ever held that a general was "what we in English should call a 'thing' " (1.27n). This is why he denies that the controversy in the middle ages had "anything to do with Platonic ideas" (8.17). On the other hand, Peirce has a rebuke for the schoolmen: he feels they were so misled by "ordinary language" that they thought all predicates indicate an objective generality (6.361, 5.430). As he points out in connection with the dropping of the stone, the object of a representation is not *ipso facto* real: it is just as general a formula that all stones rise when released (5.96). That such a formula is a fiction can be determined only by trying the experiment. He continues:

On the other hand, and by the same token, the fact that I *know* that this stone will fall to the floor when I let it go . . . is proof that the formula, or uniformity, as furnishing a safe basis for prediction, is, or if you like it better, *corresponds to*, a reality [5.96].

Clearly enough, Peirce does not think that a real general is an existing thing to be found among other existing (and individual) things. The last quotation, however, introduces us to a more positive approach: Peirce finds the evidence for real generality in uniformities, and the generalizations based upon them. In the light of our earlier discussion, we should expect to find that there are objective and subjective generalizations; and the passage just quoted would suggest that only those which furnish a basis for prediction will be called objective and real.

Subjective Generalization [22]

It takes a bit of looking, but it does turn out that Peirce uses the phrase 'subjective generalization'; and the passage in which it occurs

[21] In this context Peirce says that pragmatism on its metaphysical side is an attempt to solve the problem: "In what way can a general be unaffected by any thought about it?" (5.503) The idealism involved in this is evidenced in 8.191. It should also be mentioned here that Peirce says Scotus' realism should "be adapted to modern culture, under continual wholesome reminders of nominalistic criticism" (1.6).

[22] Not to be confused with, although related to, subjective generality. See p. 72, below.

is well worth the search. Before looking at the passage, let me point out that the absence of the phrase 'objective generalization' is not a disappointment. In its place we find 'law of nature,' and Peirce tells us elsewhere that he considers this phrase a proper rendering of what in Latin is simply 'nature.' [23] The last part of the paragraph in which Peirce sets up the distinction is worth quoting at length:

> But the expression "subjective generalization" calls for an explanation. Augustus DeMorgan very simply demonstrated that, taking any selection of observations whatever, propositions without number can always be found which shall be strictly true of all those observations (and it may be added that they may be propositions not going beyond the matter of the observations), and yet no one of them likely to be true of any other observations which the same principle of selection might add to the collection. Such a generalization, a mere fabrication of ingenuity, which I term a subjective generalization, is often proposed by an amateur in science as an induction. "Bode's Law" was a subjective generalization. Let the artificers of such false inductions dare to set up predictions upon them, and the first blast of nature's verity will bring them down, houses of cards that they are.[24]

Perhaps an illustration will help tie some of these matters together. Suppose that, in addition to the accepted scientific class-names, a scientist has given a proper name to every object in his laboratory. Suppose further that he has not always used a different proper name: not only are there many things called gold, for example, but also many things called Harry. Now, what is the difference between the group of things called Harry and the group of things called gold?

First of all, consider the similarities between the proper name and the class-name. Both terms can be applied to many different things; that is, there is more than one individual thing of which it is true to say, "This is Harry" and (of the same or different things) "This is gold." Then again, both names are in some sense conventional. If our scientist discovers a new metal, he is as free to call it "thalium" as he is to call the first lump of it "Thales."

---

[23] Wiener, *Values in a Universe of Chance*, p. 292; see also 2.409n2, where Peirce equates "essence" with "law of being."

[24] The passage is not included in the *Collected Papers*. Fortunately, it appears in Wiener, pp. 290–91. Professor Wiener has also supplied a helpful explanation (p. 290, n. 17): "Bode's Law (1772) has the form $d = 4 + 3.2^n$, where d is the distance of a planet from the sun, taking the earth's distance as 10, and n as the order of the planets. The 'law' fails badly for Neptune and Pluto." See also 2.739 and, for a more complicated case, 7.468–69.

There is some objection, of course, to calling a common noun as well as a proper noun a *name*. Peirce himself feels that the former should be treated as part of the verb, and the latter as a pronoun or demonstrative (as in 2.328, 3.419). For my present purposes, I should like to play down this distinction so that I can stress a particular way in which the group of things called Harry differs from the group of things called gold. One way to express *this* difference is to say that in the case of things called gold, the same term is applied to each member of the group because of something about the group; in the other case, the very grouping itself results only from the fact that the same name was used for each thing. The problem is to put this distinction in a more practical form.

Let me point out, first of all, that it is not simply the logical or grammatical behavior of a term which grounds the distinction; that is, it is not the fact that a group bears a class-name that makes it different.[25] Establishing whether a group is of one kind or the other may require a complicated experimental inquiry; nor need there be any claim that we can achieve a definite result in every instance. I have chosen gold and "Harry" in order to draw the lines as strongly as possible.

Suppose, then, that we run a test on some of the things called gold; for example, we might look for the Prussian Blue reaction. Now we take some of the things called Harry (the cat, an old rubber stopper, and a bar of soap), and we find that they all float in water. The next thing called Harry that we select *may* float in water, but we would bet on it about as we would on a run of sixes with dice. As for the next piece of gold, that it will give the Prussian Blue reaction seems to deserve something much closer to the "one hundred to one" bet that Peirce offered his Harvard audience.

[25] Recall Peirce's criticism of the schoolmen in 6.361 (p. 26, above). He holds that all collections have some character, at least that of being selected for that collection (4.171, 4.649). But suppose even that the Harrys, in the example that follows, all give the Prussian Blue reaction. The point is, what is to prevent the next Harry from being the cat or the stopper? In short, what answer does the scientist give to the question: How do you know that x is a Harry? Because I called it so?

Nominalism

Could it not be, however, that our scientist is a very regular fellow? The question is an important one, for we will find that it reflects pretty nearly what Peirce thinks of as the nominalist position. Could it not be, then, that the group of things called Harry should give evidence of a uniformity as strong as that which we find in the group of things called gold, *and* that this uniformity results from the regularity of the naming habits of our hypothetical scientist?

If this regularity is due to the scientist's giving the same name to *similar* objects, the question at best misses the point. What Peirce finds important is precisely the original similarity.[26] An analogous situation arises in connection with the theory that common nouns resulted from the use of proper nouns to refer to more than one object. As a theory about the genesis of common nouns, it may have its points; but in its general statement, it does not as yet touch the issue between the realist and the nominalist. The problem still remains why the same term was applied to certain things.[27]

But the question may intend to suggest that the very similarity of the objects results from the regularity of the namer. All generalization, on such a view, will be "subjective generalization," and the unity of any group of objects will ultimately derive from the fact that one name had been given to all of the objects. Thus:

> . . . while from this standpoint it may be admitted to be true as a rough state-ment that one man is like another, the exact sense being that the realities external to the mind produce sensations which may be embraced under one conception, yet it can by no means be admitted that the two real men have really anything in common, for to say that they are both men is only to say that the one mental term or thought-sign "man" stands indifferently for either of the sensible objects caused by the two external realities . . . [8.12].

Later on in the same article, Peirce says of Ockham:

> He allows that things without the mind are similar, but this similarity consists merely in the fact that the mind can abstract one notion from the contemplation

[26] Peirce's attitude toward the relation of similarity is typical of realists: he considers it a problem and not a solution.

[27] It may be that in some cases we are interested specifically in the regularity of the namer. It can be important, for example, that we know what things Caesar calls Caesar's.

of them. A resemblance, therefore, consists solely in the property of the mind by which it naturally imposes one mental sign upon the resembling things [8.20].[28]

In terms of our illustration, the view that Peirce is attacking here maintains that the group of things called gold should be treated on the model of the group of things called Harry. If for that reason it is called Nominalism (that is, name-ism), no charge is being made that the theory has confused names and predicates in any simple logical or grammatical sense. The real issue is whether the similarity, regularity, or uniformity of events (or members of a group) is grounded "objectively" or "subjectively." [29] In saying that a general term is a name, the nominalist is opting for the latter.

Strictly speaking, the nominalist should hold that there is no similarity in things apart from the mind; however,

. . . [he] may admit that there is in the events themselves an agreement consisting in the uniformity with which all stones dropped from the hand fall to the ground; but if he admits that there is anything at all, except the mere fact that they happen to do so, that should in any sense *determine* the different stones to fall every time they are dropped, he ceases to be a good nominalist and becomes a mediaeval realist [6.377].

And in another place:

The man who takes the [nominalist] position ought to admit no general law as really operative. . . . He ought to abstain from all prediction, however qualified by a confession of fallibility. But that position can practically not be maintained [5.210].

Prediction

Throughout all these discussions, scientific prediction is the prominent feature. Somehow the fact of prediction requires an explanation that involves admitting to the reality of generals. Peirce says it explicitly: "My argument to show that law is reality and not figment— is in nature independently of any connivance of ours—is that predictions are verified" (8.153).[30]

[28] "Upon the nominalistic theory, there . . . are not even any real agreements or likenesses between individuals; for likeness consists merely in the calling of several individuals by one name, or (in some systems) in their exciting one idea" (6.593).

[29] "The nature of the *fundamentum universalitatis* distinguishes the mediaeval realist from the nominalist" (6.377).

[30] See also 1.26, and Wiener, *Values in a Universe of Chance*, p. 291.

Peirce was neither the first nor the last philosopher to hold that prediction has a particular significance for scientific inquiry. What I want to bring out is the special way prediction figures in Peirce's setting forth of the problem of realism. Perhaps he can best speak for himself:

If I have tried the experiment with a million stones and have found that every one of them fell when allowed to drop, it may be very natural for me to believe that almost any stone will act in the same way. But if it can be proved that there is no real connection between the behaviour of different stones, then there is nothing for it but to say that it was a chance coincidence that those million stones all behaved in the same way; for if there was any *reason* for it, and they *really* dropped, there was a *real reason*, that is, a real general. Now if it is mere chance that they all dropped, that affords no more reason for supposing that the next will drop than my throwing three double sixes successively with a pair of dice is a reason for thinking that the next throw will be double sixes [6.99].

In the light of this, Peirce's little experiment in the Harvard lectures is more than just a bit of showmanship. If he can get his audience to admit to a certitude about a prediction, then he can ask what kind of fact allows them to transcend the limits of their experience of past, actual events. In carrying out the whole investigation, Peirce feels that the burden of proof is upon the realist; nominalism is the simpler hypothesis (2.166, 4.35), and one should relinquish it only in the face of the *force majeur* of facts (4.1). But one should not hide from these facts,[31] and ". . . after physical science has discovered so many general principles in Nature, nominalism becomes a disgraceful habitude of thought" (6.175).[32]

It might be well to follow such an extreme statement with a reminder of what this chapter is about. I have been trying to indicate the problem that gives rise to Peirce's realism, and I hope to have shown

[31] "I beg you will not take offence at a truth which is just as plain to me as is the truth that children do not understand human life. To be a nominalist consists in the underdeveloped state in one's mind of the apprehension of [active law]" (5.121; see also 1.359, 5.61–64, 6.590).

[32] "So if you believe that modern science has made any general discovery at all, you believe that general so discovered to be real, and so you are a *scholastic realist* whether you are aware of it or not"; *Letters to Lady Welby*, p. 39. "The concepts of science—that is, its laws and classes—are not figments of the mind. Given sufficient investigation and these ideas are destined to force themselves upon every mind through observation. Now that constitutes them as real; for that is all that reality consists in"; Widener I C 1b, c, p. 4. On figments and the fictive, see 5.152.

that this problem centers upon the explanation of scientific prediction. The problem is not, in a trivial sense, how we talk; it is—though not in a mystical sense—a problem of how the world is. Of course, Peirce had already opted for realism before he set pen to paper to tell us what the problem was. Consequently, it has been impossible, without distorting Peirce's expression, to present the problem apart from the terms of its solution and the resultant value-connotation of 'realism' and 'nominalism.' But this is not the place to present counterarguments to Peirce's interpretation, if only because the full formulation of Peirce's realism must wait upon the development of other conceptions.[33]

Up to this point, all we have learned about Peirce's realism is that it is a position he finds it necessary to maintain in order to account for our ability to predict. He does not think that the nominalist wants to deny scientific prediction, but he objects strenuously that nominalism does not *explain* it (in 6.273, for example). How realism does "explain" it, and how this is connected with pragmatism, will be the special concern of Chapter IV.

The Unknowable Thing-in-Itself

One of Peirce's criticisms of nominalism, although somewhat strange, does reveal a basic attitude. Peirce says that the nominalist must ultimately maintain that reality is made up of unknowable things-in-themselves: "The unknowable is a nominalistic heresy" (6.492). The allusion is obviously to the difficulties involved in the Kantian notion of a *Ding an sich*. Peirce's treatment of this aspect of Kant's philosophy is hardly sympathetic, but it is not to our present purpose to discuss its adequacy.[34] Inasmuch as he uses his interpretation of Kant as a model with which to explain the nominalist-realist problem, we must take the interpretation on Peirce's own terms.

As Peirce sees it, Kant holds that our conceptions are produced by the mind in organizing the manifold of sensation. The world independent of the mind is, in that independence, unlike our mind-con-

---

[33] For example, Peirce's realism is often formulated in terms of his categories; see 5.103 ff. Cf. n. 10, above.

[34] For a more subtle account, see 5.525, 6.95; and cf. 5.452 and 6.556.

structed conceptions and essentially incognizable: it is the realm of the *Ding an sich*. This results in what might be called two worlds: one a product of the mind and intelligible, the other independent and unintelligible.

Presented this way, the doctrine of the *Ding an sich* is obviously open to the charge of being empty. To whatever extent the *Ding an sich* acquires content as, say, a cause of phenomena or a ground for objectivity (or even coherence), it becomes to that extent intelligible. If it can affect man, if it can "make a difference," then it can be known at least as that which makes such a difference.

At this point, two alternatives are open: either we can simply drop the *Ding an sich* and say that there is no reality beyond our own mental constructs, or we can insist that we do know things in themselves. In either case, of course, it will be maintained that the object of our knowledge is what is achieved by the process of mental activity; but the second alternative contends that this object consists in the real things themselves. To choose the first alternative is to run the risk of scepticism, for it amounts to saying that there is nothing real except what is dependent upon my mind. On such a view, it should not be said that a man comes to understand the real world; in effect, it is the world which comes to be the way he understands it. Peirce concludes that we must take the second alternative.[35]

Now consider the proposition 'This is sulphur,' where the individual subject-term 'this' stands for a real thing and the general predicate-term '——— is sulphur' represents a scientific conception. The nominalist, says Peirce, holds that the individual indicated by the subject-term is real; and he also admits that the predicate is general, that is, that the predicate can be true of another "this." But the nominalist wants to say that the predicate in its generality is a factor of our mental operations without any objective correlate. That is, if it is true that x

---

[35] Peirce does not set out the alternatives explicitly, but see 6.95. In his thesis, Metaphysics and Pragmatism in Peirce, Moore says (p. 71) that Peirce contradicts himself when he talks sometimes of our knowledge and sometimes of our lack of knowledge of things in themselves. I think Moore misses the import of what I have called the second alternative, whereby Peirce can say that the Kantian *Ding an sich* is unknowable (e.g., 6.108), but that things in themselves are knowable (e.g., 5.312, 6.95). See also 5.553 and 8.13.

is sulphur and that y is sulphur, on the nominalist account this can only mean that I call them both sulphur and not that there is something common to both x and y which makes them so.[36]

Such a view, according to Peirce, is quite analogous to the theory of an unknowable *Ding an sich* (5.312), for it makes all scientific predicates to be mental constructions that are essentially unlike the real world of individual things. Therefore, nominalism also results in two worlds: the world of predicates, which owe their identity and interrelation to the way the thinker applies names, and a world of individual things saddled with common predicates to which they are, in themselves, indifferent.

The nominalist cannot save himself by denying that there are real objects independent of our thoughts to which these predicates would be applicable. As in the case of the first alternative to the theory of the *Ding an sich*, this would seriously risk scepticism. Moreover, it would destroy the very nominalism it meant to save, for then only the general predicates would be real.[37]

Peirce admits that the nominalist does not set up the problem this way. While the realist bases his stand on the objective reality of our general conceptions, the nominalist bases his arguments on the independent reality of things—upon a *res extra animam* (8.17). This was understandable in the historical context; scholastic realism had degenerated to the point where "idle logical distinctions" precluded physical inquiry (6.361), and it was to be expected that philosophy would react by stressing the independence of the real world and the need for experiment.

But this channeling of interest was unfortunate. The real came to be viewed as that which is so independent from and outside our minds that it is but a stimulus to the mental process. As a result, the treatment of the *product* of our mental activity became more and more separated from that of the real as the *source* of knowledge (cf. 5.525 and 8.12 ff.). Peirce feels that the good reasons for this view are distorted by its overemphasis, but that these can be preserved if the real is taken as the normal term or goal of our mental processes: that is, if

---

[36] See pp. 29–30, above.
[37] I am extrapolating from 1.422.

we hold that our mental activity leads into the real world rather than away from it (8.15).

In 1871 Peirce said that Kant's Copernican Revolution was a step toward realism because it aimed at establishing just this sort of conception of reality (8.15). Of course, one would have to strike out the doctrine of the unknowable *Ding an sich* and make the necessary corrections for that throughout Kant's writings (5.452). F. E. Abbot, on the other hand, who is very much like Peirce in pairing science with realism and scepticism with nominalism, considers Kant the arch-nominalist.[38] He attacks the Copernican Revolution because it makes objects conform to our ideas rather than vice versa. Peirce does not mention this difference of interpretation when he praises Abbot's book, but perhaps he did not want to draw attention away from the strong case that Abbot makes for the realism of science (1.20, 4.1, 4.50, 5.423).

For our purposes, the difference should not be allowed to slip by unnoticed. We have already suggested that the meaning of *reality* has an important bearing on Peirce's realism, and that it bears traces of both pragmatism and idealism.[39] In Peirce's later writings there is no direct mention of Kant's Copernican Revolution in connection with realism.[40] He does continue to associate nominalism with the theory of an unknowable *Ding an sich*—a point in which he and Abbot are in agreement.[41] But most important, he continues to insist that the proper conception of reality is essential to the solution of the nominalist-realist controversy (5.313, 5.431). That is to say, whether he can refer the theory to Kant or not, Peirce continues to defend the idea that reality must be that which draws our opinions and not that which triggers them.[42]

Let me summarize the main points about Peirce's attitude toward realism that I have tried to bring out in this chapter.

[38] Abbot, *Scientific Theism*, Introduction, but esp. pp. 4–5.

[39] See above, pp. 13 ff.

[40] Peirce always thought that Kant's philosophy was nominalistic (1.19, 6.506), but he felt that Kant did not appreciate the import of his own doctrine. 6.95 is an interesting attempt to get Kant out of what Peirce considers to be the difficulties in his system.

[41] Abbot, *Scientific Theism*, p. 26.

[42] For a somewhat simplified résumé, see *Letters to Lady Welby*, pp. 34–39.

First: realism, an important issue for him, has both a logical and metaphysical aspect as well as ramifications in areas of vital concern. However much we may have to go into the technicalities of logic and grammar, we should not forget Peirce's insistence that the nominalist-realist controversy is a question about real things. *Second:* the problem which *gives rise* to realism is the need to account for or explain scientific knowledge, especially prediction. Peirce's realism cannot be properly understood if it is treated apart from this problem. *Third:* Peirce contends that a good deal of the controversy results from a misunderstanding, due historically to a shift in emphasis. The medieval realist was interested in an objective ground for general conceptions, while the modern nominalist wants to stress that a "thing" exists apart from the mind. *Fourth:* a realist need not hold that all conceptions involve a real (that is, objective) generality, or that any universal is a "thing." *Fifth:* nominalists are right in stressing the thought-like character of generals. *Sixth:* a proper definition of *reality* is essential to any adequate solution of the problem.

Admittedly, none of this reveals much positive information about what Peirce's realism consists in except that it is a solution to a problem. It seemed important to stress the problem, however, because the controversy is not always set out in the way Peirce has done it. There are difficulties, to be sure, in talking about a problem apart from its solution. In going on with the study of Peirce's position, I can only hope that the problem and solution will clarify one another reciprocally.

The transition to an analysis of Peirce's solution is faced with another complication. Although I am inclined to find more structure in Peirce's realism than Professor Buchler does,[43] I certainly cannot insist that it is very clearly expressed in Peirce's writings. But Peirce has at least provided a significant clue in calling himself a Scotistic realist; so this seems the proper place to "break the repose of the schoolman" (8.12). By spending some time on the analysis of Scotus' position, we can treat the historical backgrounds of Peirce's realism, and at the same time develop a model to aid in the understanding of that realism.

[43] Buchler, *Charles Peirce's Empiricism*, p. 123.

II

The Realism of John Duns Scotus

ANYONE acquainted with Peirce's philosophy could hardly expect him to choose as his patron the most naive of scholastic writers; on that account alone the Subtle Doctor,[1] as Scotus came to be called, would seem a likely candidate. It is particularly unfortunate, therefore, that there is no critical edition of the works of Scotus available. Recent scholarship has shown that significant portions of the hitherto accepted corpus are unauthentic, and the question of authenticity has only added to the controversy over the proper interpretation of Scotus' thought.[2]

Fortunately, almost all of Peirce's references are to the accepted works of Scotus.[3] Besides, many of the issues that bear on Peirce's

[1] Cf. F. Copleston, *A History of Philosophy* (5 vols.; London: Burns, Cates and Washbourne, Ltd., 1946–59), II: "Augustine to Scotus," p. 567. See Peirce's description of Scotus in 1.29, 3.404, 8.11.

[2] For a résumé of the views on authenticity of the works contained in the *Opera*, see E. Gilson, *Jean Duns Scot: introduction à ses positions fondamentales* (Paris: J. Vrin, 1952), pp. 672–75. For an example of the relation of textual criticism to interpretation in Scotus, see Copleston, pp. 478–91.

[3] Cf. C. K. McKeon, "Peirce's Scotistic Realism," in *Studies in the Philosophy of Peirce*, pp. 240–41 and notes. It is known that Peirce was acquainted with at least a considerable portion of the works of Scotus, which was included in the volumes he sold to Johns Hopkins University; the fact that the volumes are underscored and that errata were noted in the indexes suggests they were closely read by Peirce. (Cf. M. Fisch and J. Cope, "Peirce at Johns Hopkins University," *ibid.*, p. 293.) I have inspected these volumes, but unfortunately Peirce's marginal notes are scarce and uninformative. It is interesting, however, that one of the

realism are relatively well established by Scotistic commentators. But it is important to warn the reader that to find the Scotistic position developed from within, he must look beyond this study. Our concern is with the influence of Scotus on Peirce, so the problem of establishing *the* thought of Scotus can to some extent be avoided.[4]

Scholastic Realism

In its general outline, Scotus' solution to the problem of universals is properly described as a moderate realism—what is often called "scholastic" realism.[5] But it must be pointed out that, while Scotus concludes with a moderate realism substantially like that, say, of St. Thomas Aquinas, he arrives at this conclusion in a significantly different way.[6] In advocating a realism even more extreme than that of Scotus (8.208), Peirce retains only some of Scotus' ideas, and even these are transformed when they are fitted into Peirce's own solution. For this reason special attention must be paid to Scotus' particular position as distinct from the general scheme of scholastic realism. Per-

---

incunabula has the name of Peirce's father, Benjamin Peirce, written on the inside cover. This suggests that Charles may have been introduced to Scotus through his father's library.

Aside from the direct quotations and citations of the writings of Scotus by Peirce, it should be mentioned that the résumé of Scotus' position on universals, which appears in Peirce's review of Fraser's *Berkeley* (8.18), is a very brief but obvious condensation of Scotus *In Metaph.*, VII, q. 18 (Vives VII, 452b ff.).

[4] It might also be pointed out that I am not treating the whole question of Scotus' influence on Peirce. Josiah Royce, for example, has said that Peirce's theory of "interpretation" derives, to a considerable extent, from Peirce's study of scholastic logic: *The Problem of Christianity* (New York: The Macmillan Co., 1914), II, 116. There is also the interesting issue of the alleged "voluntarism" of Scotus, which might have some connection with Peirce's theory of the primacy of the "normative" sciences.

[5] Turner, whose account Peirce had commended (see n. 14, intro.), calls Scotus a moderate realist (*History of Philosophy*, p. 390). Peirce's remark that his own realism is more extreme would indicate that he, too, read Scotus as a moderate realist.

[6] See B. Landry, *La Philosophie de Duns Scot* (Paris: Librairie Felix Alcan, 1922), p. vii. While Landry argues an extreme case, it is difficult to dismiss him completely (see Copleston, *History of Philosophy*, II, 48). The opposite extreme is perhaps best represented by P. Minges: see, for example, "Der angebliche excessive realismus des Duns Skotus," *Beitraege zur Geschichte der Philosophie des Mittelalters*, VII (Münster, 1908). But even Minges admits that the *approaches* of the two philosophers are different.

haps a brief statement of the general scholastic position will help in orienting the solution that Scotus proposes.

Broadly speaking, the scholastics held that only individual *things* (what they called "supposits") exist. But these supposits have an intelligible structure (what the scholastics called a "nature"), which is not simply identical with the supposit as an individual. When a carpenter makes a bed, it is possible for him to have given the same structure to another thing. When someone looks at the bed, he sees that it could have been made with other materials—or better, he realizes that there could be other beds. It does not seem unreasonable to say, then, that it is the same structure, or nature, that is (1) in the mind of the maker, (2) in the bed, and (3) in the mind of the viewer. The scholastics, holding that the world was created by an intelligent God, viewed the intelligible structure of the world in a framework analogous to this example.[7]

Notice, however, that while any and every bed will have a certain structure, the structure is not identical with any individual bed or group of beds; the structure is a sort of plan, whereas this or that bed is an execution or instance of the plan. In the world of supposits, however, we do not find plans existing alongside the instances of those plans. Still, the mind of man can "abstract" the plan or structure and consider it "in itself"; that is, it can consider the structure or plan as it is applicable indeterminately to many individuals. In order to guarantee the truth of our conceptions, the scholastics were concerned

---

[7] Sometimes the three possibilities are called *universale ante rem, in re,* and *post rem,* respectively. While moderate realism entails a special interpretation of each of the three, some early scholastics seem to have held a theory of *"post rem"* or *"in re"* only. Consequently, Peirce makes a distinction between early and late scholasticism when he treats the problem (1.27n1). A full treatment requires an analysis of the *universale ante rem,* which involves the notion of ideas in the mind of God. For an interesting discussion of the contrast between Scotus and Aquinas on this aspect of the problem, see Gilson, *Jean Duns Scot,* pp. 279–305. I have not made much of it in my presentation of Scotus because the issue arises only obliquely in Peirce: see 5.107, 5.119, 6.502, and Wiener, *Values in a Universe of Chance,* p. 300, n. 45. (But see also my discussion on p. 130, below.)

I should make it clear that my use of the "maker" analogy does not mean that the scholastics began with such an image and then expanded it to include the problem of universals.

to show that such abstraction does not produce a mere fiction; [8] but because of the primary importance of the supposit, or existent thing, in their philosophy (at least the later) scholastics insisted that any nature must be individuated in the existent individual thing.

Although this is the briefest possible sketch of the general position, it should make clear the questions we must ask of any scholastic realist: What is the status of the nature "in itself"? What is involved in saying that the nature is "individuated" in a physical object? What is the process of "abstraction"?

On Terminology

Philosophical style in the middle ages required the citing of certain authorities and, consequently, the use of certain terminology. Uniformity of style, however, does not mean that all scholastics said the same thing. By the late thirteenth century the problem of universals had been pretty definitely cast into Aristotelian terms, and Scotus will abide by the definition of a universal as that which is in many and predicable of many (in multis et de multis).[9] But his position will not be clear until we have followed him through a lengthy analysis of what it means to say that a universal is in things.

While I am on the topic, I should mention a slight complication of usage which seems to make 'essence' or 'nature' an alternative for 'universal.' In general, when the emphasis was upon predicability, 'universal' was more often used, and the basis in the thing for that predication was also considered a type of universal (that is, in multis). Conversely, when investigation began from things, 'nature' was more likely to be used, and the concept was then treated as a type of nature (the "abstracted nature"). We shall soon have reason to make this distinction of universal and nature even more definite.

Among other terms of particular interest will be 'abstraction' and 'common nature.' These terms occur in many scholastic discussions, but they are not always used in the same way.[10] Here especially, it is

---

[8] See Peirce's defense of abstraction in 1.549n1 and 5.329; see also 5.181, 5.301.

[9] In Metaph., VII, q. 18, n.5 (VII, 455b); q. 13, n. 19 (419b–420a).

[10] This is nicely brought out by J. Owens, The Common Nature, a Study in

very easy for the common terminology of the scholastics to obscure the distinctiveness of their solutions. Bearing this in mind, we can observe Scotus as he sets forth the problem of universals.[11]

Scotus on the Problem

Scotus begins his presentation by examining two extreme positions, one holding that the universal as such is to be found in things, and the other that the universal is found only in the mind.[12] He is thinking of positions actually defended by philosophers, probably of the twelfth century and before; and if we are to understand how these positions were extremes and not simply alternatives, we must recognize the significance in Scotus' phrase, the universal *as such*. The "nominalism" involved in the second position should be clear enough for our present purposes. But notice that the peculiarity of the early realisms to which Scotus objects requires that the universal as such— one thing that is predicated of many things—be actual in many things apart from the mind. The extent of Scotus' disagreement with this early realism will, I hope, become clearer as we proceed.

Scotus marshals a set of arguments, some highly technical, for and against each position. The basic problem, however, can be brought out more strongly if we allow ourselves to be somewhat selective, and draw from arguments to be used later in the same question. Perhaps the notion of a universal as an *unum in multis et de multis* provides the most convenient framework. The first position stresses the universal as one *in* many. When we say that Socrates is a man, we mean that Socrates really has some character, attribute, quality, or whatever,

---

St. Thomas Aquinas and Duns Scotus, unpublished Licentiate dissertation, The Pontifical Institute of Medieval Studies, Toronto, 1946. A much-abbreviated version, under the title, "Common Nature: a Point of Comparison between Thomistic and Scotistic Metaphysics," appears in *Medieval Studies* (Pont. Inst. of Med. St., Toronto), Vol. XIX (1957), pp. 1–14.

[11] In general, I am following the format of *In Metaph.*, VII, q. 18 ("*Utrum universale sit aliquid in rebus?*"), although I have taken considerable liberties with the order of the question and the arguments given, in order to incorporate material from q. 13 ("*Utrum natura lapidis de se sit haec, vel per aliquid extrinsecum?*") and from *Oxon.*, II, d. 3, q. 1 ("*Utrum materialis substantia ex se, sive ex natura sua sit individua vel singularis?*").

[12] *In Metaph.*, VII, q. 18, n. 4 (VII, 454b).

which is *in* him and is the same *in* other men.[13] If the universal were only in the mind, the real world could change without affecting the truth of general predicates; [14] and conversely, it would no longer be necessary to look at the world to determine whether a particular proposition is true, for predicates would refer only to our mental operations and not to things. The early realists concluded, then, that the universal is really in things.[15]

The other extreme position stresses the predicability of the universal (*de multis*).[16] According to this approach, universality pertains to the relation of a predicate to a subject, and that relation occurs only in the mind.[17] When you see Socrates, you do not see a subject and a predicate, but the man Socrates (that is, the supposit).[18] The act of relating a subject and predicate in a judgment takes place only in the mind, thus the universal exists only in the mind and not in things (supposits) apart from the mind.

Behind all of this, of course, is a basic distinction between existence outside the mind (*esse extra anima*) and existence within the mind (*esse in anima*).[19] For Scotus, anything which exists outside the mind can also have existence in the mind simply by being known; [20] but the reverse is not true: one cannot conclude from existence within the mind to real existence apart from the mind.[21] It is in light of this that we must understand the distinction between a real being (*ens reale*)

---

[13] *Ibid.*, and cf. 1.27n1.

[14] *Ibid.*, n. 10 (459b–60a).

[15] *Ibid.*, n. 4 (454b–55a).

[16] *Ibid.*, n. 5 (455b).

[17] *Ibid.*

[18] On a somewhat similar issue of the relation of words to perceptual images, see 1.538, 2.27, 2.141, 4.332, 5.115, 6.95. See also Goudge's remark: "A perceptual proposition *symbolizes* some feature of a percept, but does not *picture* it" ("Peirce's Theory of Abstraction," *Studies in the Philosophy of Peirce*, p. 123).

[19] Cf. Gilson, *Jean Duns Scot*, pp. 106 ff. It would be dangerous to conclude from the prepositions used that this is a spatial metaphor. See Peirce on the "external" and the "mental": 6.328.

[20] *Oxon.*, I, d. 36, q. *unica*, n. 9 (X, 576b); see Gilson, pp. 105–6.

[21] *Oxon.*, Scotus, like most of the scholastics, was an epistemological realist, and held to the maxim that sensible experience was a prerequisite to knowledge. Cf. Gilson, p. 776, n. 67. In this context one might also mention P. C. Vier, *Evidence and its Function According to John Duns Scotus* (St. Bonaventure, New York: The Franciscan Institute, 1951).

and a being of reason (*ens rationis*). It is possible for a real being to "have existence in the mind," simply by being known.[22] An *ens rationis*, however, can have existence only in the mind.

For the problem of universals the major import of this distinction lies not so much with the difference between real things and thoughts about them, as with the difference between concepts that refer to real things and those that do not. It is in the latter usage that one might say that a dream is *unreal* without at all intending to deny that someone has really dreamed.[23] In fact, the reality of any concept is twofold: its reality in itself (the fact that someone has that concept), and its reference to a real thing (the fact that there is something real of which the concept is true). It is the latter sort of reality that is involved in the distinction between first and second intention. First intention is thought about the real world; second intention is thought about first intention. Notice that first and second intentional concepts are equally mental. The objects of first intentional concepts, however, are real things, while the objects of second intention are the first intentional concepts themselves. Thus although first intentional concepts are, in a sense, *entia rationis*, they have real things for their objects. Second intention can be defined, then, as having for its *objects* only *entia rationis*.[24]

If the same distinction is applied to the "sciences," then biology is a "real" science whereas grammar is not. This is no insult to the grammarian who knew all along he was not talking of plants and animals but of 'plants' and 'animals.' And, of course, *both* kinds of science use concepts: the biologist uses *plant* and *animal*, and the grammarian uses *subject* and *predicate*. But the biologist is still concerned with "real" things: things that exist independently of how we talk or think about them. What the grammarian talks *about* is precisely the way we

[22] See Peirce's remarks in 8.16.

[23] "[The medieval] realists did not fall into any confusion between the real fact of having a dream and the illusory object dreamed" (1.27).

[24] For a general discussion, see P. Coffey, *The Science of Logic* (London: Longmans, Green and Co., 1912), pp. 30–33. For a detailed study of Scotus' account, see Stephan Swiezawski, "Les intentions premières et les intentions secondes chez Jean Duns Scot," *Archives d'Histoire Doctrinale et Littéraire du Moyen Age*, IX (1934), pp. 205–60.

do talk about things. I shall return again (and again) to this special sense of 'real,' for it is quite prominent in Peirce.[25]

Now when we say, "This is a stone" and "That is a stone," although we are using subjects and predicates, we seem to be talking about real things and saying something about their real make-up. If universality is a feature only of our concepts (that is, is second intentional), does this mean that everything which exists apart from the mind is individual?

Scotus evinces the common concern of realists that such a dichotomy, unqualifiedly accepted, would undermine the applicability of our conceptions to the real world.[26]

The Two Questions of Realism

Scotus approaches the solution of this problem by distinguishing two uses of the term 'universal.'[27] In the first sense the universal is the relation of a predicate to a subject, and thus is a matter of second intention. When the logician says that 'man' is a universal, he is indicating that 'man' can be predicated of many different subjects; and it is in the relation which a term bears to many subjects that universality is to be found.[28] The scholastics held that a term may be predicated of its subject in five ways: as genus, species, accident, property, and (specific) difference.[29] These five, called the predicables, are then types of relations of predicate to subject, and strictly speaking (that is, within the first use of 'universal') they are the only universals.[30] It must be pointed out, of course, that predicates (such as

---

[25] Cf. 1.559, 3.94, 5.430, 6.328, 6.495.

[26] Compare with Peirce's discussion of nominalism and the unknowable thing-in-itself, chap. i, pp. 32–35.

[27] In Metaph., VII, q. 18, n. 6. The second sense is again divided, so that Scotus here speaks of a threefold use (tripliciter). See Swiezawski, "Les intentions premières et secondes chez Scot," and Gilson, Jean Duns Scot, p. 536.

[28] In Metaph., VII, q. 18, n. 6 (VII, 456b), Oxon., II, d. 3, q. 1, n. 7 (XII, 48b).

[29] The technical terms used for the predicables must not be confused with any other use (logical, biological, or whatever) of the same words. 'Species,' as I have used it in some examples (pp. 81–83), is a predicable and not a biologist's term. When Peirce adds a sixth predicable, law, he gives a much overworked term a new meaning; but it is parallel, in its confusion, to the other predicables.

[30] In Metaph., VII, q. 16, n. 5 (VII, 466a); Super Universalis Porphyrum,

'animal,' 'white,' 'risible,' and 'rational') are also called universals. Strictly speaking, however, such terms should be called universal (here used adjectivally) since they possess the character of universality: they are fit to be predicated of many subjects.

The universal in its first sense Scotus calls the logical universal or universal in act. It does not exist in things because its object is the relation of predicate to subject and that relation occurs only in the mind. But sometimes, Scotus says, 'universal' is also used to refer to the ground or basis for a concept like *man*—or to what Peirce calls the *fundamentum universalitatis* (6.377).[31] To keep these two uses clear, it seems advisable to have a different set of terms for each. We have been discussing the logical universal, an *unum de multis*, which concerns the *universality* of a predicate and is investigated by a *second intentional* science like logic.[32] The next moment in Scotus' position is directed at the Common Nature, an *unum in multis*, which concerns the real *commonness* of a nature and is investigated by a *first intentional* science like biology.[33] The relation of these two "universals" is to some extent like that between *ens reale* and *ens rationis;* that is, whatever is really common will be universally predicable, but one cannot legitimately infer from a universal predicate to a real commonness.[34]

Before going on to examine Scotus' theory of real commonness, the distinction between the two kinds of universals deserves special com-

---

q. 12 (I, 154a ff.); q. 34, n. 2 (384a/b); q. 36, n. 5 (420a/b). See Peirce, 2.367–68, 4.5.

[31] *In Metaph.*, VII, q. 18, n. 6 (VII, 456b).

[32] *Ibid.*, n. 7 (VII, 457a); *Oxon.*, d. 3, q. 1, n. 8 (XII, 546). Scotus himself does not use the word 'common' very much, but the distinction between the commonness of the nature and the universality of the predicate is quite important: see Owens' article, "Common Nature: a Point of Comparison," *Medieval Studies*, p. 8, n. 28; Gilson, *Jean Duns Scot*, pp. 108–10; M. Grajewski, *The Formal Distinction of Duns Scotus* (Washington, D.C.: Catholic University of America Press, 1944), pp. 141 ff.; A. B. Wolter, *The Transcendentals and their Function in the Metaphysics of Duns Scotus* (St. Bonaventure, N.Y.: The Franciscan Institute, 1946), pp. 108–9; see also nn. 33, 46, and 62.

[33] *In Metaph.*, VII, q. 18, n. 6 (VII, 456b); cf. q. 13, n. 19 (419b–20a) and *Oxon.*, II, d. 3, q. 1, n. 7 (XII, 48b).

[34] Note Peirce's remark that the "object of a representation is not *ipso facto* real" (5.96). For a discussion of the relation of logic to metaphysics in Scotus, see Gilson, pp. 105–10. Cf. *Oxon.*, II, d. 3, q. 1, nn. 8–9 (XII, 54a–55a).

ment. Peirce insists, and I think rightly so, that scholastic realism is essentially a question of real commonness.[35] This is undoubtedly related to the question of logical predicability, but it is not solved by the same sort of inquiry. It is only by distinguishing the two questions that we can appreciate the reasons Peirce has for treating realism as a solution to the problem of accounting for scientific prediction. In terms of our present analysis, Peirce is making the second question of realism the definitive one. Scotus' discussion of real commonness can be seen, I think, as analogous to that of "objective generality," which Peirce finds implied in scientific inquiry.

The Lesser Unity

To understand Scotus' position on real commonness (or the "universal" in its second sense), we must transfer our attention to the question of whether the nature of a material thing is of itself a "this" (that is, is *de se haec*).[36] Socrates, as this man, is simply different from Plato; and the parts that make up Socrates are also distinct from the parts that make up Plato. What then are we to say of Socrates' nature, which is in some sense a part of him? Must it be as distinct from Plato's nature as Socrates and Plato? Scotus contends that if this were the case, Socrates would be as different from Plato as he is from a line.[37] If we want to say that Socrates and Plato have the same nature in a sense in which Socrates and the line do not—maintaining all the while that all three are distinct things—then the nature which is "the same" in two of these things must have a peculiar unity of its own.[38]

---

[35] "The nature of the *fundamentum universalitatis* distinguishes the mediaeval realist from the nominalist" (6.377). Note also his use of "really . . . common" in 8.12.

[36] *In Metaph.*, VII, p. 13 (VII, 402b ff.); cf. also *Oxon.*, I, d. 3, q. 1 (XII, 6a ff.).

[37] *In Metaph.*, VII, q. 13, n. 1 (VII, 403a/b); q. 18, n. 1 (453a). On the latter reference, see Peirce, 8.18. See also *Oxon.*, II, d. 3, q. 1, n. 4 (XII, 9a), *Rep. Par.*, II, d. 12, q. 5, n. 13 (XXIII, 31b).

[38] Scotus proposes to prove a real "lesser unity" in "five or six ways": *Oxon.*, II, d. 3, q. 1, nn. 3–4 (XII, 8a–9b); *In Metaph.*, VII, q. 18, nn. 1–2 (VII, 452a–453b). For a discussion of the proofs, see Gilson, *Jean Duns Scotus*, pp. 106–7; J. Kraus, *Die Lehre des J. Duns Skotus von der Natura Communis* (Freiburg: Studia Friburgensia, 1927), pp. 76–93; and Minges, "Der Angebliche," pp. 54 ff. Note Peirce's remark on the unity proper to "Molecular Structure" in 4.530; see also 8.18.

The significant phrase in Scotus' original statement of the question is *de se haec* (of itself this). Scotus does hold that Socrates' nature, as *this* nature, cannot without contradiction exist in another. But the question at hand is whether the nature is a *this* of itself or made a this (that is, individuated) by something extrinsic to itself. If Socrates is a man and Plato is a man and the line is not a man, then the nature is not *de se haec* (for it is the same nature in two distinct things) and yet it is real (for Socrates and Plato really have the same nature where Socrates and the line do not).[39]

It should be clear even from the way Scotus states the problem that he does not intend to treat a nature as another "thing" (like Socrates, Plato, and the line). In order to appreciate his position, however, we will have to follow the characteristically Scotistic plan of treating the problem in terms of unity and distinction. For Scotus maintains that Socrates and Plato are "numerically distinct," and consequently if they have the same nature, that nature must have a "less than numerical unity."

Scotus is well within the Aristotelian-scholastic tradition for the primary position he assigns to the supposit. The highest form of unity, says Scotus, is exemplified in the supposit; and he calls this "numerical unity." [40] But the use of 'numerical' may not be particularly clear. Scotus does not think that supposits are numbers, nor in calling numerical unity a "perfect unity" does he mean that supposits are simple beings (having no parts).[41] There is some reference to a supposit's being countable, but this is due, I think, to the fact

---

[39] Clearly enough, Scotus does not consider similarity a sufficient answer to the problem, for it is the similarity he is trying to account for. The conflict between realist and nominalist does not really arise until the question is asked, Why do we say that A and B are similar in a way that A and C are not? If the answer is, Because of something about the things, the realist then wants to know if this "something" is the individuality of the things (which does not seem enough to distinguish any pair as opposed to another). Scotus, of course, does not wait for our answers, but goes on to discuss what this something must be, namely, the Common Nature.

[40] *Oxon.*, I, d. 23, q. *unica*, n. 2 (X, 259a); II, d. 3, q. 2, n. 4 (XII, 809b). See Peirce, 1.451, 4.159, 6.374, 6.377.

[41] It is true that Scotus, along with other scholastics, held that an individual could be designated as that which has no "subjective parts." But a discussion of this would lead us rather far afield. See Wolter, *The Transcendentals*, p. 104, n. 22.

that Aristotle's notion of first substance as the subject par excellence lies pretty close to the surface of the whole discussion.[42] In general, we must recognize that Scotus' conception of "unity" is not mathematical but metaphysical. The status of a numerical unity is a function of the status of the supposit as a being.[43]

The next question, then, is whether all difference is numerical and all unity is numerical (as a numerical one or a plurality of numerical ones).[44] But we have already seen Scotus' answer: if in any real sense Socrates and Plato have the same nature, that nature will not be numerically one. For the two men do not have the same nature in the way in which they might carry the same pail; consequently, if the nature as common is real, it must have a unity which is "less than numerical."

If it were maintained that this lesser unity is a contribution of the mind, and that the only real difference was the numerical one, it would follow that our scientific conceptions would not give us information about the real world. For the world would be composed of things numerically one, equally diverse (or equally the same), which would not in themselves have the uniformities and differences reflected in our conceptions. I think that Peirce is making the same point when he says that the nominalist makes the real to be an unknowable thing-in-itself.[45]

It is particularly important, both for Peirce and for Scotus, that the theory of the logical universal is not sufficient to solve the whole problem. Scotus says that such an attempt would turn all science into logic.[46] He seems to mean that if the commonness reflected in scientific classifications were a feature solely of the organization of our concepts apart from a real ground for this in things, the commonness

---

[42] Aristotle, *Metaphysics* (1017 [b]13); *Categories* (2 [a]11).

[43] One of the factors lurking about the whole discussion is the theory of transcendentals (being, one, good, etc.). Thus the question of the unity of a nature arises quite naturally in Fr. Wolter's study of the transcendentals.

[44] *In Metaph.*, VII, q. 13, n. 1 (VII, 403a/b); q. 18, n. 1 (453a) See Peirce, 8.18.

[45] See pp. 32 ff., above.

[46] See *Oxon.*, I, d. 3, q. 5, n. 10; *In Metaph.*, VI, q. 3, n. 15 (VIII, 346a), and Gilson, *Jean Duns Scot*, pp. 106–7, Wolter, *The Transcendentals*, p. 69. Peirce's attitude is similar: see 5.209–10.

itself would be only a matter of second intention—pertaining, then, to how we talk about things rather than to the things themselves.[47]

Any existent man or horse is, of course, an individual thing; and if all the horses in the world are destroyed, horseness does not hang around like the smile of the Cheshire cat.[48] Scotus is quite clear about this much: if Plato meant what Aristotle says he did, then Plato is wrong. For the nature cannot itself be a supposit, that is, be numerically one.[49] If the numerically one nature were separate from Dobbin, then Dobbin would not be a horse; and if the nature were in Dobbin, then he would be the one and only horse—indeed, horseness itself.

It is the unwillingness of the scholastics generally to treat a nature as a separate thing or supposit that is indicated by the term 'moderate realism.' Consequently, Scotus' remark that the nature has a real unity, and therefore a corresponding real being, had led some early critics to attack him for maintaining an extreme realism. We shall have more to say of this later, but for the present a few remarks are due about the lesser unity.

[47] Ockham, if I understand him correctly, is unhappy at the introduction of real "objects" if they are something other than Socrates, this tree, or that shoe; and if one is at all concerned about cluttering the landscape with odd entities, it is not too hard to feel a certain sympathy for his stand. When it comes to the notion of the "object" of scientific inquiry, Ockham grants that Aristotle was right to say that science was concerned with generals; it is only that these generals are not things but the "natural" signs of things which the mind has abstracted. Of course, the notion of a "natural sign" is Ockham's peculiar subtlety: is it a sign of an individual as individual (and if not, why not?) and what accounts for its "naturalness"? I must agree with Peirce that in the final analysis Ockham holds that the objects of science are terms (words, concepts, or mental signs, depending on one's definition). The account seems to satisfy many philosophers who protests that realists are being obtuse when they insist that science is therefore second intentional. While I am somewhat disturbed by the use to which Peirce and Scotus put the extramental "object" of science, I must admit to sharing the realist's belief that Ockham's answer won't quite cover the necessary ground. That science is made up of terms (or, perhaps, propositions) is reasonable enough, but that it is about terms seems odd to me. Of course, the troublesome notion of the "object" of a science is involved here; and I might be closer to Ockham in my own analysis of that. It is clear enough that Ockham wants science to be first intentional; as I see it, however, in order to carry such an analysis through he is going to have to deal with a *fundamentum* that is not a term.

[48] Scotus holds that if every individual of a species were destroyed, the nature would *ipso facto* be destroyed. *In Metaph.*, VII, q. 13, nn. 2–3 (VII, 424a/b).

[49] *Oxon.*, II, d. 3, q. 1, n. 10 (XII, 55a/b); *In Metaph.*, VII, q. 18, n. 3 (VII, 454a/b; q. 13, n. 6, 416a).

By a nature's lesser unity Scotus does not mean something having the viscosity of taffy; the nature is not spread out in a physicalistic sense. As a matter of fact, he emphasizes that the so-called common nature is real in one object and not in two.[50] The word 'common,' then, may be misleading.[51] Actually, Socrates has a Common Nature even if he is the only man existing, for he is still a man and not man-ness itself.[52] The Common Nature lacks a numerical unity precisely because it can be real without being determined to exist in any one thing. Although individuated in any existent thing—in Socrates, the nature is his in the sense of being this nature rather than that—the nature is of itself indeterminant with respect to this thing and that.[53]

Avicenna's Horse

It is evident that we must inquire further into the status of the Common Nature. But first let us ask whether such a nature is a universal. Scotus gives a negative answer, citing Avicenna's statement: "Horseness is just horseness, neither of itself one nor many, neither universal nor particular." [54] Scotus explains that this means, first of all, that a nature is not a numerical one nor a plurality of numerical ones, and this for the reasons we have been considering. Second, a nature is neither a "universal in act" (that is, as it occurs in predication) nor simply the individual in which it exists (that is, Dobbin).[55]

[50] *Oxon.*, II, d. 3, q. 6, n. 10. As Peirce puts it, true generality is distributive and not collective (5.532, 5.447n1).

[51] According to Grajewski: ". . . a certain nature which is ordinarily referred to as common or universal nature but which, in reality, is not common, nor universal, nor particular"; *The Formal Distinction of Duns Scotus*, p. 143.

[52] See Peirce, 5.103. I am capitalizing 'Common Nature' when I talk of Scotus' theory, lest the reader lose sight of the fact that many of the arguments that follow turn upon this specialized notion.

[53] It may occur to the reader that the only way to describe the Common Nature is as that funny-looking piece which solves the puzzle. He would not be too far wrong. But this should not be taken as a deprecation of Scotus' theory. It seems to me that one of the strong points of scholastic "method" is just that when they lacked ostensible "things" to account for a solution, they generally proceeded by refining the problem. The failure to grasp the significance of such an approach has led both critics (*and* defenders) to present unfortunate caricatures of medieval thought.

[54] *Oxon.*, II, d. 3, q. 1, n. 7 (XII, 48a). Notice that 'universal' is being used in the special sense described above: n. 32.

[55] *Ibid.* (48a–49a).

The second point calls for some explanation. It is the same nature that is in the individual and in the mind considering it, but Scotus maintains that in both cases something happens (*accidit*) to the nature in itself.[56] The nature of itself is not determined to any particular individual: it is not contradictory for the one nature to exist in many things. As such, however, the nature does not have the unity which allows it to be predicated as one thing of many things; that is, the nature is an *unum in multis* but not truly an *unum de multis*. The latter property it receives only in the mind.[57] We shall have more to say of this later (pp. 59–63).

In the individual, too, something must happen to the nature in itself, for in Socrates the nature becomes peculiarly his.[58] To preserve the status of the individual, Scotus holds that there must be a principle whereby the Common Nature, as well as all the other "common" attributes of a thing, becomes ultimately real in the one, unique, integral thing that is the supposit. This "principle of individuation" Scotus calls "haecceity" and its operation "contraction."[59] Precisely how it operates is not easy to describe. Scotus attempted only one metaphor and that he found inadequate.[60]

At this point, it might be helpful to pause for a moment to get our bearings. Scotus feels that his position solves the problem of universals by taking into account the true elements of the two extreme

---

[56] "*Et sicut secundum illud esse* [*in intellectu*], *non est natura de se universalis, sed quasi universalitas accidit illi naturae secundum primam rationem ejus, secundum quam objectum, ita etiam in re extra*" (*ibid.*).

[57] *Ibid.*, n. 9 (54a/b). Cf. Kraus, *Die Lehre des Skotus*, pp. 129 ff.

[58] "*Respondeo, si loquimur realiter, humanitas, quae est in Socrate, non est humanitas, quae est in Platone. . . .*" *In Metaph.*, VII, q. 13, n. 21 (VII, 421b). Peirce has simply changed the cast of characters for 2.415.

[59] There is some question as to whether Scotus himself uses the term 'haecceitas,' but the theory that bears the name is clearly his. See Kraus, *Die Lehre des Skotus*, pp. 93–100.

[60] ". . . *sicut si in manu multa corpora ponantur, et ex perfecta compressione manus fiant omnis unum corpus, nullius ratio per se perit. Sed exemplum non est in omnino simile.*" *In Metaph.*, VII, q. 2, n. 28 (VII, 175a). So far as I can tell, no commentator has done much better. Copleston suggests that the *haecceity* "seals a being as this being" (*History of Philosophy*, II, 517). My own effort is to describe "contraction" as the operation whereby haecceity makes a being real and unique. One hesitates to simplify further since, however mysterious it may be, the doctrine is central to Scotus' philosophy.

positions, described on pp. 41–42. In its strictly logical sense the universal *is* a creation of the mind and cannot exist apart from the mind. But it is not necessarily a fiction, for it can be based on a real commonness which is the nature in itself. Since the same nature is universalized in the mind and contracted in the individual, the uniqueness of individual existents is maintained without impugning the objectivity of our conception.[61] Universality is of course an element of our way of thinking, but the commonness upon which it is based is not.[62]

Once having said that the nature is the same thing undergoing two different processes, contraction in the individual and universalization in the mind, Scotus must give an account of the status of the nature in itself and of our way of coming to understand it. It is in this account that the doctrine of formalities and the theory of abstraction are set forth; and it is these doctrines which are particularly important for understanding Peirce's Scotism.[63]

Haecceity

To get a clearer idea of Scotus' answer to the second question of realism, then, we must take up in more detail the relation between Common Nature and haecceity. If Socrates is truly a man, there must be something "in" Socrates which is the basis for that assertion.[64] In addition, there must be a principle by which Socrates is the real, unique individual that he is.[65] Scotus calls the first principle the Common Nature and the second the haecceity. A Common Nature is not a class

[61] The importance to Scotus of preserving the objectivity of our conceptions is brought out by many commentators; see, for example, Copleston, *ibid.*, p. 512, and Wolter, *The Transcendentals*, chap. ii.

[62] *Oxon.*, II, d. 3, q. 1, nn. 8–9 (XII, 54a–55a). See Gilson, *Jean Duns Scot*, pp. 108–10; Kraus, *Die Lehre des Skotus*, p. 143, and n. 32, above.

[63] See 1.549n, 2.428, 8.319.

[64] It should be remembered that not all predicates imply a real commonness. I have used *man* because the scholastics considered it a specifiable natural class. See Peirce, 6.361.

[65] C. R. S. Harris points out that St. Thomas asks two questions—What makes a thing exist? What makes a thing an individual?—while Scotus tends to merge them. The issue is a large one, but Harris' remark seems to me substantially correct and brings out an important difference between the two thinkers on the strict use of the term 'individual.' *Duns Scotus* (2 vols.; Oxford: Clarendon Press, 1927), II, 15–16.

but a specific perfection.[66] And haecceity should not be understood as another form or essence; [67] it is not a nature added to other natures. The word 'haecceity' functions like 'uniqueness': to speak of the uniqueness of an object should not involve the paradox that the object is not unique for its having uniqueness in common with other things. Besides, Scotus does not think of haecceity as adding to the character of a thing, as if Socrates were a man and a philosopher and a this. The haecceity is the "ultimate actualizing entity," but actuality is not another character on the same footing with humanity, hardness, and the like.[68]

At any rate, we are now approaching the central problem of Scotus' realism. If the Common Nature is individuated in any existent thing, is there any sense in saying that the Common Nature is real? Scotus wants to protect both the primary status of the individual (as a supposit) and the real Common Nature as a ground for our conceptions. But can Socrates, for example, have at one and the same time an individuated nature and a common nature? To resolve this problem, Scotus introduces his famous "formal distinction": the Common Nature and haecceity are not two separate things in an existent individual, but they are formally distinct.[69]

The whole notion of the formal distinction is not an easy one.[70] In fact, to suggest that it is a simple idea would really be unfair to Scotus —common sense can go only so far. But since the doctrine is essential to Scotus' realism, it will be necessary to be as clear about it as possible.

We find no explicit definition of the formal distinction in Scotus' writings. However, Grajewski has managed to reconstruct a definition out of various passages in which Scotus applies the distinction. It is very nearly a composite quotation from Scotus:

[66] A comprehensional rather than extensional treatment is involved here. See Peirce's remarks in 3.43.

[67] *Oxon.*, II, d. 3, q. 6, n. 19 (XII, 147a). See Kraus, *Die Lehre des Skotus*, p. 104; cf. Peirce, 3.460, 6.318, 6.595 (last sentence).

[68] Cf. *Oxon.*, II, d. 3, q. 6, n. 15 (XII, 144a). See Grajewski, *The Formal Distinction of Duns Scotus*, pp. 151–52.

[69] See Peirce's remarks in 1.549n1.

[70] Scotus uses the distinction in many places, but I am considering it only in its application to the problem of universals. For a sensitive account of the doctrine's application to the problem, see Wolter, *The Transcendentals*, pp. 14–24.

A formal distinction is a distinction from the nature of the thing occurring between two or more really identical formalities, of which one, before the operation of the intellect, is conceivable without the others though inseparable from them even by divine power.[71]

By 'really identical' Scotus means that the Common Nature and haecceity are neither separate nor separable supposits: they are not distinct as *res et res*. But the Common Nature and haecceity are not merely logically distinct, and therefore Scotus says that they are distinct as *realitas et realitas*.[72] Consequently, the terms of a formal distinction are called equivalently realities or formalities.[73] The phrases 'from the nature of the thing' and 'before the operation of the intellect' are meant to indicate that the distinction is objective and lies primarily in the real thing. But it is also an essential part of the definition that the formalities are *conceivable* as distinct.

If we are to find out in what sense the Common Nature is real, we must determine the sense in which a formality is real; and to do that, we must determine the sense in which two formalities are distinct. Consider, as a preliminary example, Sir Walter Scott, who wrote *Ivanhoe* and *Rob Roy*. *Ivanhoe* and *Rob Roy* are two really distinct works: the world is somehow "bigger" for having these two things in it. But the man who wrote *Ivanhoe* and the man who wrote *Rob Roy* are not really distinct; the world has only the one object, Sir Walter Scott, who can be referred to in either way. In scholastic terminology, the man who wrote *Ivanhoe* is logically distinct from the man who wrote *Rob Roy*. A logical distinction, like a logical being (*ens rationis*), is one that exists only in the mind. It refers not to things in the world, but to our way of representing those things.[74]

In order to maintain his realism, Scotus must hold that the distinction of Common Nature and haecceity is more than a logical one.[75]

---

[71] Grajewski, *The Formal Distinction of Duns Scotus*, p. 93.

[72] *Oxon.*, I, d. 2, q. 7, n. 45 (VIII, 604a), *Oxon.*, II, d. 3, q. 6, n. 15 (XII, 144a/b): Grajewski, pp. 80–81.

[73] See Gilson, *Jean Duns Scot*, pp. 73 and 110; Grajewski, pp. 74 ff., 78, 80.

[74] If we were to construe 'the man who wrote, etc.' as a name, we might say that in a logical distinction only the names are distinct, whereas in a real distinction the things named are also distinct.

[75] Grajewski, pp. 65, 74. Recall our discussion of "name-ism" in the example given in chap. i (pp. 29–30). And notice Peirce's remark: "Whether or not

If the Common Nature and haecceity are distinct only in the mind, the less-than-numerical unity of the Common Nature could not be real. Consequently, although the formal distinction is not a distinction between supposits, it is also not a logical one. An *entredeux* of this sort is nothing new to the scholastic discussion of distinctions; the peculiarity of the formal distinction is that it is somehow relative to the mind, that is, the terms are *conceivable* as distinct.

A bitter controversy has raged around the formal distinction, and Scotists have apparently never been allowed the peace to come to an agreement among themselves. Thomists, among others, have consistently complained that a distinction relative to the mind is a logical one and that a real distinction is not relative to the mind.[76] As a result, they feel that the subtlety of the doctrine consists in its affirming two contradictory positions at the same time. The pressure has been strong enough to make some commentators try to bring Scotus' distinction into line with those of Aquinas; quite naturally, these commentators

---

there be in reality any definite separation between the haecceity-element and the idea-element is a question of metaphysics, not of logic" (3.462).

[76] Notice that Peirce identifies the objection as Ockham's, and says that it begs the question (5.312); see also 5.430, 6.361, 8.14. However, "relative to the mind" can mean (1) that something is dependent either upon the way we think or the way we think about it—in which case it is either mental or not real (see the analysis of these terms on pp. 82–83, below)—or (2) that it is "knowable," that is, capable of being related to a knowing mind. It is the latter sort of "relatedness" that Peirce is concerned with in 8.14; the former seems to me to be second intentional, on Peirce's account as well as Scotus'. In 5.430, Peirce speaks of what is relative to *thought* (which can have a definitely objective status for Peirce). Hence 5.312 can be treated as parallel to the other passages where Peirce criticizes the nominalist for begging the question in concluding from the fact that generals are thoughtlike to their not being objectively real (cf. 1.26, 8.144–48, 8.153).

It is on the basis of the attitude reflected in passages like these that I have formulated my interpretation of Peirce's "objective idealism" as related to the problem of realism. I might mention, however, that Peirce's reasoning on this point seems to me a good deal more subtle than the doctrine that results. If generals as thoughtlike are relative to the mind in just the way that anything known is relative to the mind, how can Peirce be so sure that the controversy has nothing to do with Platonic archetypes (8.17)? By making everything thoughtlike (in his panpsychism), Peirce has, it seems to me, changed only the terminology of the problem and not its substance. Of course, I must admit that in arriving eventually at what I find to be a doctrine not unlike the Hegelian "concrete universal," Peirce has reintroduced subtlety enough to satisfy most any reader. (See pp. 131–43 below.)

find Scotus' position on universals to be very nearly the same as that of Aquinas.[77]

The Metaphysical Mode

It would be rash to suppose that this brief study could supply a complete solution to the problem of interpreting the formal distinction. Yet it does seem that some of the difficulties in Scotus' treatment can be avoided if we treat him as approaching an "objective idealism." Most commentators on medieval philosophy are loath to characterize any scholastic as an idealist; and there are good reasons for such an attitude.[78] But there are at least some grounds for treating Scotus as approaching idealism, and good grounds for holding that Peirce read him in this way.[79]

After all, Scotus is much more interested in showing that the Common Nature is an objective reality than he is in showing it to be non-psychic or unlike an idea. As we have seen, he insists that a formality is what the mind correctly *conceives* of the real thing. Of course, Scotus does not consider a formality to be my idea or the idea of any person; his statements that it is discovered rather than made indicate that he thinks of a formality as something objective. But if a thing is intelligible, then the conceptions which a truly knowing mind would have of it deserve to be called objective. These conceptions are neither physical parts of the object nor conventional names; they are "metaphysical realities." [80]

In his very interesting study of the doctrine of the common nature in Scotus and Aquinas, Joseph Owens suggests that Thomists have been unable to find a real correlate to Scotus' formalities because there is nothing in the Thomistic framework that corresponds to one

---

[77] Notice that it affects the thesis of E. C. Moore that he has selected Minges as his guide. See Grajewski, *The Formal Distinction of Duns Scotus*, p. 1, n. 1, and Kraus, *Die Lehre des Skotus*, p. 138.

[78] See, for example, Gilson, *The Spirit of Mediaeval Philosophy* (New York: Charles Scribners' Sons, 1936), pp. 239 ff.

[79] See n. 76, above. I hope to show that Peirce's definition of "reality" is very nearly a pragmatic reformulation of Scotus' "formality": see p. 128 and n. 44.

[80] The exact phrase is mine, but see Gilson, *Jean Duns Scot*, p. 86; Grajewski, *The Formal Distinction of Duns Scotus*, p. 76; and Wolter, *The Transcendentals*, p. 100.

entire mode of being which Scotus calls the "metaphysical." [81] The Thomist recognizes only two modes of being, the real and the logical. Scotus recognizes, in addition to the logical mode, two modes of the real: the physical and the metaphysical. The physical mode is that made up of real individuals (supposits); the objects of the logical mode are the ways the mind uses to refer to the real world. The objects of the former are real and independent of the mind, while the objects of the latter are found only in the mind. The objects of the metaphysical mode are like those of logic, for they are not supposits; but they are also like those of the physical mode, for they are real. The metaphysical mode consists, to use a barbarism, in the intelligibilities of real objects, which are objective, in the sense of being discovered rather than made.

The importance as well as the subtlety of the status of formalities can be seen in the controversy among expositers of Scotus. Minges, in his monograph on the alleged excessive realism of Scotus, has stressed the fact that Scotus did not hold that universals are real substances. [82] Kraus, while agreeing with this, criticizes Minges for failing to recognize that Scotus differed from Aquinas in insisting upon the real commonness of the nature (as a reality). [83] Owens then takes Kraus to task for putting the Common Nature in the physical mode in order to make it real. [84]

The Importance of the Individual

Owens is right, I think, in insisting that the proper understanding of Scotus depends upon our taking the metaphysical mode as real. Only in this way can we account for Scotus' statement that the Common Nature has a real existence apart from the mind. [85] On the other

---

[81] Owens' thesis, The Common Nature, pp. 30 ff.

[82] Minges, "Der Angebliche," pp. 103 ad fin.

[83] Kraus, Die Lehre des Skotus, pp. 70–72, 137 ff.

[84] Owens' thesis, The Common Nature, p. 54; Wolter, The Transcendentals, p. 110, n. 40. Kraus does not put much faith in what he calls the "abstract metaphysical order" (Die Lehre des Skotus, p. 134).

[85] Of the Common Nature, Scotus says: "Et sicut objectum in intellectu secundum illam entitatem ejus et universalitatem habet vere esse intelligibile, ita etiam in rerum natura secundum illam entitatem habet verum esse extra animam reale"; Oxon., II, d. 3, q. 1, n. 7 (XII, 49a).

hand, the independent reality of the Common Nature in the metaphysical mode must not overshadow Scotus' contention that the haecceity in a real existent thing contracts all other formalities. It is on the
latter point that Minges quite rightly bases his presentation of Scotus
as a moderate realist. The existent object is not a mosaic of common
attributes held together, as it were, by the "cement" of haecceity.[86]
The existent supposit is one, integral individual, and Scotus says that
the nature in the supposit is more individual than universal.[87]

Perhaps I can bring out in a different way the difficulty of interpreting the metaphysical mode. Suppose we grant Scotus that an individual is an integral, unique thing that can be known through a
variety of well-founded conceptions. And we might go even further,
granting that all the characters of an individual, though they do not
require a separate, thing-like status (which would make of the individual a plurality rather than a unique unity), are yet distinct
enough to be called realities. I am not sure how many philosophers
would want to hold this position, but I think that most of them could
understand it, especially if these dangerous entities are confined to a
special "mode." [88]

A certain confusion arises, however, if we let haecceity run with the
common herd of formalities. For where the other formalities are
"common," haecceity is not. In fact, haecceity is precisely what accounts for a nature's not being common in its mode of existence in the
individual thing. If the Common Nature has a real status apart from
the mind (even granting that it is not a *res*, and that it has only a
lesser unity), there is going to be some difficulty in finding a place for
it. Scotus himself makes it clear that there is no room in the world of
supposits, for here haecceity rules; that is, in the world of supposits,
natures are without exception contracted or individuated.

---

[86] See Gilson's defense of Scotus against the charge that he makes of the existent
thing a mosaic of entities: *Jean Duns Scot*, pp. 471 ff., 476, n. 1.

[87] *In Metaph.*, VII, q. 13, n. 23 (VII, 424a).

[88] The temptation to speak of idealism (something akin to the metaphysical
idealism I discussed in the Introduction) is particularly strong here, because the
formalities seem to be (1) by definition, something conceivable, (2) real before
the operation of the intellect, and (3) somehow independent of the individual
(contracted) thing. That is, while "less" than real things (as *realitas* versus *res*),
formalities are more than conceptions of things.

At this point, the defense of Scotus rests pretty squarely on the notion of a formal distinction. For in one sense, a formality is relative to the mind—that is, something which can be *conceived* of as distinct from another formality—while in another sense, the distinction is grounded *a parte rei*, before any act of intellection. Unquestionably, this is a subtle doctrine. But as Minges aptly points out, one should expect nothing less as the solution to a subtle problem.[89] If for the present I abandon the effort to inquire further into the nature of the formal distinction, it is only because I want to stress the problem.[90]

Let me put this in another way. It is evidently difficult for the expositor of Scotus to bring the notion of a Common Nature as a reality into line with the position of importance that Scotus assigns the individual. But that difficulty should not be allowed to cause trouble (retroactively, so to speak) with some important things about which Scotus is clear. First of all, Scotus nowhere treats a nature, common or contracted, as a universal in the strict sense. Second, he never claims, and even explicitly rejects the idea, that a Common Nature is a supposit. And third, Scotus insists that any nature must be contracted or individuated in the existent individual thing; to say anything else would be to miss what is surely a cardinal element in Scotus' thought.

From the point of view of Scotus' realism, this insistence upon contraction is what creates the difficulty that the formal distinction is intended to solve. My reason for stressing the problem in this way should be obvious: it is precisely the matter of contraction to which Peirce objects.

Metaphysical Abstraction and Second Intention

Before concluding my presentation of Scotus, I must keep my promise to say something more about the issue of our knowledge of the Common Nature and the universalization of it by the mind. Here it might be helpful to compare Scotus and Aquinas, especially since it seems to be the position of St. Thomas (or an approximation thereto) which is usually presented as "scholastic" or "moderate" realism. For St. Thomas, the individuating principle is matter, a potential and

[89] Minges, "Der Angebliche," p. 108.
[90] See below, n. 102.

limiting principle. As a result, the nature in the individual is limited, or, to use a metaphor, scarred. To abstract a nature is not simply to disentangle it from other elements; the nature has to be "restored" to its unlimited state. The power required for that operation is supplied by the agent intellect. This is, of course, a very brief and oversimplified statement, but it should be adequate to our purpose.[91]

Scotus has many reasons for disagreeing with the Thomistic principle of individuation; [92] but in the particular context of abstraction, Scotus seems to feel that the Thomistic account does not sufficiently safeguard the objectivity of our conceptions. For Scotus, the Common Nature must come across whole—which is why the formality must be real before the operation of the intellect.[93] But since the Common Nature is not of itself a universal, the nature as known is still only potentially a universal.[94] To be predicable as one thing of many things it must be given the numerical unity, and *this* is the work of the agent intellect.[95] That is to say, the nature, even as understood, still retains its "commonness." Since, as we have seen, there is only a lesser unity to the Common Nature, that nature cannot function as one thing which is predicated of many. It is necessary, therefore, that the mind make a representative object (a sign) which can be so predicated.[96]

The full process of abstraction, then, contains two steps: (1) the nature, which is already (before the operation of the intellect) distinct from the haecceity and therefore "common," is considered in it-

[91] For thirteenth and fourteenth century scholastics, the problem of universals is not an isolated topic, but is bound up with an entire metaphysics. I mentioned this earlier but it is worth repeating. For St. Thomas especially, the discussion of natures (*what* things are as distinct from the fact *that* they are) involves the question both of existence and of limitation within a species. Consequently, a comparison of Aquinas and Scotus would require some analysis of "the real distinction" and, even on this level I think, of the place of analogy.

[92] See esp. *In Metaph.*, VII, q. 13, nn. 5–7 (VII, 406b–408b). For a general discussion, see Kraus, *Die Lehre des Skotus*, pp. 93–100, and Gilson, *Jean Duns Scot*, pp. 451–66.

[93] See Gilson, *ibid.*, p. 536; and Owens' thesis, The Common Nature, pp. 19–21.

[94] *Oxon.*, II, d. 3, q. 1, n. 9 (XII, 54b); *In Metaph.*, VII, q. 18, n. 10 (VII, 460a).

[95] *Oxon.*, II, d. 3, q. 1, n. 8 (XII, 54a/b). See n. 47, chap. iii, for a parallel in Peirce's theory of hypostatic abstraction.

[96] *Oxon.*, II, d. 3, q. 1, n. 8 (XII, 54b); *In Metaph.*, VII, q. 18, n. 6 (VII, 457a).

self; and (2) the nature thus in the mind is given a numerical unity so that it can be predicated as one thing of many things. By insisting upon this first step, and maintaining that the nature is real before the operation of an intellect, Scotus feels that he can better account for the objectivity of our conceptions. Then, by holding that the Common Nature is contracted in the individual, he is able to conclude with a moderate realism similar to that of St. Thomas. As we saw earlier, Scotus does this only by positing a third mode, the metaphysical, in which Common Nature is real.

Scotus' attitude is reflected in the fact that he refers to the Common Nature by words like 'humanity.' [97] We are thus reminded that the Common Nature, which is a formality, cannot be directly predicated of a supposit; that is, we say that Socrates *has* humanity and not that he *is* humanity. Maritain calls such terms as 'humanity' and 'whiteness' abstract to the second power,[98] for they refer directly to the perfection of being a man or being white, and only indirectly to men and white things.

Such abstractions, however, should not be confused with second intention; for Scotus, this would be confusing metaphysics with logic.[99] 'Humanity' may refer directly to *being a man*, but if Socrates is a man, then 'humanity' refers at least indirectly to Socrates as he possesses this character. However much an *abstraction* of this sort is a construction of the mind, it is a construction done with an eye on the real object. In second intention, 'predicate' would refer to 'being a man' without reference to any object beyond that predicate itself. In short, Scotus holds that metaphysics is like logic in that its objects are abstractions of a second order; but it is like physics because its objects are real.[100] We shall see in the next chapter that this is of particular importance for Peirce.

[97] Peirce, too, is inclined to use 'humanity' and 'whiteness' rather than 'man' and 'white.'

[98] J. Maritain, *An Introduction to Logic*, p. 33.

[99] See Gilson, *Jean Duns Scot*, pp. 106–8; see n. 32, above. See esp. Grajewski, *The Formal Distinction of Duns Scotus*, p. 81, where he points out that the mind does not create formalities but discovers them. See also Harris, *Duns Scotus*, II, 2 ff.

[100] Here again the notion of a real "object" for science comes up. If there is a touch of "Platonism" about Scotus (and Peirce), it is, I think, a result of insisting

The metaphysical mode, then, is one referred to by abstractions, although these are in some sense discovered. The objects of this mode are the conceivable aspects of the world of supposits, but these aspects are there to be conceived of before the operation of the intellect. Gilson asks whether Scotus is then a platonist, and his answer is not unequivocal:

> One can see in what the error consisted with which Aristotle charged Plato; it consisted in reifying a universal under the name of the Idea—that is to say, of making a universal, whose being is that of an object of the intellect, to be a singular, external reality [*Oxon.*, II, d. 3, q. 1, n. 10]. Thus one has reason to deny that Scotus is a Platonist, if this requires him to admit a doctrine of Ideas which he himself is not certain that Plato maintained; but it is not impossible to maintain that our doctor "platonizes" in attributing to the common nature *etiam in rerum natura a verum esse extra animam reale.* And we have just seen that he does this is so many words [*Oxon.*, n. 7].[101, 102]

We can now try to bring together some of the uses of 'universal' in Scotus' theory. In one sense the universal is the relation of a predicate to a subject; it is a thing of second intention, and therefore exists only in the mind. In this sense there are strictly speaking only five universals: the predicables. But an abstracted concept, such as *humanity*, is itself called a universal; it is made by the mind as a representative object and is one thing that can be predicated of many. In another sense, however, 'universal' is used to designate the Common Nature, which is the ground of a true concept. In the individual thing

---

that the question be put in just this way. See the remark of Gilson quoted below, p. 62.

[101] Gilson, *Jean Duns Scot*, p. 451, n. 2.

[102] For an alternative view, see E. Bettoni, *Duns Scotus: The Basic Principles of His Philosophy*, trans. B. Bonansea (Washington, D.C.: Catholic University of America Press, 1961) pp. 53–58. Fr. Bettoni makes the "metaphysical universal" the mediator between the "physical universal" (which he says is the Common Nature) and the "logical universal" (p. 57). While I am not persuaded that this view does justice to the Common Nature as a formality, it nevertheless seems to me to capture the spirit of Scotus' theory. (I readily admit that my own stress upon Scotus' "idealism" is done with Peirce's interpretation in mind.) For there is little doubt that Scotus means to capture with his "metaphysical mode" the idea that the "object" known is partially constituted by the activity of the understanding and yet is not therefore false or "unreal." This aspect of the "moderateness" of Scotus' position can also be found in Peirce, but I feel that what is valuable in such an analysis has been brought out by other studies. Besides, it still seems to me that Peirce—if not Scotus—involves himself in special difficulties in his effort to clarify the status of such an "object."

the Common Nature is contracted by the haecceity, so that it is really identical with the individual. As a result, it is contradictory for Socrates' nature to exist in Plato. In itself, however, the Common Nature is indifferent to being in any one supposit; it has a less-than-numerical unity and cannot be predicated as one thing of many things. But since it is not *de se haec*, it can serve as the basis for the actual universal.[103] As a formality or reality, the Common Nature has a distinct and therefore real existence apart from the mind.

The basic distinction of the logical predicability of the universal from the commonness of the nature deserves special mention. The 'real' in Scotus' realism has to do with the reality of the Common Nature and not that of the logical universal. It is, I think, necessary for the moderate realist to distinguish the universal in its strictly logical sense from the nature as a *fundamentum*. And it is also typical of him to treat the abstracted concept as a sign in some sense made by the mind. But it would be a serious mistake in emphasis to consider either of these aspects the definitive character of moderate realism. In the case at hand, the reason why Scotus' realism is moderate is not because he holds that the *universal* is made by the mind, but because he insists that the *nature* is contracted in the existent individual.

Peirce's Denial of Contraction

Peirce's description of his divergence from Scotus' position should now have a little more meaning: "Even Duns Scotus is too nominalistic when he says that universals are contracted to the mode of individuality in singulars, meaning as he does, by singulars, ordinary existing things. The pragmaticist cannot admit that" (8.208).[104] The full significance of this rather cryptic passage will not be evident until we have examined Peirce's theory in detail, but it should be clear why I object so strongly to presenting Peirce in terms of scholastic and not

---

[103] Of course, Scotus does not mean that the "actual universal" (more properly, "universal in act") is something that exists in *rerum natura*.

[104] Before the publication of vol. VIII of the *Collected Papers*, we had only a general idea of Peirce's dissatisfaction with Scotus' realism. Scotus "inclined toward nominalism" (1.560), defended a "halting realism" (6.175), was separated from nominalism "by a hair" (8.11, which was in the review of Fraser's *Berkeley*), and was not infallible: "We all make our blunders" (6.95). For praise of Scotus, see 4.28, 5.84, 8.11.

Scotistic realism. The import of contraction for Scotus lies with his conviction that the existent thing, the individual supposit, has in a unique and integral way all the richness and fullness that the formalities express in their multiplicity. When Peirce denies the contraction in the individual, he is giving to Scotus' metaphysical mode (that is, to the formalities and specifically the Common Nature) a more distinct reality; thus Peirce has, as he says, a more extreme form of realism. At the same time, however, he is emptying the physical mode of its content.[105]

The denigration of the individual is no mere by-product of Peirce's theory; it is just what he wants.[106] He says at one point that the heart of the nominalist-realist controversy is simply this: which are more important, the laws or the individuals under those laws (4.1). Perhaps Aquinas could have accepted this statement, for he holds that the principle of individuation is a negative and limiting one. But aside from the fact that St. Thomas uses 'individual' in two senses,[107] he has a quite different scheme for treating the whole problem. Scotus, however, would surely deny the statement, holding as he does that the individual contains all the perfections of the contracted formalities.

As we shall see, Peirce gives a special status to some things ordinarily called individuals—notably the human person. Ultimately, such individuals are for Peirce living laws and thus essentially general.[108]

---

[105] When we come to examine the category of secondness, which for Peirce is the category of the individual and actual, we will see that it is totally devoid of character or quality and is constituted by the event of reaction. See chap. v, pp. 120–24 and 131–43.

[106] See pp. 138 ff.

[107] See n. 91, above. If matter is the principle of individuation, nonmaterial things (as Aquinas considers angels to be) are not individuals in the strict sense. If angels are spoken of as individuals (as opposed to universals), a distinction in the notion of individual seems to be involved. I cite the instance of angels to make explicit a distinction that would also occur in things like Socrates, which evidence "individuality" as unique things and "individuation" as limited expressions of a nature. (The quoted terms are from G. Klubertanz's presentation in *Introduction to the Philosophy of Being* [New York: Appleton-Century-Crofts, Inc., 1955], p. 86, n. 10. The difficulty of comparing St. Thomas and Scotus requires, of course, something more complex than just making a distinction in the notion of individuation; and I feel sure Fr. Klubertanz would agree to that.)

[108] When I first began to study Peirce's statements on realism, I was inclined to think that Peirce was making use of two kinds of *individual* as a sort of "Thomistic" criticism of Scotus (see n. 65, above). As the study shows, I have

But this step in his theory does not take place until after he has gone beyond what he thinks are the limitations of Scotus' presentation. At the risk of overrepetition, let me say again that Peirce is a Scotist not for working out from Scotus' conclusions, but for adapting the Scotistic framework of the solution. In fact, he denies just that operation of contraction which Scotus had held in order to be a moderate realist.

Peirce's Scotism: a Projection

To understand the organization of the following chapters, it might be helpful to look ahead to the general character of Peirce's transformed Scotism. In the first place, Peirce follows Scotus in taking the universal in a twofold sense: one involving the predicability of general concepts and the other involving a real commonness in things. Although the two issues are related, the problems behind them are distinct. Most important of all, the discussion of how predicates are related to subjects will not by itself answer the question of whether there is real commonness in the world apart from the knowing mind. This problem, which is behind Scotus' notion of a real but less-than-numerical unity and Peirce's treatment of real modality, is the central issue for the realism that Peirce calls scholastic. In the process of solving this problem, Peirce makes use of three postscholastic developments: the logic of relatives, the pragmatic analysis of scientific method, and a special conception of the reality of ideas.

New developments in logic, Peirce feels, make the whole question of universals easier to express and to solve. Abstractions like *humanity* turn out to be simple forms—the limiting cases—in a general process whereby relations are treated as things (hypostatized) in order to serve as the terms for higher order relations. Pragmatism shows that scientific formulas take the form of such relations. When successful prediction indicates that these formulas are not fictions, they are called

---

since changed my mind on the topic, one of the main reasons being Peirce's own remark in 8.208. So I would now have to say that Thompson's guess at what Peirce meant by Scotus' "halting realism" is wrong. (See "The Paradox of Peirce's Realism," in *Studies in the Philosophy of Peirce*, p. 342, n. 8.) I would like to suggest, however, that the reasons Thompson gives for his interpretation are still eminently worth considering when one is trying to get an adequate picture of the whole of Peirce's thought. The same can be said for Goudge's discussion, *Thought of Peirce*, p. 101.

laws. Laws are manifested in things as real powers, or, in pragmatic terms, as real "would-be's."

But pragmatism also indicates that the would-be is independent of the individual actualities, and therefore that the law is not contracted in the individual. The laws are not simply other individual things: they are of a different mode of being. Relative to the mind—indeed, idea-like in character—they are nevertheless real; and Peirce follows Scotus in calling them realities. Other investigations by Peirce, notably concerning continuity and signs, suggest that these laws are but one manifestation of a category he calls thirdness.

Unfortunately, Peirce's own words apply here, for no realist ever set out his position so straightforwardly (cf. 8.17). But the framework of our investigation can be based on the preceding analysis of Scotus,[109] in which the major issues centered around (1) the nature of the logical universal, (2) the notion of a real but less-than-numerical unity, and (3) the status of the nature in itself. The next three chapters will be devoted to these areas, and will allow us to take account respectively of the three "new" developments in Peirce mentioned above: the logic of relatives, pragmatism and scientific method, and the reality of ideas.

---

[109] I am not claiming that Peirce began (in a chronological sense) with the position of Scotus and then adapted it point for point under the pressure of the "new developments" I have mentioned. I am using Scotus more as a model through which the structure of Peirce's position can be more readily understood.

III

Realism and Logic

My plan for defeating nominalism is not simple nor direct; but it seems to me sure to be decisive, and to afford no difficulties except the mathematical toil that it requires. For as soon as you have once mounted the vantage-ground of the logic of relatives, which is related to ordinary logic precisely as the geometry of three dimensions is to the geometry of points on a line, as soon as you have scaled this height, I say, you find that you command the whole citadel of nominalism, which must thereupon fall almost without another blow [4.1].

WHAT follows this rather remarkable passage is, as promised, neither simple nor direct. The editors of the *Collected Papers* included only five paragraphs of the original manuscript (which, in their defense, is not the clearest of Peirce's writings).

Yet the manuscript does contain a direct statement of what Peirce thinks the logic of relatives accomplishes toward bringing about the easy overthrow of nominalism. The logic of relatives, he says, changes the question of whether there are real generals into the question, Are there real continua? [1] Whether the new question strikes fear in the heart of the nominalist is something of which I am not altogether convinced, but it surely has a bearing on the structure of Peirce's realism. In the present chapter I shall be content merely to bring to light the relation of continuity and generality, as well as some other elements in Peirce's logic that reflect upon the structure of his realism.

Even this limited project is not without its difficulties; for the dif-

[1] Widener I B 2 (#10): Detached Ideas on Vitally Important Topics, Lecture II, "Detached Ideas," p. 27. This is the manuscript from which 4.1–5 was selected —a passage well worth studying.

ferences between Peirce and Scotus are as important as the similarities. For example, one of the major aspects of Peirce's more extreme realism is the close connection he establishes between metaphysics and logic.[2] As we shall see, Peirce does not think that one can determine real commonness without experimental evidence; but he does attribute more of the idea-like characteristics of the logical universal to the (law of) nature which, for him, is the really common.[3]

Another warning might be appropriate here. Throughout this chapter I shall be speaking of logic in what Peirce calls the "broader sense." That is:

. . . it is the science of the necessary laws of thought, or, still better (thought always taking place by means of signs), it is general semiotic, treating not merely of truth, but also of the general conditions of signs being signs (which Duns Scotus called *grammatica speculativa*), also of the laws of the evolution of thought . . . which I content myself with inaccurately calling *objective logic*, because that conveys the correct idea that it is like Hegel's logic [1.444].[4]

Peirce also calls it "the philosophy of representation" (1.539) and "significs" (8.342).[5]

I bring up the issue of "objective logic" only to suggest that Peirce's logic extends beyond purely formal considerations. In this sense, then, I take objective logic to be like the "material logic" of the middle ages (as Peirce does in 2.544, 2.549). The more difficult notion of logic as a "normative science" is an issue I should prefer to avoid as far as possible.[6]

---

[2] "The question of realism and nominalism . . . means the question of how far real facts are analogous to logical relations and why" (4.68). "Metaphysics consists in the results of the absolute acceptance of logical principles not merely as regulatively valid, but as truths of being" (1.487). See also 7.580, 8.113.

[3] I continue to use "really common" after the manner of Scotus; see pp. 45 ff., above.

[4] On speculative grammar, see 2.83, 2.206, 2.229, 2.332, 3.430–42, 8.342. Recent scholarship has shown that Scotus did not write the *Grammatica Speculativa* contained in most editions of his works; but actually Peirce never quotes from it or makes references to it in detail. Cf. McKeon, "Peirce's Scotistic Realism," in *Studies in the Philosophy of Peirce*, pp. 240–41.

[5] For further remarks on the nature of logic, see 1.559, 2.227, 4.9, 8.342 (logic and the study of signs); 1.559, 4.80 (logic and second intention); 1.442, 2.191, 2.532, 4.134, 4.244 (logic and mathematics). See also Goudge, *Thought of Peirce*, chap. v, B.

[6] For a discussion of Peirce's contention that logic is normative, see Thompson, *Pragmatic Philosophy of Peirce*, esp. pp. 194–201, 241. While the issue is not

These warnings out of the way, we can proceed to examine some of the basic features of Peirce's logic. Quite in keeping with his love of triads (and, in this happy case, with a logical tradition), Peirce considers the basic logical elements to be term, proposition, and argument.[7] Of these, the argument is not only the most important but the most fundamental form.[8] It is not, strictly speaking, composed of propositions in turn composed of terms (4.572); on the contrary, insofar as propositions can stand alone, they are implicit arguments (2.344, 2.346), while terms are implicit propositions.[9]

In the proposition [10] 'Socrates is a man,' the predicate is '——— is a man,' a form that Peirce calls a *rhema* (2.95, 4.438) or *rheme* (2.272, 4.560). The logical subject of a proposition is what is placed in the blank space of a rhema to make a proposition. Of course the logical and grammatical subjects will not always coincide; in the example 'Anthony gave a ring to Cleopatra,' the underlined words are the logical subjects (5.542)—a reasonable enough position which leads Peirce to frequent attacks upon the status of the common noun according to grammarians.[11] Peirce brings grammar into line with logic by taking the basic grammatical forms as subject and verb (2.328), the subject being a demonstrative or something that can take its place (2.296, 3.419), adjectives and common nouns being parts of the verb (2.328, 4.157).[12]

In speaking of the rhema, Peirce says that it is obtained by *erasing* the logical subject(s) of a proposition (2.272, 4.354), which shows perhaps as well as anything why the term is a derived form rather

---

irrelevant to Peirce's realism, I feel that it does not affect the major structure of my analysis.

[7] 1.471, 1.515, 1.559, 2.95, 4.572.

[8] 2.340–44, 4.9; see also 5.76, 7.580.

[9] 2.341, 4.48, 4.56; see also 2.356, 4.583, 8.183.

[10] For Peirce, the proposition is not identical with the written or spoken expression (4.354n1, 5.424n1). But every proposition has a (possible) concrete expression (2.315). The relation of proposition to its expression is an instance of the general case of the relation of thirdness to secondness, which will be discussed in chap. v.

[11] 2.69, 2.211, 2.287n, 2.341, 4.438n1, 8.337. On medieval usage, see 2.201, 4.354. For Peirce's more positive presentations, see 2.338, 2.439, 4.58, 8.183.

[12] It is worth noting that pragmatism was designed to deal only with predicates (symbols) and not with subjects (indices): 5.8, 5.429, 5.467. For more on subjects and predicates: 2.312, 2.357–58, 3.419, 3.434, 3.439, 4.438n.

than a building block for propositions. That the proposition itself is an implicit argument requires a more complicated explanation—one involving Peirce's contention that the copula is illative (3.440).

First of all, Peirce denies that the copula is 'is,' holding instead that 'is' is a part of the predicate.[13] Still, he insists that a proposition cannot adequately be treated in terms of subject and predicate alone: for "*composition* is itself a triadic relationship, between two (or more) components and the composite whole" (6.321).[14] Second, Peirce denies that the link between subject and predicate is identity, for he considers identity to be in reality only another general predicate.[15] And finally, he affirms that the link, that is, the copula, is a form called *consequence*.[16]

Peirce holds that the relation of premiss(es) to conclusion is the same as that of antecedent to consequent. Consequence, then, is the prototype of argument; it is the "one primary and fundamental logical relation, that of illation, expressed by *ergo*" (3.440). Note particularly that the consequence is the *relation* of consequent to antecedent, not just a consequent and an antecedent.[17] An argument is somehow more than just its premisses and conclusion, just as a proposition is more than its terms. Peirce tells us that a proposition is an assertion or predication of a predicate of a subject.[18] Consequence, in which the copula is explicit, is the basic (what might be called the "normal") predicational and inferential form (2.472, 3.440, 7.104).[19]

---

[13] 2.319, 2.328 (see 3.459), 2.343.

[14] "The triadic clause of the law of logic recognizes three elements in truth, the idea, or predicate, the fact or subject, the thought which originally put them together . . ." (1.485).

[15] 2.341, 2.440, 5.151.

[16] 2.354, 2.415, 2.435 ff., 2.444 and note, 2.581, 3.165, 3.440, 7.104–7; for the bearing of this on metaphysics, see 3.173n2, 3.435.

[17] "In the language of logic, 'consequence' does not mean that which follows, which is called the consequent, but means the fact that a consequent follows from an antecedent" (4.435n1; see also 2.669, 4.51). The application to pragmatism is well made by Moore in his Metaphysics and Pragmatism in the Philosophy of Peirce; see also his *American Pragmatism: Peirce, James and Dewey* (New York: Columbia University Press, 1961), pp. 44 f.

[18] 5.546–48; see also 3.621, 5.543.

[19] For an apt discussion of the copula, see 3.621. On the importance of illation, see 2.44n, 3.472, 4.375. Regarding the latter, the following passage is interesting (if somewhat spooky): "The mode of being of the composition of thought, which is always of the nature of the attribution of a predicate to a subject, is the living

For Peirce, then, predication is essentially a form of consequence (4.3). We might note in passing two rather important effects of this doctrine. First, even the perceptual judgment is but a limiting case of hypothetical inference (4.541).[20] Second, categorical propositions in their basic (or normal) form are, without exception, conditionals (3.439, 4.3).[21] The latter point in particular has a bearing on Peirce's pragmatism.

The Generality of the Predicate

It is scarcely an innovation in Peirce that generality is associated with the predicate (5.151).[22] He calls attention to the fact that the definition of *universal* used by the scholastics was: "what is fit to be predicated of many" (1.27n, 2.367, 5.102). Actually, he holds that the predicate is general in two ways (1.420, 5.429). In the first place, the predicate as a word exhibits the peculiarity of any word, which Peirce refers to by the now familiar distinction of token and type. The token, the sound or inscription, is an individual and actual thing; the type is a general form which the token signifies [23] and to which it conforms (5.429). Peirce takes this back one more step to "concepts":

. . . which are such objects as those each of which is related to equivalent words in different languages, e.g., *horse, Pferd, equus*, as any one of these is related to the spoken and to the written word, or as the latter is related to the series of ink-marks that represent it on a particular line of a particular page of a particular copy of a book. . . .[24]

In his existential graphs Peirce seems usually to be dealing with inscriptions only (4.514). When he talks of the characteristics of a word or idea, however, it is pretty evident that he is talking of the concept.

---

intelligence which is the creator of all intelligible reality, as well as of the knowledge of such reality. It is the *entelechy*, or perfection of being" (6.341).

[20] It is no surprise, then, to find Peirce criticizing the "analytic-synthetic" distinction in Kant: 2.451n1 (see 4.87 in this regard), 2.690 ff., 3.641, 4.51 f., 4.85, 5.45, 5.175 ff., 5.348.

[21] For a criticism of this, see W. V. Quine's review of the *Collected Papers*, Vol. IV, in *Isis*, No. 22 (1934), p. 292.

[22] On the importance of the predicate: 2.278; see also n. 12, above.

[23] The token is a sign of the type which is a sign of the object (4.537). For more on token and type, see 2.246, 2.261, 2.292, 3.433, 4.447, 4.544, 8.334.

[24] Widener I B 3 (1b): "Neglected Argument for the Existence of God," MSS-G, p. 128.

The distinction between type and concept is not so clear, especially when we consider the case of demonstratives. Apparently, although the token-type distinction is applicable to demonstratives (5.138, 5.429), the latter do not have corresponding concepts.[25] A demonstrative (or index) and a verb (or symbol) do not refer in the same way. An index draws attention to an individual thing—an haecceity, as Peirce sometimes calls it (3.434, 3.460) [26]—which has an identity in space and time and for which the index stands (2.287, 2.305); but ". . . contrast this with the signification of the verb, which is sometimes in my thought and sometimes in yours, and which has no other identity than the agreement between its several manifestations" (3.460).

The first way in which a predicate can be general, then, is for its signification to be in many minds. Peirce calls this subjective generality.[27] The objective generality of a predicate lies in its signifying many things,[28] which needs some explanation—indeed, it is the major concern of the rest of the chapter. But subjective generality cannot be just forgotten. As we know from the first chapter, Peirce is going to say that real generals are of the nature of a word or idea.[29] That is, once he has shown to his satisfaction that there are real generals, he will go on to discuss the nature of these entities; and the primary analogate for this will be the notion of subjective generality. We

---

[25] Cf. 5.467. Although a "mental representation of the index is produced" (5.473), it cannot function as does the concept which constitutes the predicate. It must be remembered that Peirce holds the individual to be "unintelligible": that is, experienced but not represented qua individual in a concept. See Thompson, *Pragmatic Philosophy of Peirce*, p. 252, and the discussion of secondness below: chap. vi (esp. n. 22).

[26] This is a revealing barbarism. For a Scotist, *haecceitas* is an important aspect of a thing. The phrase 'an haecceity,' however, reflects Peirce's own attitude toward the individual as a second that contains no thirdness at all. See the discussion in chap. v, pp. 131–43.

[27] 5.429; see also 1.420, 2.301, 8.357. For the relation to tokens and habits, 3.360.

[28] Even when there is only one thing of which the predicate is true, the predicate is still general in its signification (5.103). And the question realism asks concerns not what a word stands for, but what it signifies (1.27). On "signification," see 1.27n, 2.249, 2.293, 2.431 ff., 5.138, 5.471. Peirce criticizes Mill's usage of "connote": 2.317n, 2.431.

[29] Pp. 11 ff., above.

would do well, then, to stay on the lookout for information that will contribute to our understanding of subjective generality.[30]

Relatives

We must now determine what Peirce means by calling the rheme a "relative," for it is in terms of relatives that he will ultimately explain the generality of the predicate. A relative, he says, is "the equivalent of a word or phrase which either as it is [a complete relative] or else when the verb 'is' is attached [a nominal relative] becomes a sentence with some number of proper names left blank" (3.466). A complete proposition, without blanks, is a medadic relative (3.465); [31] a proposition with one blank is a monadic relative, with two blanks a dyadic relative, and so on. A relationship, or *fundamentum relationis*, is "a fact relative to a number of objects, considered apart from those objects, as if, after the statement of the fact, the designation of those objects had been erased" (3.466, 3.638, 6.318). Peirce reserved 'relation' to indicate a relationship said to be true of one of the objects (usually the noun-subject), the others not being considered (3.466).[32]

In treating the order and independence of relatives, Peirce finds that a triad cannot be reduced to dyads nor a dyad to monads. He does discover, however, that all relatives higher than triads can be reduced to triads, and so he makes of them all one group which he sometimes calls "plural relatives" (3.421).[33]

To speak of a complete proposition as a medadic relative is to indicate that its subject(s) could be erased to allow for the formation of a higher relative. There is no difficulty in thinking of the proposition as a relative if at least two names can be erased in every proposi-

---

[30] The token-type relation comes very close to being the prototype of Peirce's realism; see 5.502, 3.360, and chap. v, below (esp. pp. 135–36).

[31] But see 3.420 f., 4.354, and 4.438, where medads and monads are rhemas but not relatives.

[32] Peirce eventually confessed that he had gone against his own rules for terminology in changing DeMorgan's 'logic of relations' to 'logic of relatives' (3.574n2). Consequently, his use of 'relation' after this time must be treated with some care. I am following the earlier usage, however, in order to distinguish a relative as a predicate from a relation as a *fundamentum* or species of relationship.

[33] See Quine's criticism in *Isis*, No. 19 (1933), p. 224.

tion. The real oddity of nonrelational relatives lies in the notion of a monadic predicate, for it seems to imply there is a *fundamentum relationis* that is not relational.[34] The way Peirce handles the problem will be of some interest to us.

If categorical propositions are virtual hypotheticals, it might be that all monadic predicates are virtual relations. To some extent, Peirce's pragmatism reflects such an attitude: a predicate like 'is hard' signifies a relation of test to response. We shall be discussing this notion when we come to Peirce's pragmatism, but as a solution to the present problem it amounts to saying that there are no monadic predicates.[35] A more plausible suggestion is that monadic predicates are simply limiting cases of higher relatives. A nonrelative character, then, is a limiting case of a relative character.

The import of Peirce's attitude comes through somewhat more clearly if we follow him one step further in his analysis of the predicate. Corresponding to every rhema is a collection, whose members have a certain character (4.171, 4.649). In the case of monadic predicates, we might call the character simple (for example, being blue or blueness), and in dyadic and higher predicates complex (for example, the father-son relationship). A predicate signifies the character and denotes the members of the collection; in other words, a predicate has an extension and a comprehension.[36] But we should pause for a moment here to examine Peirce's use of 'kind,' 'class,' and 'collection.'

Of the three, Peirce is most consistent in his use of 'kind.' A kind is a character, specifically one that is not sometimes true and sometimes false of the same individuals (4.647). Clearly, *kind* is always a matter of comprehension. *Class*, on the other hand, is exclusively a matter of extension; it is:

---

[34] See n. 31, above. It never comes quite clear to me whether Peirce thinks that some characters are nonrelational, or that every character has a relational and a nonrelational aspect (cf. 3.417, 4.235). In its metaphysical aspect the same problem arises concerning the status of firstness and thirdness: see chap. v, pp. 124–28.

[35] In fact, Peirce comes very close to saying this. It is a part of the problem referred to in the previous footnote.

[36] For Peirce's account of the history of the distinction, see 2.391–408. I have chosen 'comprehension' in order to avoid confusion between 'intension' and 'intention.'

. . . the totality of all those singulars that possess a definite existent character, which is the *essential character* of the class. Should observation show that two classes having different essential characters embraced the very same singulars, then since it is the singulars, and not the kinds, that constitute the existence of the class, we should say that the two classes, though *entitatively*, that is, in their possibilities, they were diverse, were yet *existentially* one. Such, I think, is the modern notion of a class, though I must confess that it appears to me to be rather hazy. The characters which go to define a class are not necessarily permanent characters of the singulars, as a kind is [4.648, 6.384].

Peirce's favorite term is 'collection,' which he defines as a whole whose members are all and only the singulars having a certain quality.[37] This quality, peculiar and common to all the members of a collection, may be a trivial one: for example, that the members were selected for this collection. Apparently, Peirce's major objection to the "modern notion" of a class is that it allows for a class such as adolescents, which would be made up now of certain individuals and now of others (4.648); he wants to insure that collections are not treated this way. Of course, there is a collection of those who are adolescents at a specified time, and another collection of all who are, were, or will be adolescents; but in these cases there is no individual who is at one time a member of the collection and another time not.

Unfortunately, Peirce's own use of 'collection' is a little hazy. There are times when he seems to use 'class' and 'collection' interchangeably,[38] and yet he speaks of a collection as "virtually a quality or class-character" (3.537n). He never treats a clear case of two collections where the classes are the same and the characters are different. He does say that the collection of all phoenixes that were, are, or will be is identical with the collection of cockatrices that exist now (4.650), and that would suggest rather strongly the extensional use of collection. He also says that we can move by *different operations* from 'All men are mortal' to (1) 'The collection of men is a collection of mortals,' and (2) 'The character of mortality is possessed by every man' (6.382). If it is this parallelism of possibilities which makes a collec-

---

[37] On collections: 3.537n, 3.637, 4.99, 4.170–71, 4.647–51, 6.174, 6.384.

[38] I am thinking particularly of his use of 'natural class,' which, though perhaps historically justified, does not seem to be in keeping with his purely extensional use of 'class.' His remark that genus and species are "in our nineteenth century dialect" classes (4.5) seems inappropriate for the same reasons.

tion a "virtual" class-character, then the extensional use of collection is not destroyed. That is at least the way in which I shall construe it.[39]

System and Relational Generality

We can now return to the problem of relating monadic predicates to higher relatives. Peirce's solution is reflected in three points which he makes about collections. First, the older logic had reached its limit in treating things that are similar to one another as a collection; the logic of relatives provides the notion of a *system* that can be constituted by any relation of its members (3.454, 4.5). Cause and effect, symptom and disease, the triadic relation of a sign to its object and interpreter, and, most important, a scientific law or mathematical formula—all constitute systems whose members are not necessarily similar to one another. The contribution of the logic of relatives, according to Peirce, is to treat a class or collection as a degenerate form of system (3.454).

Let us examine this in the context of our original problem of monadic predicates. The predicate 'is a man' defines a collection whose members are similar in that they all possess the character *humanity*. Relational predicates can be treated in the same way by taking the subjects that fill the blanks in any plural rhema as a set:[40] for example, [Peter, Peter, Jr.] in the proposition 'Peter is the father of Peter, Jr.' Then, just as the character *humanity* defines a collection of similar subjects Peter, Paul, and so on, so the character *father-son-ness* defines a collection of similar sets [Peter, Peter, Jr.], [Paul, Paul, Jr.], and so on. Generality, on this account, revolves around the similarity of the members of a collection, which can be subjects or subject-sets.

---

[39] I readily admit, however, that Peirce's constant insistence on a common character for all members of a collection is pretty suspiciously "un-extensional" activity. The editors of the *Collected Papers* seem to feel that a collection *is* a rhema or propositional function (3.537n), and that a class is the extension of a collection (3.66n). I am inclined to think that Peirce's use of 'collection' and 'class' is much sloppier than his use of 'virtually': see 3.537n.

[40] 4.543. A set is distinguished from a collection in that the serial arrangement of the members of a set is essential: the collection of Peter and Peter, Jr., and Peter, Jr. and Peter, are the same collection but different sets. See Peirce on the "ordered pair": 1.442 and 3.571.

The lesson to be learned from the logic of relatives, Peirce insists, is that this scheme must be turned around. That is, the most significant generality is that of the set itself. Odd as it seems at first glance, what Peirce is saying here is that '_____ gives _____ to _____' is general because it ranges over many subjects; and he means here *not* the various three-member sets, but the members of any one set: for example, Anthony, a ring, and Cleopatra. The power of the new logic, on such an interpretation, is that it allows us to move not just from a sample to a collection, but from a fragment of a system to a whole system. In the case at hand, Peirce apparently means that we can move to things like the jeweler, the banker, and the attraction of women to shiny things and not simply to the set [George, a ring, Louise]. A collection, as made up of similar members, is considered the simplest form of system.

We can approach the same idea from a slightly different angle by examining Peirce's second point about collections: the distinction between discrete and continuous collections. The collection of the books on my desk is a discrete one; the collection of drops of water in the ocean is not (4.172). The most important kind of nondiscrete collection is that of possible objects:

If you and I talk of the great tragedians who have acted in New York within the last ten years, a definite list can be drawn up of them, and each of them has his or her proper name. But suppose we open the question of how far the general influences of the theatrical world at present favor the development of female stars rather than of male stars. In order to discuss that, we have to go beyond our *completed* experience, which may have been determined by accidental influences, and have to consider the possible or probable stars of the immediate future. We can no longer assign proper names to each. The individual actors to which our discourse now relates become largely merged into general varieties; and their separate identities are partially lost. . . . When we say that of all possible throws of a pair of dice one thirty-sixth part will show sixes, the collection of possible throws which have not been made is a collection of which the individual units have no distinct identity. It is impossible so to designate a single one of those possible throws that have not been thrown that the designation shall be applicable to only one definite possible throw; and this impossibility does not spring from any incapacity of ours, but from the fact that in their own nature these throws are not individually distinct [4.172].

The relevance of possibility to realism is indicated by Peirce in what follows:

The possible is necessarily general; and no amount of general specification can reduce a general class of possibilities to an individual case. It is only actuality, the force of existence, which bursts the fluidity of the general and produces a discrete unit [4.172].

Peirce eventually comes to hold that every predicate specifies a continuous collection of possible objects. The collection of animals specified by the biologist's classification includes not only the discrete individuals, which are the actually existent animals, but a continuous range of possible cases between any two of these (5.103). Here again, monadic predicates (like '———— is an animal') are being treated as the limiting case of higher relatives. The quality spectrum that corresponds to monadic predicates is a simple form of the more complex continuity of a process. The events in a process are related not by being similar to one another, but by being ordered to, or successively realizing the end of, the process.

We shall see more of the contrast between the continuity of quality and that of process in Chapter V; the notion of possibility will figure centrally in the next chapter when we examine Peirce's efforts to show that there is "real" generality in the world. But the foregoing discussion should be enough to suggest the importance of Peirce's remark that generality in the logic of relatives, that is, relational generality, is continuity (6.190).[41]

Hypostatic Abstraction

There remains a third point about collections, which leads into the next important feature of Peirce's logic. Peirce points out that a collection is not the same as its members. Even the collection whose sole member is Julius Caesar is not identical with Julius Caesar:

[41] See also n. 1. One might note here, however, an ambiguity in Peirce's treatment: it is not clear whether he has only reformulated the problem or changed it. Usually the problem of generality revolves around the defining character of a collection, *humanity* being general because it is the same in Peter and in Paul. But the same thing holds true of plural relatives: the father-son relationship is the same in Peter and Peter, Jr., and in Paul and Paul, Jr. In this sense the logic of relatives does no more toward exposing generality than did the simpler logic of monadic predicates. Does Peirce think he has solved this problem by treating similarity as a subspecies of continuity? I think he does, for, as I hope to show, he is aiming at a notion very much like the Hegelian "concrete universal" (cf. 4.50). The reader, like myself, may not be ready to grant that the two issues are the same.

. . . the latter was a man of immense force of intellect who was brought into the world by a grossly unskillful operation of surgery, while the former is nothing but an *ens rationis* brought into being by the idea of that man being chosen without any surgery at all and utterly deprived of any force of intellect or life [4.650].

Peirce comes to define a collection as a fictitious entity made up of less fictitious entities; but he points out that 'fictitious' is taken in a special sense (6.382, 3.637). What that special sense is must be examined now.

As we have already seen, Peirce contends that the common noun is an accident of Indo-European grammar, being in reality only a part of the verb or predicate; the same is true of adjectives. But if 'man' is an unessential grammatical form, 'humanity' and 'mankind' are not. For the latter are not parts of the predicate at all: they are the predicate made into a subject by a process called "subjectification" (2.428, 4.332) or, more often, "hypostatic abstraction" (as in 4.235).

Peirce holds that the term 'abstraction' has been misleadingly applied to two different operations which he calls prescisive and hypostatic abstraction, or sometimes prescission and abstraction.[42] In prescisive abstraction a thing is thought of through one of its aspects indifferently to the others, as in: 'The library building is large,' where nothing is said about color, position, and so forth. In hypostatic abstraction the aspect selected is converted into another logical subject, and thus changes from something we think through to something we think about: 'The library building has largeness' (4.332).[43]

Some have held that abstraction is a mere grammatical change with no logical significance, but Peirce thinks this is a serious mistake (2.428, 3.462, 4.235). Consider the rhema which each statement allows: 'The library building is large' and 'The library building has largeness.' In the second case *largeness* has become a logical subject, a change that

[42] 2.364, 2.428, 4.234–35, 4.332, 5.534; for particular reference to Scotus, 1.549n, 2.428. Peirce explains his peculiar spelling of 'prescission' in 5.449 (cf. 2.364).

[43] Something that is not itself a "thing" comes to be treated as a "thing"— this seems to be the definitive element of hypostatic abstraction: 2.364, 2.428, 4.235, 4.332, 4.549, 5.449, 6.595. Peirce often uses a terminology that he picked up from William James, and describes abstraction as making "substantive" the "transitory" elements of thought (the "birds on the wing"): 3.642, 8.89–90; see also 1.83, 3.424. However, Peirce emphasizes that abstraction is not to be taken as a psychological process: 2.44, 2.428.

is obscured if we think of it only as an adjective becoming a noun. The change allows now for further predicates to be applied to *largeness;* for example, that it is impressive (4.332, 4.235).[44]

Nominalists have railed against abstraction, and Peirce thinks they were justified inasmuch as many scholastic abstractions were empty formulas—the results of idle logical distinctions (6.361, 8.193). But this does not justify the attack on the process of abstraction itself (3.509). Peirce considers abstraction one of the most powerful tools of the human understanding (1.383, 3.509, 5.162).[45] It is through abstraction that the mathematician is able to treat operations as themselves the subject of further operations (1.83).[46] Equally important is the fact that the language of science abounds in abstractions: *velocity, density, weight,* and the like. Biological and chemical classifications likewise require that the scientist deal with collections and their relations; and scientific laws and formulas are themselves the essential characters of collections. As a result, Peirce holds that the proper procedure is not to refrain from abstracting, but to do it intelligently (1.383).

Peirce's insistence on the importance of subjectification is one reason why he rightly calls himself a Scotist. As we saw in the last chapter, Scotus considers abstraction proper to be the process whereby the mind operates on the Common Nature as known, giving it a numerical unity it did not of itself possess. Only the predicables, the second intentional notions like genus and species, are universals in the strict sense; but second order abstractions like *humanity* and *whiteness* are also universals (in a sense) because they are "fit to be predicated": that is, they have a unity allowing them to be predicated of many individuals (see 2.368).[47]

The same scheme can be found in Peirce. As Goudge points out,

---

[44] Peirce insists that although abstraction is more removed from the perceptual object than is the "*Vorstellung* or composite of images," its intellectual purport is the same (5.534). See also 1.549n, where he quotes Scotus approvingly in showing that abstraction is not distortion, and 5.327.

[45] "[Symbols] enable us, for example, to create Abstractions, without which we should lack a great engine of discovery. . . . In many respects they are the very warp of reason" (4.531).

[46] 1.383, 2.227, 2.364, 3.462, 3.509, 3.642, 4.235, 5.449, 5.534.

[47] See the discussion on pp. 60 ff., above.

although a general term like 'large' first occurs in the perceptual judgment, a universal is, strictly speaking, not present until after the process of hypostatic abstraction (cf. 5.448n).[48] Peirce devotes so much time to the logical process of abstraction because he feels the older logics were unable to handle it adequately;[49] and he finds that he must add a sixth predicable: law (4.1). From our earlier discussion of relatives, we can see that *law* is needed to handle the complex characters of dyadic and higher predicates.

Abstraction and Second Intention

For both Scotus and Peirce, abstractions can be treated in terms of either their logical behavior or their real reference. A biologist, for example, may use abstractions in speaking of a collection of animals or the differentiating character of sentient things, but he is not doing logic. Conversely, a logician may talk of the collection of fairies as an "empty" collection, but it is not a logical inquiry which establishes that there are no fairies; actually the logician is not interested in fairies but in collections.[50] The same reasoning applies to the distinction of trivial and nontrivial characters. In general, although any predicate can be made a subject by a logico-grammatical process, that process does not of itself determine that a collection or a character is real.

Consequently, it is important to distinguish in Peirce, as we did in Scotus, between second intention and abstraction.[51] Second intention is "thought about thought as symbol" (4.465), and thus requires an act of abstraction: our thinking about things is itself made a thing to be thought about. Both logic and grammar make use of the process:

[48] T. A. Goudge, "Peirce's Theory of Abstraction" (*Studies in the Philosophy of Peirce*, p. 123). Goudge suggests that Peirce should never have used the term 'abstraction' for this process; but he has missed the Scotistic precedent for it by considering the "classical Aristotelian theory of abstraction" as all of one piece.

[49] It is apparently the logic of relatives' ability to handle abstractions that gives it the vantage point over nominalism (cf. 4.1, 3.642).

[50] See 2.54, 2.64, 2.548.

[51] Peirce himself is not too careful with his terminology. It is possible to speak of "*entia rationis* some of which are real," since all abstractions are concepts though some have a real reference (4.463). But sometimes he seems to treat second intentional concepts as real (4.549, 6.593), and this tends to blur the distinction between abstractions like *predicate* and those like *humanity*.

'subject,' 'predicate,' 'noun,' 'verb,' and the like are all second intentional terms. Take for example, 'This is a man,' and then move to the comprehensional abstraction, 'This has humanity.' If our interest is in the logical or grammatical function of the term ("as symbol"), we can proceed to 'Humanity is a species' and then, repeating the operation, to 'Species is a predicable.' Similarly, the grammarian might say, 'Humanity is a noun,' 'Noun is a part of speech.'

Peirce calls attention to an analogous process in the extensional treatment. We can move from '——— is a man' to 'mankind,' that is, the collection of things which are men; and from this we could go on to a collection of collections (number), and from that to higher order collections like multitude (3.43, 5.534). The peculiarity of second intention in both the comprehensional and extensional treatment is that it has for its object the abstraction precisely as abstraction. In the examples used the interest is directed not at men and their properties, but at characters and collections and *their* properties.

Now consider the move from the collection of Indians to the collection of men that includes it and is, in turn, included in the collection of animals. Although it can be talked *about* in terms of second intention, the transition to "higher," that is, more inclusive, collections remains in the same logical order. While it is important to the logician because it relates to the behavior of collections, the process is used by biologists or anthropologists for saying something about Indians, men, and animals.

The same thing can be found, in a comprehensional treatment, in the move from 'The library building is large' to 'The library building has largeness' and then to 'The largeness of the building is impressive.' This, too, has interesting logical and grammatical aspects; Peirce himself brings up the example to talk *about* abstractions (4.332). But it is not as an abstraction that largeness is impressive, nor would it be a logical inquiry to investigate, say, the preconscious ground for man's susceptibility to being impressed by largeness.

For an interesting example of a complex predicate treated in a first intentional, comprehensional way, consider the pragmatic explication of *hardness*. A thing is hard if it responds in a certain way to a certain test; and 'hardness' names the hypostatic abstraction of the relation between test and response. Then *hardness* can be correlated to high "polemerization" of the molecule or some other character or complex of characters (5.457). As we reach the higher level relations of hypostatized relations, we sometimes lack names for the relations and use instead scientific formulas or laws. Even where we have the names at hand, the explicitly relational form of the law can be substituted. Such would seem to be the reasoning behind Peirce's contention that what the scholastics called a nature was in reality a law of nature: the nature of a diamond, for example, consisting in a higher order character, a relation of relations, or law.[52]

One reason for spending time on the distinction between second intention and abstraction is to clear up a possible confusion about "moderate realism" and its applicability to Scotus and Peirce. Scotus, as we saw, is a moderate realist for insisting that the Common Nature is contracted to the mode of individuality in the existent thing; but that pertains to the second question of realism.[53] We are dealing here with Peirce's answer to the first question, and the fact that he, like Scotus, contends that the universal concept is a construct or *ens rationis* does not necessarily indicate that he is a moderate realist—or for that matter, a conceptualist.

Universals, as concepts predicable of many, are abstractions and therefore *entia rationis* (5.447n); collections and characters, as objects of logic, are constructs of the mind. When Peirce says that some abstractions are real, he does not mean that they have the same mode of being as existing physical objects.[54] 'Real' has a specific meaning in the context of the problem, and Peirce claims to use it in its original scholastic sense (6.453). The real is that which does not change regardless of what anyone thinks about it; the characters of a fiction—which is properly opposed to the real—depend upon what someone has

---

[52] If one goes in for dispositional analyses in the first place, I see no reason why he cannot hold that the scholastic substantial form is *the* disposition of a thing, in the sense that it is the disposition of the qualities (themselves dispositional) of a thing. See Peirce's remarks in Wiener, *Values in a Universe of Chance*, p. 292.

[53] For the two questions of realism, see above, chap. ii, pp. 44 ff.

[54] Notice that Peirce explicitly distinguishes *existence* and *reality*: e.g., in 5.503.

attributed to that fiction (5.405, 5.430). The substance of a dream is not real, for it depends on the fact that the dreamer so dreamed it (6.453). The fact of the dream, that it has been so dreamed, is real although mental and not external. The mental depends for its reality on someone's thinking it, but then it has its characters as a mental reality despite what anyone thinks *about* it (6.327–28).

The fact that someone has made an abstraction is as real as the fact that someone has dreamed. And just as this is not the issue when it is said that a dream is unreal, so it is also not the issue when it is said that an abstraction is real. The reality in question here is the reference of the abstraction; and this must, I think, be the interpretation of the otherwise shocking phrase: "The real is that which signifies something real" (5.320).

Real abstractions are distinguished first of all from second intentions, for the latter refer *only* to *entia rationis*. A real abstraction, though itself an *ens rationis*, refers to something that does not depend on what someone thinks or thinks about it. Second, real abstractions are to be distinguished from abstractions which purport to refer to the real. Bode's Law,[55] for example, was not proposed as a second intentional notion, but it turns out to be a fiction. Notice that only experimental inquiry will establish the latter distinction. The relational predicate that Bode devised is a real mental fact; just as a dream is a real mental fact, and just as all abstractions are real mental facts. The question of real collections and characters is something beyond this.

Is there something general in the world, corresponding to some abstractions? How do we find out? And what is the nature of these things? These are all part of the second question of realism. As yet, we have not actually considered Peirce's solution—although it was suggested in the first chapter, where Peirce's statement of the problem was presented, that scientific prediction has something to do with it. What I want to stress here is that Peirce's insistence that abstractions are *entia rationis*, whose reality consists in their reference to something real, should not be taken as proof positive that he holds to a moderate realism. As a matter of fact, Peirce is only dissociating himself from what he considers to be a caricature of scholastic thought (6.361) and,

---

[55] See our discussion, pp. 27 ff., above.

at the same time, distinguishing the issue of logical predicability from that of metaphysical commonness.

Abduction

The discussion of real abstractions has forced us to look beyond the limits of logic to the question of real commonness. Before going on to that, however, we must examine another aspect of Peirce's logical theory, which will lead us to the same point in a slightly different way; that doctrine is Peirce's notion of abduction.[56]

Peirce holds that there are three forms of inference: deduction, induction, and abduction, of which only abduction provides a new idea.[57] We say to the deductive logician: Never mind whether the premises are true or not, tell me whether the conclusion follows from them. In somewhat the same way, we might say to the inductive logician: Never mind why I picked these characters, tell me how many A's are also B's.[58] As Peirce puts it, all that induction contributes is a ratio of a frequency (5.194, 2.775, 5.145).

It is particularly important to keep abduction separate from induction,[59] even in what might seem to be "obvious" cases. By induction one may find that all or nearly all A's are B's, but to conclude that being an A has something to do with being a B is a matter not of inductive but of abductive inference (2.636). For example, we may establish that nearly all people who have taken opium have gone to sleep, and from this we may obtain an inductive ratio. But if we go on to say that opium puts people to sleep, we are no longer giving a ratio but suggesting a connection. We might find that five and a half hours before any person has gone to sleep, someone in China had sneezed (5.8, 5.172). The inductive logician could find a ratio between these two characters as well.

We tend to overlook the fact that in any experimental situation

---

[56] An adequate study of Peirce's theory of abduction would require a book of its own. For a brief but illuminating discussion, see Arthur Burks, "Peirce's Theory of Abduction," *Philosophy of Science*, pp. 301–6.

[57] 2.96, 2.777, 5.145; see also 5.171, 5.591, 1.383.

[58] See 1.630, 5.145, 5.580.

[59] Peirce admits that he confused the two in some of his own writings (2.102); but straightening out the details of this would be a topic in itself.

there are a large number of characters involved (1.92). Because of funded experience, we narrow our concern immediately to a few characters that seem significant; but Peirce is pointing out that this is already an act of inference (6.409).[60] Even more important, we are inclined to take for granted the separate step of inference in concluding to a connection when we have found a high statistical correlation; but from the point of view of induction, that added inference (which is abduction) is simply the fallacy of *post hoc ergo propter hoc* (7.114).[61] To put it in another way, a real connection cannot be the conclusion of an inductive process alone.[62]

It is in these terms, apparently, that we are to understand Peirce's contention that only abduction provides a "new idea." It is true that induction can give us more information; [63] if we reason from the character of a sample to that of a whole, we are talking of more *things* in the conclusion than we were in the premisses. But we are not introducing any new *idea* in the conclusion; the idea we began with is now simply applied to more things. An act of prescission is required in the inductive process, for things are considered inasmuch as they are A's or B's, irrespective of their other characters; but strictly speaking no act of abstraction is involved (2.364).[64]

[60] Peirce adopts Whewell's term 'colligation,' and says that it is "all that calls for sagacity in deductive reasoning" and "is then no part of the syllogism" (2.553). "It is plain that colligation is half the battle in ratiocination" (4.45); see also 2.442, 2.451. Notice, too, that many hypotheses are possible to account for a given fact: 5.172, 7.38, 7.680.

[61] "An efficient cause, detached from a final cause in the form of a law, would not even possess efficiency: it might exert itself, and something might follow *post hoc*, but not *propter hoc*; for *propter* implies potential regularity" (1.213).

[62] "By induction, we conclude that facts, similar to observed facts, are true in cases not examined. By hypothesis, we conclude the existence of a fact quite different from anything observed, from which, according to known laws, something observed would necessarily result. The former is reasoning from particulars to the general law; the latter, from effect to cause. The former classifies, the latter explains" (2.636). On the significance of abduction for the illative copula, see 4.3.

[63] 'Information' is a technical term in Peirce; see, for example, 2.418–19. Although I have the technical use in mind, I am satisfied in the present context with the ordinary meaning of the term.

[64] As we go to higher level abstractions, the abstracted character can then be prescinded at each level. And so it may be that there is an induction which has for its subjects not things with characters but hypostatized characters with characters. I suspect this is what is involved in the "induction of characters" that Peirce

In moving from sample to collection, induction is likewise limited to the relation of similarity (2.642). The step from fragment to system, which we have seen to be so important to Peirce, must be a matter of abduction. And since any plural relative defines a system, the discovery of relations or laws (as relations of relations) must involve abduction.[65] The first step in the framing of a scientific theory is an abductive one (6.525). Peirce sometimes calls abduction "hypothesis" (2.96, 5.272): more often, however, he says that the *framing* of an hypothesis is an abductive inference: the scientist then deduces certain results of his hypothesis and tests these by experiment.

Peirce is even tempted to say that only abduction *explains*, although he modifies this to some extent.[66] He feels that an explanation requires something other than the facts to be explained (6.273), and since neither deduction nor induction supplies a new idea, each fails to do anything more than restate the facts themselves. If it is objected that induction does explain by showing that an event belongs to a larger collection of similar events, Peirce replies that precisely what needs explaining is the similarity.[67]

The prime example of restating the facts without explaining them is the doctrine of the uniformity of nature.[68] If I wonder why it is that people always go to sleep after taking opium, it is not much help to be told that this is because nature is uniform; after all, it was the uni-

---

earlier identified with abduction and later came to see as only a special mode of induction; see 8.233.

[65] See 1.35, where Peirce objects to Kant's sharp demarcation of the intuitive and discursive operations.

[66] Cf. 2.636 and 7.581. In 2.716–17 and 6.612n1, Peirce seems to allow for a looser sense of explanation that includes induction.

[67] Except where Peirce allows that unexpected events need some explanation (see 7.202), he nearly always insists that what needs explaining is uniformity: 1.405, 6.60, 6.612–13, 7.189. Such an attitude seems to me slightly unfair, unless we grant him a technical usage of 'explain.' His contrast in 6.612n of *reason* and *explanation* seems somewhat forced. There are times when we "explain" something by saying, "They always act like that." For example, "I explained to my fellow passenger that fire always comes out of the exhaust of airplane motors." In defense of Peirce, however, it must be said that this is not a very strong sense of *explain*.

[68] See 1.92, 2.633–34, 2.749 f., 2.756n1, 5.342–43, 5.508, 6.35 ff., 6.395, 6.411–14. The sense in which the notion of uniformity of nature is helpful is really scholastic realism with a different emphasis: 6.99 ff., 7.131–38, in Wiener, *Values in a Universe of Chance*, p. 295.

formity that got me interested in the first place. Besides, the doctrine puts all uniformities on the same footing. At least in Molière's time, people regularly went to sleep after putting on nightcaps; and maybe it *is* the case that someone in China had sneezed just five and a half hours before anyone has gone to sleep.[69] But if someone suggests that there is a real connection between taking opium and going to sleep, that there is "something about opium" which accounts for the fact that people always go to sleep after taking it (5.534), then, although such a suggestion "carries vagueness to its last extreme" (4.234), at least it starts me on the way to an explanation. It suggests, for example, that I might study the chemical structure of opium and other soporifics to explain what this "something about" opium is.

Virtus Dormitiva

The interesting thing about Peirce's treatment of Molière's famous burlesque of scholastic explanations is that it occurs in discussions not of abduction but of abstraction (4.234, 4.463, 5.534). Though he does not take up the connection of abstraction and abduction in any detail, there is a hint in his remark that abstraction is "the only kind of thinking that has ever advanced human culture" (3.509); for, as we have seen, Peirce insists that abduction is the only mode of inference that provides a new idea. The same attitude is reflected even more strongly in the following statement: "Intuition is the regarding of the abstract in concrete form, by the realistic hypostatization of relations; that is the one sole method of valuable thought" (1.383).

Apparently the unimaginative medical student has made a realistic hypostatization of a relation. He was asked why opium puts people to sleep: "*causam et rationem quare facit dormire*"; and he replies that it is because opium has a dormitive power: "*virtus dormitiva*" (5.534). Peirce has this to say:

It is an answer that no doubt carries vagueness to its last extreme. Yet, invented as the story was to show how little meaning there might be in an abstraction, nevertheless the physician's answer does contain a truth that modern philosophy has generally denied; it does assert that there really is in opium *something* which

---

[69] "Still, the solar system is moving through space at a great rate, and there is a bare possibility that it may have just then entered a region in which sneezing has a very surprising force" (5.8).

explains its always putting people to sleep. This has, I say, been denied by modern philosophers generally. Not, of course, explicitly; but when they say that the different events of going to sleep after taking opium have really nothing in common, but only that the mind classes them together—and this is what they virtually do say in denying the reality of generals—they do implicitly deny that there is any true explanation of opium's generally putting people to sleep [4.234].

There are actually a number of issues involved in the passage just quoted, which must be straightened out if we are to understand Peirce's position. We might begin by making explicit the nominalistic account that Peirce opposes.

In holding that there is nothing common to the various cases where going to sleep follows taking opium, the nominalist is forced to treat the uniformity involved as he does the uniformity between someone sneezing in China and people going to sleep.[70] "Opium puts people to

[70] D. C. Williams has rather gently suggested that a considerable weight is being placed here on the distinction between "accidental" and "essential" qualities. The point is an important and unfortunately complicated one. In the first place, Peirce seems to suggest that it is by prediction that we make the distinction betwen accidental uniformities and "real connections." But if all crows happen to be black, prediction alone will not suffice to show whether blackness is an "essential quality" of crows. The same criticism holds for the general contention that prediction is the definitive element in scientific method. Actually, I agree with Williams, for Peirce seems to me to be trading on a more or less uncritical, but surely unaccounted for, notion of causality (see pp. 108 ff.). In another place, however, I have suggested that the proper distinction of accidental and essential quality for Peirce should be made on the basis of the various levels or orders of predicates (n. 52 and p. 105).

Now the further question arises, is an "accidental" similarity any less a problem of universals than an "essential" one? Here again, I think Professor Williams and I, while far from holding the same solution, agree on the nature of the problem. For Peirce, however, a "real connection" (causal?) has the special status of a system. As I have tried to explain, Peirce is interested in the generality of a system, not because there can be similar sets of things so systematized, but because a system itself consists in a special interrelatedness of more than one thing. However odd this may be, it seems to me to be a very important part of Peirce's realism. And I think Professor Williams and I would also agree that Peirce is providing more of a subtle shift in the problem than a subtle solution to the age-old chestnut about universals.

Finally, there is the question of whether any nominalist would say that "there is nothing really in common about the different events, etc." (or, for that matter, about different black crows). Peirce claims that the nominalist's account is ultimately contradictory precisely because he cannot say this although his position involves it. The nominalist seems to rest his case on a distinction between things and concepts (or mental signs); to Peirce this answers only the first question of realism (see above, pp. 46, 48, 61 and 63 f.). Peirce's solution requires some distinction between individuality and commonness if not *in re* at least *a parte rei*;

sleep," says the nominalist, means only: "It happens regularly that people go to sleep after taking opium." When asked for an explanation of the regularity, the nominalist replies that nature is uniform—an answer which Peirce says is typical of nominalism for not explaining anything (6.273).

We have still to see how the student's answer explains anything. How does 'Opium has a dormitive power' suggest something that 'Opium puts people to sleep' does not? The nominalist finds the student's answer so funny because it simply says in other words that opium puts people to sleep. To a certain extent, Peirce admits this. That is to say, although he holds that it is a true inference to conclude from 'Opium causes people to sleep' that 'Opium possesses the power of causing people to sleep,' he nevertheless maintains that the rational purport of the two propositions is the same.[71] "The peculiarity of such inference," says Peirce, "is that the conclusion relates to something—in this case a power—that the premiss says nothing about" (4.463). The rhema of the conclusion contains an additional subject.

What the student has done is to perform an hypostatic abstraction. That is, just as one changes 'The building is large' to 'The building has largeness' (4.332), or 'Honey is sweet' to 'Honey possesses sweetness' (4.235), the student has changed 'Opium puts people to sleep' to 'Opium has a putting-to-sleep character.' 'Dormitive power' adds nothing to the putting-to-sleep character; it only indicates a special relation. As we saw, Peirce uses 'relation' to indicate a relationship said to be true of one of the objects related, usually the noun-subject, the others not being considered (3.466). In much the same way, 'power' seems to indicate a lawlike relationship which is said to be true of the noun-subject or, in this case, what is usually called the cause.

What a power explains is the special regularity involved. When we say, for example, that a charged battery has a power which an uncharged battery does not, we imply that it is not a mere chance sim-

---

and I think Professor Williams and I, each in his own way, agree with Peirce. But the choice array of exotic landscapes that we offer will probably not stimulate the nominalist, with his taste for simplicity, to choose.

[71] 5.534; see also 3.417, 4.235, 1.549n, 4.463. Note also Peirce's remarks that abstraction is not distortion: 5.329.

ilarity that a motor attached to the battery will start. We feel that there is some reason why a motor attached to one battery will start while, when attached to the other, it will not. As a matter of fact, we feel that there is something about the charged battery even when it is not attached to the motor which makes it different from the uncharged battery. To explain the difference by a power is admittedly not a very good explanation.[72] What Peirce claims is that it goes a step beyond nominalism (4.234), which denies that there is a real reason for the regular behavior of batteries or opium; that is, Peirce feels that nominalism can make no distinction between a chance similarity (like a run of sixes with honest dice) and such regularities as the behavior of opium.

But cannot the nominalist maintain a *propter hoc* relation without becoming a realist? Can he not maintain that this piece of opium causes this person to sleep (which distinguishes the case from chance similarities), and still deny that there is anything common and real to the various events? The expected reply is that the nominalist has not yet explained why *all* pieces of opium cause people to go to sleep. Peirce may seem to say this, but I think his real reply is that the logic of relatives shows that to admit a real connection between taking opium and going to sleep is to admit a real general: a system whose members are the taking-opium event and the going-to-sleep event. That is, the reason he brings up the fact that opium always puts people to sleep is primarily to show that there is a real connection involved. That is why prediction is so important to Peirce's realism: in order to defeat the nominalist, Peirce has to show that there is a real difference between the similarity of a chance succession and the regularity of a real connection.

If my interpretation is correct, there is some subtlety in describing pragmatism as a method for understanding abstractions. The pragmatic maxim transforms 'x is hard' into 'If x were scratched by carborundum, it would not leave a mark'; the *hardness* is the hypostatization of the relation between test and response. The would-be, which

---

[72] See 4.235, where Peirce points out that even so simple an abstraction as *sweetness* is helpful in order to make the move to relations of relations.

Peirce insists upon in his later writings, is but the pragmatic equivalent of 'power' in the sense we have just discussed.[73] In short, pragmatism is not just a matter of changing abstract terms into concrete ones; it is the very logic of abduction (5.196–97).

Insight

At this point some remarks should be made about the noetic of abduction. From the above discussion it should be obvious that there is some analogy between abductive inference and "seeing connections" (as in 1.47–48). Indeed, Peirce calls abduction insight, instinct (5.173), and perhaps even intuition (1.383). But his own attacks on intuitive cognition (5.213 ff.) suggest that something slightly more complicated is at work here.

The stimulus for abductive inference is some experience,[74] but the abduction is not based on the past experience; ultimately, abduction is a guess.[75] Sometimes Peirce seems to hold that abduction needs no justification because it commits us to nothing more than a suggestion of what might be (5.171, 5.602). At other times he speaks as if its justification lay in its being our only hope of coming to understand the world (2.777, 5.145). The fact that, out of an infinity of possibilities, the scientist can achieve his purposes with relatively few guesses suggests to Peirce that we have an instinct for the truth and that the mind and nature must be pretty much of whole cloth.[76]

For our purposes, the significant aspect of such an analysis of abduction is its relation to the theory of reality and our knowledge of the real, which Peirce suggested in the *Berkeley* review of 1871. There he said that reality must be viewed as the goal of our mental activity and not its source. The hypotheses that man constructs do not lead

[73] And habit: 5.493; see also 2.664–66. Note also the reference to law: "To say that a body is hard, or red, or heavy, or of a given weight, or has any other property, is to say that it is subject to law and therefore is a statement referring to the future" (5.545). See chap. iv, pp. 99–101.

[74] See 2.755, 5.212, 7.43.

[75] 5.591. But see 2.638, where Peirce says that scientific hypotheses are not pure guesses, but are guided by reason.

[76] For guesses indicating an instinct for truth: 1.80, 1.630, 2.25, 2.86, 2.753, 5.431, 5.591, 7.220, 7.679–80, 7.687. For the notion of the "whole cloth": 1.81, 1.121, 1.316, 2.22, 2.34, 2.750, 2.753–54, 2.776, 4.157, 5.586, 5.591, 6.491.

away from the real but toward it, so that the origin of an hypothesis is never so important as where it leads. Abductive inference, then, is verified not by tracing it back to sensory impulse but by experimental testing of its predictions.

Although I have had to extend my analysis beyond it, the major issue in this chapter has been Peirce's treatment of the first problem of realism: the notion of logical predicability. The similarity to Scotus is particularly striking in Peirce's theory of abstraction, which involves his use of 'real' and of the distinction between first and second intention.

Needless to say, Peirce does not simply adopt the whole Scotistic framework, nor does he leave unchanged what he has used. The logic of relatives provides not only the relational treatment of law, but the even more important issue of continuity as relational generality. As a matter of fact, the peculiar way in which Peirce uses the notion of system and collection raises the suspicion that he has changed not only the solution but maybe even the problem itself.

IV

Realism and Pragmatism

Of all the topics in the philosophy of Peirce, none has received so much attention as his pragmatism. While I hope that what follows will add something to a better understanding of this complex doctrine, I must point out that I am discussing it only for what it has to do with Peirce's realism. It is in the context of his pragmatism that Peirce brings up the issue of real possibility (as well as the notion of virtual prediction), which is involved in some cases of our attribution of a character to a thing. In discussing his pragmatism, I am therefore returning to the problem of realism as it was presented in Chapter I. In the light of my discussion of Scotus, that problem can now be seen as the central issue of what I call the second question of realism: whether there is something real and general apart from the representation of the world in terms of subjects and predicates.

Except for the presentation of scholastic realism in the *Berkeley* review, the most prominent treatment of realism by Peirce occurs in the critical remarks he makes about his own early formulation of pragmatism.

From Pragmatism to Pragmaticism

In a discussion of his view that reality is the ultimate object of inquiry, apparently written about 1873,[1] he says the following about the hardness of a diamond:

[1] Burks feels that the manuscript belongs to the logical writings of 1873; see 7.336n10. The absence of an explicit use of 'would-be' and of reference to pragmatism suggests that it is an early work.

94

We say that a diamond is hard. And in what does this hardness consist? It consists merely in the fact that nothing will scratch it; therefore its hardness is entirely constituted by the fact of something rubbing against it with force without scratching it. And were it impossible that anything should rub against it in this way, it would be quite without meaning, to say that it is hard, just as it is entirely without meaning to say that virtue or any other abstraction is hard. But though the hardness is entirely constituted by the fact of another stone rubbing against the diamond, yet we do not conceive of it as beginning to be hard when the other stone is rubbed against it; on the contrary, we say that it is really hard the whole time, and has been hard since it began to be a diamond. And yet there was no fact, no event, nothing whatsoever, which made it different from any other thing which is not so hard, until the other stone rubbed against it [7.340; cf. 7.341–45].

In the article "How to Make Our Ideas Clear," published in 1878, Peirce takes up the issue again. It is here that he makes his famous statement of the pragmatic maxim: [2] "Consider what effects, that might conceivably have practical bearings, we conceive the object of our conception to have, then, our conception of these effects is the whole of our conception of the object" (5.402). Applying the maxim to the conception of a thing as hard, Peirce suggests that we mean that the thing will not be scratched by many other substances. Then he adds: "There is absolutely no difference between a hard thing and a soft thing so long as they are not brought to the test" (5.403).

Later in the same article he applies his new maxim to our conception of "reality," [3] and along the way he has this to say: "Propositions . . . like that about a diamond being hard when it is not pressed, concern much more the arrangement of our language than they do the meaning of our ideas" (5.409). It is this passage which Peirce later came to criticize, remarking that it is a barbarous abuse of our ordinary meaning of 'real' to deny real hardness to a diamond because of the *accident* of the nonarrival of carborundum (5.457).[4] By 1905 he was able to describe the error:

[2] At the time, Peirce did not call his doctrine "pragmatism," but see 5.11 ff., 5.438. The same form of the maxim is used in 5.2; and see 5.9.

[3] See 5.405 ff. It is important to keep in mind that the question of untested diamonds involves the meaning of both *hardness* and *reality*.

[4] Peirce had defended realism before he wrote "How to Make Our Ideas Clear," but he apparently had not yet made the correlation of realism and pragmatism through the notion of real possibility (5.453).

I myself went too far in the direction of nominalism when I said that it was a mere question of convenience of speech whether we say that a diamond is hard when it is not pressed upon, or whether we say that it is soft until it is pressed upon. I *now* say that experiment will prove that the diamond is hard, as a positive fact. That is, it is a real fact that it *would* resist pressure, which amounts to extreme scholastic realism [8.208].[5]

Where William James praised pragmatism for its nominalism in reducing the meaning of a conception to particular experimental actions,[6] Peirce says again and again that pragmatism involves realism.[7]

It is a commonplace now that the pragmatism that James was able to bring to the notice of such a wide circle of readers was really not the same as the theory of Peirce to which James had acknowledged his debt.[8] Peirce himself remarks that he and James would likely have developed their philosophies pretty much as they did even if pragmatism had never been heard of (5.466).[9] But the popularity that pragmatism enjoyed in the writings of James and of others, such as Schiller, was surely responsible for the re-evaluation of his own doctrine that occupied Peirce at the turn of the century (5.414).[10]

Peirce felt that pragmatism's success had done much to clarify

---

[5] See 1.422 (c. 1896) and 1.615 (1903). Concerning "How to Make Our Ideas Clear": "The error of the Essay lies in its *nominalism*" (8.214n1; cf. 8.216). Peirce had also criticized the article for its nominalism and stoicism where it implied that "the end of man is action" (5.3), but he later retracted this as unjustified (5.402n3). It might also be noted that, although the editors feel that it refers to 5.402n2, 5.402n1 could as easily refer to 5.403 ff.

[6] W. James, *Pragmatism: A New Name for Some Old Ways of Thinking* (London: Longmans, Green and Co., 1943), p. 53.

[7] "For pragmatism could hardly have entered a head that was not already convinced that there are real generals" (5.503). See also 5.423, 5.439, 5.453, 6.485, 8.208, 8.258. See John Dewey, "The Pragmatism of Peirce," *Chance, Love and Logic*, pp. 303, 307; and Morris Cohen, in the same volume, pp. xv–xxi.

[8] Cf. James, *Pragmatism*, p. 47. Perry remarks that "the modern movement known as pragmatism is largely the result of James's misunderstanding of Peirce": *Thought and Character of James*, II, 409. Of course, this does not mean that James's doctrine itself is an error. See intro., n. 33, above.

[9] Peirce sometimes stresses his affinities to James and sometimes his differences: compare 5.504n1 and 5.494 with 5.3, 5.358n. Mostly he criticizes James for his lack of precision in expressing his pragmatism (and other notions): 5.466, 6.482, 6.485.

[10] Peirce criticizes the "nominalism" of both James and Schiller in a letter to James; Perry, II, 430.

terminology and thus end empty disputation (5.207). But that was only one of the purposes for which he had designed pragmatism (5.206); the other and more positive goal was to lend support to difficult ideas, particularly thirdness, which is the category of active law or reasonableness—the category that includes his scholastic realism (5.208). The failure of other pragmatisms to assert the positive side —or, what is perhaps the same thing, the stunted development of the doctrine in its exclusively negative aspects—led Peirce to rename his theory pragmaticism (5.414).[11] More important, Peirce was also led to emphasize the elements of his theory that had been obscured in the writings of others. Two of these elements are of particular importance for us.

In the first place it had been suggested that, according to pragmatism, the meaning of a conception is equivalent to a number of individual actions. If the "effects of our conceptions" are the beliefs upon which we would act, then such an interpretation is surely unfair to Peirce; for he clearly holds that beliefs are not individual acts but general habits of action (4.53, 5.4, 5.538). However, Peirce's rebuttal is even more direct. He points out that in his original statement of the maxim, the meaning of a *conception* was held to be equivalent to *conceptions* of actions (5.402n3).[12] He is not just balancing equations; in fact, he feels that his opponents have not allowed ideas to play a big enough part in their lives (5.12).[13] In the next chapter we shall see something more of his theory of the reality of ideas. At present we can concentrate on the notion of consequence, the second distinctive element of Peirce's pragmatism.

[11] See also 8.176n3, 8.205. For the significance of '-icism' as an ending, see 5.413. In general, I have continued to use simply 'pragmatism' to designate Peirce's doctrine as a whole.

[12] Since some people labor under a delusion about the "hardheadedness" of Peirce's empiricism, a few passages about the general aim of the pragmatic maxim might be cited: 1.339, 2.293, 4.127, 5.402n3, 5.427, 5.432, 7.360–61, 8.208, 8.212, 8.250, 8.272. And on "theory" as against "practice": 1.43–44, 1.76, 1.590, 1.619, 2.644, 5.341. See also Burks, in *Classical American Philosophers*, p. 44.

[13] I hope the reader is coming to expect that these little idealistic digs will be thrown at him from time to time. It is important to see that they come up in the midst of Peirce's discussion of pragmatism.

Consequence

According to Peirce's pragmatism, the truth of a categorical proposition in which a conception (hardness) is predicated of a subject consists in the truth of a corresponding statement in the conditional form, the antecedent of which stands for a test (rubbing with force against carborundum) and the consequent of which indicates a reaction (not being scratched) (1.615, 5.18, 5.432). The logical form of the conditional proposition is what Peirce calls a consequence. We have already seen that the consequence is not to be identified with the consequent or even with the consequent-and-antecedent. It is, rather, the relation of the consequent to the antecedent.[14]

The importance of the theory of consequence for a proper understanding of the pragmatic analysis may be obscured by the fact that the very notion of a consequent suggests a relation to an antecedent. But the event referred to by the consequent does not in itself show a relation to the event referred to by the antecedent. A listing of the events referred to by the consequents of a pragmatic reformulation would not give the meaning of a conception, if only because it is solely as reactions to or results of certain tests that these events are significant. The "conception of the effects" referred to in the pragmatic maxim cannot be a statement of an event but must be a conditional statement. For Peirce, then, pragmatism shows that hardness consists not in actions or events, but in relations of actions and events, a position quite in keeping with his logical analysis of predicates as relatives.

The stress upon the would-be, characteristic of his later writings on pragmatism, carries the relation of consequence one step further.[15] If the hardness of a diamond consists in the conditional fact that it *would* give a certain response to a test, then hardness is not just this present and actual relation which holds between this test and this re-

---

[14] It was Moore who, in his thesis, Metaphysics and Pragmatism in the Philosophy of Peirce (pp. 147–48), brought out the significance of this point for Peirce's pragmatism. See also his book, *American Pragmatism: Peirce, James and Dewey*, pp. 44 f.

[15] See esp. 5.467–68 (where Peirce speaks of "this kernel of pragmatism"); cf. 5.453, 6.485.

sponse, but a general relation that holds for all possible tests and responses of this type.

The Actual and the Potential

The notion of the would-be in Peirce's pragmatism involves two points. First, the would-be is a relation that is independent of past, present, and future events: it ranges over possible cases and is therefore general.[16] Second, and more important, the would-be in some way *controls* the events. We shall take these two points up in order.

The general principle behind the first point can be seen in Peirce's insistence that the pragmatist does indeed hold that the meaning of a conception lies in its reference to some experience: it indicates the possibility of an experience. While Peirce grants that it is important to stress the role of experience, he finds no less important the element of possibility.[17] If a diamond has been tested for hardness, it is not the past test that constitutes its hardness. If I have tested the diamond and found it hard, I do not conceive of its hardness as being something exclusively past: it is something present and future as well. Similarly, if I am now rubbing the diamond with carborundum, the would-be is not lost in what now is; the possibility is not destroyed even when it is being actualized.[18] And finally, even though the meaning of hardness has a reference to the future, it is not a reference to any particular action. When I say that it would so react, there is no particular event I could now specify: in speaking of a possibility I am not speaking of a collection of discrete acts.[19]

---

[16] "And do not overlook the fact that the pragmaticist maxim says nothing of single experiments or of single experimental phenomena (for what is conditionally true *in futuro* can hardly be singular), but only speaks of *general kinds* of experimental phenomena" (5.426). See also 6.327, 8.216–17.

[17] "You forget perhaps that a realist fully admits that a sense quality is only a possibility of sensation; but he thinks that it remains possible when it is not actual. The sensation is requisite for its apprehension; but no sensation nor sense-faculty is requisite for the possibility which is the being of the quality. Let us not put the cart before the horse, nor the evolved actuality before the possibility as if the latter *involved* what it only *evolves*. A similar answer may be made to the other nominalists" (1.422).

[18] For example, one does not lose the power of sight just because he happens, at present, to be seeing something (cf. 4.640).

[19] See 4.172 (quoted on p. 78, above), 5.436, 5.528.

Since the meaning of a conception in terms of the pragmatic re-formulation cannot be reduced to any actuality or (discrete) collection of actualities,[20] Peirce concludes that the pragmatist must admit to a theory of real possibility (5.45). Notice how the conclusion comes about: if the pragmatist holds that the meaning of a conception like *hardness* consists in the conception of a relation between two events, and if he holds that hardness is not just this single event or a specifiable and discrete series of single events, then hardness must consist in the relation of possible events; but if things are now really hard, then there must be real possibility (5.457).[21]

The theory of real possibility has a far-reaching effect on pragmatism. Peirce actually builds the theory into the logical structure of the pragmatic maxim:

Some years ago, however, when in consequence of an invitation to deliver a course of lectures in Harvard University upon Pragmatism, I was led to revise that doctrine, in which I had already found difficulties, I soon discovered, upon critical analysis, that it was absolutely necessary to insist upon and bring to the front, the truth that a mere possibility may be quite real. That admitted, it can no longer be granted that every conditional proposition whose antecedent does not happen to be realized is true . . . [4.580].[22]

Although there are scattered references in his writings to the problem of treating modalities within the framework of a formal logical system, nowhere can one find anything like a complete development of the topic.[23] However, it is a sign of how important the doctrine of real possibility is to Peirce that he makes no effort to rework the material conditional so that it might be used as the basis for the pragmatic maxim; Peirce simply says that the conditional proposition of the pragmatic reformulation has a peculiar and essentially modal structure.[24]

---

[20] See 1.615, 5.436, 5.457, 5.467.

[21] For Peirce's own remarks on the importance of real possibility to the early articles, see 5.453, 5.526 ff.

[22] See also 4.546.

[23] "This renders may-be's and must-be's very delicate objects for thought to handle, and propositions concerning them that sound absurd sometimes express plain facts. This, however, is a matter that I cannot pretend to have got to the bottom of; and logic here seems to touch metaphysics" (6.182).

[24] By the material conditional I mean one that is false only if its antecedent is true and its consequent is false; in all other cases it is true. See 3.374, 3.441–44,

The second important point about the pragmatic would-be is that in some sense it governs events. The pragmatist expresses the hardness of a diamond by saying that the diamond has a would-be; that is, the diamond is so disposed as to act in a certain way when certain conditions are realized. As we have just seen, Peirce says this involves a real possibility. We are now interested in what might be called a real potentiality: [25] the hardness of the diamond is not just a might-be but a would-be. When I say that a diamond is hard, I do not mean just that it *may* resist scratching by carborundum, I mean that it very likely will. The same is true of opium's dormitive virtue and the power of a battery.[26] The tendency to act "in a way describable in general terms upon every occasion (or upon a considerable proportion of occasions) that may present itself of a generally describable character" is what Peirce terms a habit (5.538).

Habit, however, is not limited to human activity. To say, for example, that a die has a certain would-be

is to say that it has a property quite analogous to any *habit* that a man might have. Only the "would-be" of the die is presumably as much simpler and more definite than the man's habit as the die's homogeneous composition and cubical shape is simpler than the nature of man's nervous system and soul; and just as it would be necessary, in order to define a man's habit, to describe how it would lead him to behave and upon what sort of occasion—albeit this statement would by no means imply that the habit *consists* in that action—so to define the die's "would-be," it is necessary to say how it would lead the die to behave on an occasion that would bring out the full consequence of the "would-be"; and this statement will not of itself imply that the "would-be" of the die *consists* in such behaviour [2.664].

The upshot of this is simply that Peirce's pragmatism and realism are closely connected. Pragmatism shows that the meaning of a conception like *hardness* ultimately involves the notion of would-be, habit,

---

4.435, 4.579. On modality in general, see esp. 4.552–53 and notes. See also 5.537, where Peirce criticizes Schiller, who "does not wish us to devote any attention to the effects of conditions that do not occur, or at any rate not to substitute the solution of such a problem for the true problems of nature. For my part, I think such talk shows great ignorance of the conditions of science."

[25] If 'possibility' and 'potentiality' do not seem to the reader distinct enough, he might follow Peirce's own (occasional) contrast of 'potentiality' and 'conditional necessity.' See 1.427, quoted on p. 127, below.

[26] See pp. 90 f., above.

or power. A power or habit is a nonrelational expression for a law; [27] if habits "are not mere fantasies but are real agencies" (5.493), and do not consist in the actual behavioral events, then there are real laws which govern but are not themselves individual events.[28]

Before going on to consider how his realistic pragmatism developed, we might throw more light on Peirce's attitude by comparing his "would-be" with a traditional philosophical problem: the scholastic nature or substantial form. Oddly enough, Peirce does not mention at all a very interesting forerunner to pragmatism: the scholastic maxim *operari sequitur esse*.[29] The scholastics reasoned that the operations or activities of a thing reflected a corresponding perfection in that thing, which would account for its ability to perform that sort of operation. It was on the basis of this principle that they were able to specify natures and natural classes. If a man performs an action that other animals cannot, such as reasoning, then the man has a power that other animals do not possess. If such a capacity is the distinguishing characteristic, it is dignified with the title 'nature.' [30] Peirce's only objection to the scholastic substantial form as a dispositional character—aside from the question of how scientific one is in determining distinguishing characters (6.361)—is that it fails to reveal the relational structure which is ultimately involved. That is, the scholastics were right as far as they went, but their limited logic did not allow them to see that the nature, power, or disposition represented in these monadic predicates is only a truncated image of a relational law. Apparently it was the old logic's inability to handle abstractions properly that was mainly at fault (3.642). I take this to mean that the scholastics did not realize that their most important abstractions

[27] On character and law, see 5.545; on habit and law, 2.148. See also p. 73, above.

[28] "A habit is the *general* way in which one *would* act *if* such and such a *general* kind of occasion *were* to occur. To say it really explains anything is to make a general real, and knock the pins from under every nominalistic philosophy" (Widener I B 3, "Notes on Portions of Hume's 'Treatise of Human Nature,'" p. 22). See also 2.664–67, 5.538, 6.152.

[29] See P. Coffey, *Ontology, or the Theory of Being* (London: Longmans, Green and Co., 1914), p. 137. The literal translation, "to operate follows upon to be," is perhaps not as helpful as Coffey's paraphrase: "that the properties and activities of things are our only key to the natures or essences of these things."

[30] Cf. 6.361.

were really hypostatized relations and, therefore, that real abstractions indicated real relations—laws and not forms.[31]

But notice what happens to the problem as Peirce takes it on to the "higher" stage of relations. The schoolmen were disturbed by the fact that a number of different things "have the same nature." They did not want to say that the nature is itself a "thing," in the way that the things that have the nature are. However real they make the nature (in order to account for the similarity), they hesitate to say that the nature as it exists in Socrates is general; for then it would be difficult to say how Socrates is still an individual.[32] But this problem becomes secondary for Peirce. In order to demonstrate real generals, he need only show that the actions of Socrates reveal a real relation. The answer to the question of similarity is but the limiting case of real relations, as a collection is the limiting case of a system. Consequently, Peirce will not attempt to answer the question of similarity until he has taken up the case of real relations. In order to follow Peirce's approach, I have left the problem of relating these two questions for the next chapter.

Peirce's Nominalism

We can now take up in some detail Peirce's criticism of his own "too nominalistic" discussion of the diamond that was not tested. To avoid being misled, it is very important that we be clear about what Peirce rejects and what he retains of his earlier statements. He says he probably oversimplified the case (although he admits he may have wavered in his opinion) when he dismissed the question of whether

[31] W. B. Gallie puts considerable emphasis on the fact that Peirce held a "relational realism" in contrast to the "substantival realism" of the scholastics (*Peirce and Pragmatism* [Edinburgh: R. and R. Clarke, Ltd., 1952], pp. 153, 156–57). The point is an important one (see chap. v, pp. 124 ff.), but the terminology could be misleading. The distinction has nothing to do with whether one thinks that generals are things (first substances) or not; in fact, the "substantival realism" of the middle ages was generally not as extreme on this point as Peirce's own "relational realism." I also wonder whether one who is disturbed by real generals would find Cause-of or Scratched-by much less odious than Horse or Zebra.

[32] Even Scotus, who holds that the Common Nature has an *esse reale*, insists that in the individual the nature is more individual than universal. See above, p. 58.

that diamond was really hard (5.453). Actually, it *is* a matter of classification, but ". . . classification is either true or false, and the generals to which it refers are either reals in the one case or figments in the other." [33]

In general, the error of the first article lay in the implication that it dealt with an individual and isolated event; [34] in reality, besides the unnoticed effects which that diamond's hardness may have had upon the rest of the world, there are many considerations, involving other properties of the diamond, which are in turn related to the property of hardness (5.457). The error seems to have come about because Peirce was not faithful to the statement of the pragmatic maxim at the beginning of the article, which should have made it clear that the question was one of what *would* happen (5.453).

The extent of Peirce's re-evaluation comes out a little more directly when he explains the peculiarity of the pragmatic would-be in a letter to F. A. Woods (8.380–82). Peirce imagines that an historian has said something to this effect: "If Napoleon had done such and such, he would have won the battle of Leipzig." If the statement refers to some individual event, then Peirce holds that it is meaningless: it is absurd to talk about what follows from an event that did not occur.[35] But he goes on to say that such formulations are really intended to call our attention to a general rule; for example: If anyone were in a position like that of Napoleon at Leipzig, then such and such an action would achieve victory.

The same analysis can be applied to the case of the diamond. If there has been no test from which we could learn directly or indirectly about its hardness, and if it has had no effect at all from which we might in future come upon such information, then it is meaningless to talk of that diamond's being hard or soft. Peirce never wavers on this point (1.615), any more than he does on the somewhat similar issue of the meaninglessness of probability in connection with individual events (2.652, 2.661). What he had overlooked in the original article was the possibility that the way we "choose to talk

---

[33] See also 1.27, 1.204–31, 1.249, 5.105–6.
[34] This is a "nominalistic" error, according to Peirce: 6.93, 6.593.
[35] See n. 34, above. See also 5.463, 5.543, 5.589, 7.105.

about" the individual case might reflect upon our belief in a real law. Diamondness is just as much a would-be as hardness, although on a different level.[36] For a diamond to have that power which we call its hardness, it need not be constantly pressed upon; and for us to know that it has this power, we need not be constantly running tests. What Peirce saw in his revision was that the same is true of diamondness on its own level: it is not necessary to test for the presence of every property of a diamond in order to determine whether it possesses that complex character peculiar to diamonds—a complex character that involves hardness.

In the original article Peirce had concentrated on the explication of hardness, and he wanted to emphasize that, according to pragmatism, our meanings essentially involve expectation of the results of an experiment. Peirce never changes his mind on this point either.[37] What he points out in his later writings is that it is *just because* pragmatism requires that meaning consist only in the expectation of future actualities that the pragmatist must admit that the present possibility is real (5.457). In glossing over the element of real possibility in the early article (5.453, 5.527), Peirce was open to the charge of what he had himself called the nominalistic error of holding that the possible is only what the actual makes it to be (1.422).

We can summarize Peirce's later position by stating it in terms of consequent and consequence. Peirce never denies that the consequent must be empirical,[38] although he cautions the pragmatist not to be too hasty in deciding what is capable of verification,[39] and he suggests that something can be verified without direct observation.[40] For Peirce, however, it is one thing to verify the consequent and another to verify the consequence; for the consequent specifies a certain event, while the consequence represents a general relation.[41] The failure to

---

[36] See n. 52, chap. iii.

[37] See 5.411–12, 5.427 (1905).

[38] 5.196 ff., 5.411–12, 5.427, 5.536.

[39] 1.138, 2.511n, 2.640, 5.196, 5.409, 5.542, 5.547–48, 5.597, 6.556, 8.61.

[40] 5.198, 5.597, 8.195; see also 2.640, 2.642, 5.457, 5.542, 8.61.

[41] 5.196–205, 6.327, 6.523 ff., 7.331, 8.61; see also 1.43, 6.182. Cf. the analysis of "terminating" and "non-terminating" judgments in C. I. Lewis, *Analysis of Knowledge and Valuation* (LaSalle, Illinois: The Open Court Publishing Company, 1946), pp. 184–95 and chap. viii *passim*.

distinguish consequence from consequent can result in a serious mis-understanding of the content of his empiricism.[42]

One source of confusion lies in what I think is the mistaken notion that pragmatism must be a reductionist theory. A reductionist prag-matism, as I understand it, contends that only actual events are real—powers and laws, abstractions of all sorts, are only shorthand expres-sions for actual events. On such an interpretation, pragmatism vali-dates the use of abstractions by providing a formula by which these shorthand expressions can be translated into their full, explicit form in terms of basic propositions about actual events. That is to say, the pragmatic maxim is a formula by which all statements that are not event-statements are reduced to a series of statements containing only event-statements.

It seems to me that Peirce's pragmatism was never intended to be like this at all. For him the pragmatic maxim is a reformulation, in-tended to expose the structure of our conceptions and indicate their reference to actual events. Only the actual events "exist," but they do not exhaust the "real" (6.349); [43] besides events, there are relations of events.

The distinction between a pragmatism that refers our conceptions to events and one that reduces conceptions to events is obscured, per-haps, by an unfortunate tendency to regard the logical form of the pragmatic reformulation as nonreferential and therefore somehow extraneous. If for every proposition that mentions powers, charac-ters, or laws we can find an equivalent proposition that mentions only events, then have we not exorcised these mysterious things? The upshot of Peirce's reworking of his own pragmatism is, as I see it, simply a negative answer to this question. His pragmatism has re-placed a mysterious entity by an equally mysterious relation. The gain

---

[42] While I have no doubt that there is a good deal of confusion in the way Peirce expresses himself at various times, I think it would be unfortunate if his (admittedly important) statements about the need for actual experience were to obscure what is pretty clearly a basic attitude concerning the status of theoretical knowledge. See, for example, his discussion of the three types of men (1.43–45), and the references cited in n. 12, above.

[43] "But existence is the smallest element of the reality even of those things that exist . . ."; Widener I C 1b, c, "How Did Science Originate?" p. 5. See chap. v, pp. 118 ff.

is not that we have rid the world of powers and laws, but that we have found a way of expressing our meanings so that we can tell a real law from a fiction.

Far from having no counterpart, the logical form of pragmatism is the burden of Peirce's whole theory. Our "conception of the effects" is not what is represented in the consequent, but what is represented in the consequence. The rhema of a pragmatic reformulation, however less odious are the nouns and adjectives it contains, is already "loaded" simply by its modal form; 'were to' and 'would' function as syncategorematics—ones that are just as significant as 'not.' In describing *hardness* as a would-be, Peirce calls specific attention to the fact that the complex character which issues from his pragmatic reformulation involves the structure of the consequence.

A further indication of Peirce's attitude can be found in his rather quaint talk of "occult forces" and "occult natures." [44] The occult, he tells us, was originally meant to indicate what could not be deduced from primary elements but required some experiment (6.595n1, 7.392n7). That the occult is discovered by experiment and yet cannot be directly observed does not disturb him at all:

The things that any science discovers are beyond the reach of direct observation. We cannot see energy, nor the attraction of gravitation, nor the flying molecules of gases, nor the luminiferous ether, nor the forests of the carbonaceous era, nor the explosions in the nerve cells. It is only the premises of science, not its conclusions, which are directly observed [6.2].

And again, when criticizing James, Peirce mentions the same theories and says: "All these are 'attempts to explain phenomenally given elements as products of deeper-lying entities.' In fact, this phrase describes, as well as loose language can, the general character of scientific hypothesis" (8.60).

Peirce's contention that laws and powers explain something is of itself good evidence that he does not hold a reductionist theory. A law or power hardly explains the actual events if it is merely a shorthand expression for them. Peirce finds it necessary to reformulate the law in terms of the events *not* because only the events are real, but because the only content of the law is that it explains such events.

[44] 5.440, 5.457, 5.517n1, 5.581, 6.595, 7.392.

If this means that a law or power is a cause—and I think it pretty clearly does—[45] the pragmatic would-be is even more remarkable: "But if there is any *would-be* at all, there is more or less causation; for that is all that I mean by causation" (8.225n10).

When I say that the way Peirce talks of laws and powers as explanations indicates pretty clearly that they are causes, I do not at all mean to suggest that I find what he says about causes and explanations pretty clear. He never seems to be able to make up his mind whether he should avoid talking of causes completely (as in 6.600) or whether he should use the term 'cause' in his own special sense (as in the passage just quoted).[46] As far as I can make out, however, despite his attempts to present a theory of explanation in terms of the syllogism,[47] he leans rather heavily on the ordinary notion that you explain something by citing its cause.[48]

On the other hand, Peirce is explicit about one aspect of his theory of causality: he insists that a single event cannot be a cause (6.67, 6.600). An opium-taking event does not, strictly speaking, cause a

[45] Peirce seems to be saying that we do reason from evidence to something other than the evidence, which, whether it is itself observed or not, is considered real because the evidence that it explains is real. A simple model for such investigation is the detective story. A police force may have on its hands a corpse with a hole in its head. But although no policeman ever sees or touches the murderer— that is, although the murderer is known only as what explains a hole in the head —the police do not think of the murderer *as* a hole in the head. The peculiarity of such cases, however, lies in the fact that the existence of the murderer only explains the hole in the head of the corpse because the murderer is what put the hole there. As a result, I find that Peirce's remark that abduction is reasoning from consequent to antecedent *or* from effect to cause tells me more about Peirce's notion of consequence than it does about his view of causality.

[46] See 6.66–69, where Peirce discusses the confusions in the use of 'cause' (but where he seems to mean the mechanistic analysis only). This does not stop him from using the word at other times: see 2.707 and 6.460, for example.

[47] E.g., 2.716.

[48] If, for example, you are trying to sell someone a car and he inquires about a certain noise, you might say, "Oh, all the cars of this model make that noise." But he might well object that you have not explained the noise until you tell him what *makes* it. I do not think that Peirce gets beyond this in his notion of explanation. That is, the fact that the consequent follows from the antecedent in his natural laws seems to me an extralogical consideration, which always rests upon some sort of causal sequence. I do not find such a theory particularly objectionable, except inasmuch as Peirce seems to imply that it is the syllogism and not the "causal law" that explains.

going-to-sleep event. Opium's power, which explains why a person goes to sleep after taking opium, is not itself an event. This means that Peirce uses 'cause' like 'power': as a relation for which the corresponding relationship is *law*. That is, to say that something is the cause of another thing is to say that the former is the noun-subject of a causal law.[49] Remembering from the last chapter that Peirce conceived of a collection as the limiting case of systems, we would expect that if the would-be delimits a causal system, the simple character represented by a monadic predicate will be the "cause" or "explanation" of the members of a collection. If I understand him correctly, I find Peirce saying just that in the following passage:

When we have drawn any statistical induction . . . . it is always possible to discover, by investigation sufficiently prolonged, a class of which the same predicate may be affirmed universally. . . . The truth of this principle follows immediately from the theorem that there is a character peculiar to every possible group of objects. The form in which the principle is usually stated is that *every event must have a cause* [6.414].[50]

It must be pointed out, however, that in denying that events are causes, Peirce is not denying that "individuals," in the sense that Socrates is an individual, can be causes. As we shall see in the next chapter, Peirce not only holds that Socrates is not an event, but he goes on to say that Socrates is not strictly an individual.[51] For the realist, Peirce says, "things" do not *need* reasons: they *are* reasons (4.36).

Realism and Pragmatism: a Problem

Although we have not by any means exhausted the possibilities of the topic,[52] we have seen enough of Peirce's theory of causal laws to go on to consider a more general problem concerning the compatibility of that theory with pragmatism. The problem is set out specifi-

---

[49] See above, pp. 73, 90, 102–3.

[50] For another approach to the passage, see Thompson, *Pragmatic Philosophy of Peirce*, pp. 93–95 (and his note 5).

[51] See chap. v, pp. 138 ff.

[52] There is evidently much to be done toward finding out precisely what Peirce does mean by 'cause,' 'explanation,' and related words. I am inclined to think, however, that at bottom his theory rests on a notion of "real connections." As a result, I imagine that Peirce would have approved of the statement of the issue by C. I. Lewis, *Analysis of Knowledge and Valuation*, pp. 126 ff.

cally by Arthur Burks,[53] although I think his presentation is symptomatic of a general concern. Burks suggests that we ask whether there would be a *pragmatic* difference between Peirce's theory of causal laws and the nominalist's account. A genuine dispute between the two, Burks says, can occur only if there are practical consequences to a proposition that deals solely with potentialities. But pragmatism denies this by requiring that all significant propositions have a reference to experience. Consequently, ". . . as far as action is concerned everything we need to know to guide our conduct can be stated in the indicative mood"; [54] or, to put the matter differently, ". . . action is based on actualities and not on potentialities." [55]

I think that this is one of those places where conflicting tendencies in two of Peirce's doctrines should make us ask whether perhaps "something has not escaped our notice" (5.429). As a matter of fact, the problem Burks has raised offers us a chance to see more clearly what Peirce means by both his realism and his pragmatism. To begin with, let me state the problem in a slightly different form: does the pragmatic formulation in terms of "would-be" account for any experience not accounted for by its indicative counterpart?

Notice, first of all, that the indicative form of the pragmatic maxim requires that the consequent be stated in the future tense. Unfortunately, it is the will-be that becomes ambiguous in the crucial case of prediction—which is the point of the byplay with the stone in the Harvard lectures. If I know *now* that the stone will fall—and it is essential that Peirce pick a case where I am willing to say that I do know what will happen [56]—then what is the object of my knowledge? The fact "that the stone will fall" is not a future fact but a fact about the future; and to know at present a fact about the future is just the oddity that Peirce is interested in pointing out.

If in every case we simply wait and see what does happen before we say we know anything, the nominalist is safe. Indeed, this is just what

[53] See Burks's introduction to Peirce in *Classic American Philosophers*, pp. 41–53.

[54] *Ibid.*, p. 51.

[55] *Ibid.*

[56] As in 5.93, where the audience thinks it will be a "very silly experiment." See also 2.667.

Peirce says the nominalist ought to do: abstain from all prediction (5.210). But prediction is itself a fact.[57] What Peirce charges is that the nominalist does not explain it; or, in terms of our present problem, that the pragmatic reformulation in terms of will-be does not adequately represent it. That is, if the *will-be* of a consequent is only a statement of a future actuality in the indicative mood, how is it different from any other future fact? Why do we say that we know *now* in some cases and not say that in others?

This brings us to a second ambiguity in the problem. For if we are to apply a pragmatic test to the question of nominalism and realism, it must be Peirce's pragmatism that is used; and for Peirce it is the consequence and not the consequent which is at issue. What is involved here is of considerable importance: it is the question (or one part of the question) of what a scientist is trying to find out. Is he interested only in events that happen? Then the thing for him to do is to wait and see what does happen; science becomes a matter of writing down 'x happened' and 'y happened' and so forth. What Peirce is claiming is that after a certain number of well-devised experiments, the scientist has found out more than just that a series of actual events took place: he has discovered a relation of events, and he can prove his extra knowledge by prediction.[58] Pragmatism shows that this knowledge of something extra, of powers and laws, has content only in reference to the behavior it is intended to explain. But this does not mean that only the behavior is real. The behavior alone is actual, to be sure; but Peirce's conclusion is that the pragmatist must therefore hold that some possibilities are real.[59]

The objector might reply that he has no intention of making the scientist a lover of sights and sounds; but if pragmatism insists that a

[57] ". . . it is not the fact predicted that in any degree necessitates the truth of [an] hypothesis or even renders it probable. It is the fact that it has been predicted successfully . . ." (6.527). And note that in 5.93 Peirce says: "I will *prove* that I can make a correct prediction . . ." [italics mine]. See also 1.26, 8.153.

[58] See n. 57, above.

[59] "Now what *would* be, can, it is true, only be learned through observation of what happens to be; but nevertheless no collection of happenings can constitute one trillionth of one *per cent* of what might be, and would be under supposable conditions" (6.327). On the "actual" and the "real," see 6.453.

real difference must at some point reflect a difference in experience, where is that point in the dispute between realistic law and nominalistic uniformity? The nominalist predicts on the basis of an inductively established uniformity, reasoning from the constitution of a sample to that of a class. The only actualities involved are the past events and the tests that are actually run, and the uniformity is only these similar actual events; a law is simply a particularly striking uniformity. Such is, in fact, the way Peirce conceives of the nominalist position. He says, for example, that the idea that a law admits of no exceptions is nominalistic: there cannot be exceptions to a law that consists only in what happens (6.613).[60]

Peirce's objection to the nominalists' account is that ultimately it puts all uniformities on the same footing—there is no more reason for saying that the next stone will drop because stones have dropped uniformly in the past than there is for saying that the next throw of the dice will show "sixes" because there has been a run of sixes in the past (6.99). In short, there is no *propter hoc* but only *post hoc* (1.213). But we are willing to predict from some uniformities and not from others. If we turn this reasoning around, we find the basis for Peirce's argument for the realistic interpretation of pragmatism. The would-be makes it explicit that the meaning of our conceptions involves a virtual prediction, and prediction shows there is something more than a uniformity involved.

The Via Media

In order to appreciate Peirce's position, it may be helpful to take an even broader perspective on the problem. It is undoubtedly important to recognize that pragmatism is something of a two-edged sword; and it is equally important to point out that Peirce had trouble in handling his own weapon. What is often overlooked, however, is the fact that Peirce designed his pragmatism to meet two foes and not just one. Pragmatism must be proved, Peirce says:

---

[60] Notice that the nominalistic account tends to undercut Peirce's theory of abduction as inference (6.525). That is, abduction is no longer seen as an inference to a real connection, but is only a stimulus to observations; see 2.511n on the

. . . in the teeth of Messrs. Bradley, Taylor, and other high metaphysicians, on the one hand, and of the entire nominalistic nation, with its Wundts, its Haeckels, its Karl Pearsons, and many other regiments, in their divers uniforms, on the other [5.468].

We saw something of the same attitude earlier in the twofold purpose of Peirce's pragmatism: to clear away thinking not based on experience, but at the same time to give support to difficult ideas (5.206-8). To comprehend this, the "bare definition of pragmaticism" is not enough (5.416).

Peirce admits to the nominalist that a would-be can "only be learned through observation of what happens to be" (6.327), but he insists that a would-be cannot consist simply in what happens to be actual (2.664, 4.464, 6.327). It is true that pragmatism makes thought ultimately apply to action, that is,

to *conceived* action. But between admitting that and either saying that it makes thought, in the sense of the purport of symbols, to consist in acts, or saying that the true ultimate purpose of thinking is action, there is much the same difference as there is between saying that the artist-painter's living art is applied to dabbing paint upon canvas, and saying that that art-life consists in dabbing paint, or that its ultimate aim is dabbing paint [5.402n3].

Similarly, Peirce is willing to side with the "high metaphysicians"; he holds there are real powers, habits, or laws that are occult precisely because, unlike actual events, they are not observable. But he is quick to point out that the occult state of things cannot consist in "anything but the truth of a general conditional proposition" (5.457). The only approach we have to the occult is through the kind of action it stimulates (5.457, 5.517n1), and to transcend the limits of this approach by maintaining that the occult is something "other" than the real relation of events is to cut oneself off from the only contact with the real that the human mind is capable of.[61] The "antisynechistic thinkers" get themselves all snarled up in problems of what sort of thing this "other" might be (5.440).

In a manuscript not published in the *Collected Papers*, Peirce

positivists. See also 7.331, where Peirce says that observation is not the whole of investigation.

[61] Such, I think, is the way Peirce interprets Kant's dictum that the human mind cannot transcend the limits of possible experience: see 5.525, 5.536, 6.96.

tries to set forth his pragmatic realism in opposition to the dangers of both extremes. The language is perhaps objectionable, but the import is clear enough:

Much that happens certainly happens according to Natural Law; and what is this Law but something whose being consists in its determining Matter to Form in a certain way? Many metaphysicians will answer that Law does not *make* Matter to become determined to Form but only *recognizes* in a general way, that which happens quite independently. But do these men mean to say that it is merely by chance that all stones allowed to drop have hitherto fallen? If so, there is no reason to suppose that it will be so with the next stone we may let loose. To say that would be to paralyze reason. But if it is not mere chance, then evidently it has some cause or reason. To say that this is a sign is merely to say that it has its being in producing that union of Form and Matter. Why suppose it has any further being, especially since in order to do so, you must evoke a conception that the human mind has never possessed? You might talk of such a thing, but think it you could not. Nor does anybody propose that. Those who hate to admit that anything of the nature of a sign can act upon matter imagine that they can express the phenomena with less, and do not dream of insisting upon more. Less and more are equally impossible.[62]

Toward Idealism

It is now possible to summarize my answer to Professor Burks's objection that there is no pragmatic difference between Peirce's own realism and nominalism. In the first place, I simply cannot admit that the pragmatic realist must show that propositions about potentialities alone have practical consequences.[63] In fact, all Peirce has to show is that propositions about actualities alone will not cover every real case; and he contends that one cannot state, in terms of actualities alone, what it is that one knows now which allows the prediction of the future behavior of certain things. His treatment of prediction has problems of its own, and for *some* pragmatists (that is, reductionists) the distinction between nominalism and realism might be meaningless; but I do not see that the discussion is cut off by Peirce's pragmatism.

My main objection to Burks's presentation, however, is that it tends to stop us before we examine one of the most interesting aspects of Peirce's philosophy: the way in which pragmatism affects the theory of what sort of thing a real general is. Burks's remark that

[62] Widener I A 1, "Sketch of Dichotomic Mathematics," pp. 49–50.
[63] Burks, in *Classic American Philosophers*, p. 51.

"action is based on actualities, not on potentialities" [64] is only partly true for Peirce. A power must be described in terms of events—and it is precisely that requirement which obliges the pragmatist to "subscribe to the doctrine of real Modality" (5.457)—but it is the power that explains (*viz.*, causes) the events, and not vice versa. The sense in which Peirce *does* hold that the potential is based on the actual involves the idea that the future acts upon the present (1.213, 2.86).

It is Peirce's pragmatism, then, that provides an important step in the development of his theory that laws operate in the manner of final and not efficient causes; and this is a major part of his panpsychism. It has been recognized by others that Peirce's analysis of meaning is extreme in its emphasis upon the future.[65] But as I hope to show in the next chapter, this doctrine also has a metaphysical counterpart. Indeed, pragmatism is said to support the definition of reality as the ultimate object of inquiry; [66] and Peirce can say that "the true idealism, the pragmatistic idealism, is that reality consists in the *future*" (8.284).

The major concern of this chapter has been to set forth the reasons Peirce gives for holding that there is something real and general; it is the first step in what I earlier called the second question of realism (or of real commonness). I hope to have shown that it is the pragmatic account of scientific prediction upon which Peirce bases his argument for the reality of generals. I also wanted to bring out how the conflict between realism and pragmatism has reciprocal effects upon both doctrines. It was clearly Peirce's realism that led him to revise his interpretation of the pragmatic maxim; but by keeping in mind what Peirce does *not* change in his pragmatism, we gain an insight into

---

[64] *Ibid.*

[65] See esp. 5.461. See Lovejoy's attack on Peirce in *Studies in the Philosophy of Peirce*, pp. 12 ff.; and Buchler's defense, in the same volume, p. 27.

[66] 5.4, 5.354, 5.402n2. There is also an interesting passage in the manuscripts, Widener I A 1, "Sketch of Dichotomic Mathematics," p. 51: "The true and perfect reality, the very thing, is the thing as it might be truly represented, as it would be truly represented were thought carried to its last perfection. . . . The real and true thing is the thing as it might be known to be." One cannot help but wonder whether this is not one of those places where odd statements about modalities really express only simple facts (cf. 6.182, quoted in n. 23, above).

the ultimate structure of his realism. By insisting upon the conditional analysis of our conceptions, and at the same time restricting the actual to individual events, Peirce has incorporated into his system a special theory of real potentiality, which carries with it a decided "futurism." The theory of real modality, in turn, conditions Peirce's analysis of the status of the (law of) nature in itself, and thus provides the link to his idealism.

V

Realism and Idealism

Up to now, our explicit concern has been the evidence that Peirce finds for the reality of general types and laws, and the logical or semiotic structure of our expression of that reality. That is, we have examined Peirce's analysis of predicates as general (which corresponds to Scotus' treatment of the logical universal), as well as his conception of the real modality that is reflected in certain propositions about the world (corresponding to Scotus' attempt to prove a real but less-than-numerical unity). Actually, Peirce's pragmatism overlaps these two issues. As an analysis of the meaning of our conceptions, it is primarily concerned with the structure of our expression. But in the sense that certain instances of predictive knowledge "oblige" the pragmatist to "subscribe to a doctrine of Real Modality" (5.457)—that is, in the sense that the pragmatist must hold that there is a reality of an essentially different mode of being from actual events—pragmatism can be considered the point of entry into the domain of extralinguistic generality: the domain of what I have called the second question of realism.

What remains to be discussed is the status of the real general in Peirce's philosophy, an issue I have alluded to but not examined directly. For the nominalist it is an area that can arouse only the morbid curiosity to know what kinds of things he does not have to believe in. For the realist, however, the discussion is a vital one. Once he has decided against nominalism, he is faced with a whole spectrum of solutions which purport to account for the evidence of real generality.

It is rather interesting, then, that while Peirce frequently attacks variant forms of pragmatism and idealism, his criticism of realism is rare. The reason for the discrepancy is not hard to find: when Peirce is through with the history of philosophy, there are very few realists left in it. He does object to the nominalistic tendencies in some aspiring realists, but that is not strictly a criticism of their realism. Nominalism denies real generality. The criticism of other realisms, however, is a criticism of attempted explanations of real generality.

Imperfect Realism

Throughout the *Collected Papers* there are suggestions of the line Peirce follows in his criticism of other realisms, but the most informative passage I have been able to locate unfortunately did not find its way into print. It occurs in a manuscript with the unpromising title, "Dichotomic Mathematics." [1] There Peirce speaks of "imperfect realism," which he says is a step beyond nominalism because it does not have to maintain that our hypotheses about the world contain something (generality) that is unlike anything in the real world. Such a realism is imperfect, however, because it fails to include in our hypotheses something (process) that the real world contains. [2] The whole discussion takes place within the framework of an inquiry into how many categories an adequate philosophy must have. [3] Peirce allows that imperfect realism does pretty well with two principles, but he contends that the only adequate account can be given by a system

---

[1] Widener I A 1. There is a brief reference to dichotomous mathematics in 4.368–69.

[2] "The imperfect forms of realism have this manifest superiority over nominalism, that they are not obliged to maintain the wonderful position that any hypothesis about the world can be false in the sense of involving elements the like of which does not exist or really be at all. But they are obliged to say that something can present itself, or seem to present itself to the mind, which is utterly unlike anything real and true, not by containing a positive element that the truth lacks but by not containing something that the truth contains. The philosopher who recognizes all three modes of being can alone take the sane position that nothing can be fundamentally and of its nature unlike the truth" (Dichotomic Mathematics," pp. 35–36).

[3] Compare 5.77 ff.

with three principles (which he calls here matter, form, and entelechy).[4]

The rarified atmosphere of the discussion seems more suited to "high metaphysicians" than to the "laboratory mind"; but it is worth our while to follow Peirce as far as we possibly can.[5] Let me try to explain, in terms we are familiar with, what Peirce is trying to do here.

The nominalist, as Peirce sees him, views the world as a heap of unrelated events; a law is nothing more than a uniformity, and causality is nothing more than a succession of events. As a result, continues Peirce, our general conceptions turn out to be more or less fictitious, because there is no reason on the part of the actual individual things why they should be grouped in one way instead of another.[6] The scholastic realist—for he is apparently the imperfect realist [7]—has gone a step beyond nominalism with his theory of form. A form is not an event; general in itself, it allows the realist to say that, in having forms, things objectively contain the element of generality that grounds our true general idea. However, form is "what it is within itself," [8] and although it accounts for a type of generality, it is an unfortunately static notion.

Remember that Peirce is interested in the generality which corresponds to predicates like '_____ is a cause of _____,' in the sense that the predicate delimits a two-member set. The nominalist says that y follows x; the only real things involved are x and y. The imperfect realist says that x has a power (of causing y), or possesses a

[4] Peirce sometimes seems to identify nominalism, materialism, and mechanism; see 5.59–65. Apparently Peirce uses 'entelechy' to reflect an element of final causality, both the psychic activity in nature and the drawing of the ultimate opinion to itself. He says that entelechy is what brings things together and is prominent in the notions of plan, cause, and law ("Dichotomic Mathematics," p. 37). This is also his characterization of thirdness; see the next section.

[5] While I mean to say that this aspect of Peirce's metaphysics is difficult to follow, I do not wish to imply that it is unimportant. As a matter of fact, I think it is only in the effort to understand the murkier aspects of Peirce's thought that one can really appreciate the full import of the so-called clearer parts of his philosophy.

[6] "Dichotomic Mathematics," p. 46.

[7] I say this because of Peirce's attack on the imperfect realist for attempting to account for generality through form.

[8] "Dichotomic Mathematics," p. 37.

certain form. This says something of x (what it is within itself), and helps to explain how it is similar to, say, z (as the cause of w). For Peirce, however, the predicate, if true, indicates a real relation to which the notion of form does not do justice. Form cannot "reach outside itself." It is adequate for the static generality of similar things, but for the dynamic generality of process a principle of law or entelechy is needed.[9]

We have already seen the prototype for this reasoning in Peirce's theory of the illative copula.[10] A consequence is more than an antecedent and consequent, and a proposition is more than a subject and predicate. Using the proposition as a model, we might say that in Peirce's view the nominalist holds only subjects to be real and has difficulty with the content of predicates. The imperfect realist recognizes that predicates, though they have a different mode of being from subjects, are likewise real. But a full account must acknowledge the unity of a proposition, which derives from the *assertion* that a predicate belongs to a subject.[11]

F. E. Abbot, who also emphasizes the relational structure of real generality, adds a fourth type of universal to the traditional scholastic triad: the *universale inter res*.[12] The phrase can be used to characterize Peirce's theory, but we must understand that a real general is not something like the individuals that are related; it does not lie between them, but is, rather, something of a different order which, to use Peirce's term, mediates (4.3). To understand what this involves— in fact, to appreciate the scope of Peirce's "three-principled" realism —it will be necessary to deal with what he calls the categories.

The Categories [13]

Although Peirce admits that his discovery of triads in everything he turns his attention to looks suspiciously like a mania for the number

[9] Recall our earlier discussions of characters, properties, habits, and powers as virtual laws: see the passages cited in n. 49, chap. iv, above.

[10] See pp. 70 ff., above.

[11] Recall 6.341, quoted in n. 19, chap. iii, above.

[12] Abbot, *Scientific Theism*, pp. 25 ff. For the original triad, see n. 7, chap. ii, above.

[13] It is important to recognize that throughout my analysis I am *using* the

three,[14] he argues that his analysis of the categories is "worth much more than the small sum total of the rest of my work, as time will show" (5.469).[15] These are not easy ideas to grasp,[16] and Peirce himself allows that there are peculiar difficulties of expression involved.[17] The situation is complicated even further: first, because the categories were established early in Peirce's career and he worked and reworked them; [18] and second, because he applies his triad in so many different areas that each category comes to range over cases that are, at best, analogous.[19]

It is in terms of quality, event, and law that the categories reflect most directly the structure of his realism.[20] But we can begin with a broader, if more vague, characterization of the elements of firstness, secondness, and thirdness, which Peirce says are discoverable in our experience. For the purposes of exposition, the order of the categories can be slightly transposed (as in 8.266); secondness seems the best one to begin with.

---

categories to suggest some things about Peirce's realism. As a result, my treatment is not only sketchy but selective. To make it otherwise would involve some examination of Peirce's "phenomenology"; and I can only hope that in avoiding this issue I have not distorted Peirce's realism—I am willing to bear the responsibility of not having done justice to the categories themselves.

[14] See 1.568; Peirce's own heading for the chapter is: "The author's response to the anticipated suspicion that he attaches a superstitious or fanciful importance to the number three, and forces divisions to a Procrustean bed of trichotomy"; see also 1.355, 1.369.

[15] See also 4.3, 8.213, 3.422.

[16] See also 1.353, 2.197, 4.3, 6.32.

[17] See 1.280, 2.102, 5.42, 8.263; but contrast 2.214!

[18] "On a New List of the Categories" was one of Peirce's earliest philosophical articles: CP-Bibl. G-1867-1(b); and the article referred to in n. 14, above, was written in 1910: CP-Bibl. G-1910-2.

[19] When the division is made for different purposes, the same thing can fall under different categories. See the (not always accurate) listing by Freeman: *The Categories of Charles Peirce* (Chicago: The Open Court Publishing Co., 1954), p. 57.

[20] Perhaps the concisest and most apt statement of the categories is in 1.417 ff. There is a somewhat simplified statement (in a letter to Lady Welby) in 8.328 ff., and a rather "bold" statement in 8.264–69. See also 1.23, 1.280, 1.452, 3.422, 4.157, 5.41–42, 6.18, 6.32–34. The fact that the categories are developed from both a logical and an experimental approach leads to some conflict: cf. 2.84 with 5.82. In any event, however, it would surely be "un-Peircean" to hold that matters of fact can be *deduced*.

Secondness [21] is involved in resistance and reaction (4.3), and grounds our sense of "other" (1.325). When two objects strike one another, the striking—not the *kind* of striking, but just the actual, individual striking-event—is a matter of secondness. Peirce calls it brute (1.427, 2.84), blind (1.328), unique or nonrepetitive (7.532), and contingent (1.427, 4.29). Although secondness can be experienced, it is nonconceptual,[22] a bare "thisness," and Peirce sometimes calls it an haecceity.[23] When he is watching his words closely enough to abide by his own distinctions, Peirce uses the terms 'actual' and 'existence' (and their families) exclusively of seconds.[24] Three important features of a second are particularly important for our purposes. First, an event in its secondness is totally without quality or lawlike characteristics (that is, without firstness or thirdness).[25] Then, an actual event is necessary simply because it is unalterable or irrevocable (1.427, 2.84).[26] And finally, although secondness is nonconceptual, it is an essential aspect of our experience; without it we can have no knowledge of anything apart from pure possibility.[27]

A quality, taken just in itself and without reference to any other thing, is a first (1.302, 7.528); and everything has its own peculiar *sui generis* quality in this sense (1.303, 1.426, 1.531). It is often described in aesthetic terms (1.43, 5.428); and it might be called the "tone" of experience. Peirce sometimes calls it "positive qualitative possibility" (1.25) and "pure may-be" (1.304), which is intelligible at least in the negative sense that firstness (as such) can have neither actuality nor reference without thus ceasing to be firstness.[28] It is

---

[21] On secondness, see 1.24, 1.320–26, 1.358 ff., 1.380 f., 1.419, 1.427–35, 2.84, 5.45.

[22] No general description of existence is possible: 1.35, 3.612; cf. 1.435, 2.335–37, 4.172, 5.49, 6.342. Peirce praises Scotus and Kant for their views on the "existent": 1.458, 6.95. For the implication that universals cannot *exist*: 5.502–3, 5.414.

[23] 1.341, 1.405, 1.458, 3.434. See also n. 26, chap. iii, above.

[24] 1.21, 1.325, 1.456–57, 1.532, 3.612, 4.542, 5.502–3, 6.343, 6.349, 6.495, 7.534.

[25] 1.212, 1.428, 1.478, 1.532, 5.107.

[26] See the criticism of Hegel, pp. 132–33, below.

[27] This is, after all, no more than the experimental attitude of pragmatism in a different garb.

[28] Peirce calls firstness "the tender category": 1.358; and see 1.418, 1.357.

certainly the least clear of the categories, and the one that receives the least attention. To some extent this is due to the predominance of thirdness in Peirce's treatment: almost any act of the mind leads so immediately to thirdness (1.357, 1.428) that the purity of firstness is not only left behind, but begins to seem unimportant.[29] We shall return to the contrast of firstness and thirdness in a moment.

It is thirdness that Peirce concentrates on, both because he thinks it has been neglected (5.121) and because he considers it the most important of the three (4.332). The prototype of thirdness is found in the action of a sign: "A sign stands *for* something *to* the idea which it produces or modifies" (1.339). At first he actually called the third category "representation" (4.3, 5.66, 5.89, 5.102–7); but later he realized that his characterization was not broad enough,[30] and he finally settled on 'mediation' as the proper technical term (3.422, 4.3):

I use [thirdness] as the name of that element of the phenomenon which is predominant wherever Mediation is predominant, and which reaches its fullness in Representation [5.104]. Continuity represents Thirdness almost to perfection [1.337].

For our purposes, the most significant statement of a third is that "whose being consists in active power to establish connections between different objects" (6.455). It is in this sense that a law is a third.[31] We have already seen something similar to this in pragmatism's insistence that a power is a would-be, the hypostatization of a relation which, if it is real, is a real law. And if we recall the status of the metaphysical mode in Scotus, in which the Common Nature has its reality, we find a suggestion of why Peirce might call thirdness the category of Nous or "intelligibility" (5.49).

For some more interesting discussions of firstness, see 1.43, 1.304–11, 1.427, 1.531, 2.85, 5.44.

[29] Considering the important position Peirce gives in his later writings to aesthetics (cf. 1.191), one might expect that further analysis would have led him to a more complete treatment of firstness.

[30] To sound the "breadth and depth" of Peirce's category of thirdness, it would probably be necessary to read nearly everything he wrote. For some general characterizations, see 2.86, 1.337–52, 1.420, 1.515, 1.567, 5.102–7, 5.121, 6.455, 7.535; see also *Letters to Lady Welby*, p. 7.

[31] See the discussion by Thompson: *Pragmatic Philosophy of Peirce*, p. 110 and n. 2, p. 279.

Although sketchy, this presentation of the categories does introduce us to a new set of passages that can add to our understanding of Peirce's realism. That is, if we correlate his realism with his doctrine of the categories, we can make use of Peirce's description of the relation of the categories to one another, and thus gain a better idea of the structure of his realism. We can begin by stating Peirce's objections to imperfect realism and nominalism in terms of firstness, secondness, and thirdness.

Nominalism recognizes only secondness, the brute actuality of events, although some nominalists do allow for firstness, in a limited sense, by acknowledging that some actual individuals are similar to one another. Generally, however, the nominalist is unwilling to admit any relation as real apart from the actualities that are said to be so related (5.312, 8.20). The imperfect realist, because he holds that there are real qualities not reducible to seconds, gives the category of firsts an equal status with that of seconds. But these qualities include only nonrelative characters; the only real relation that imperfect realism can handle is that of similarity. Peirce insists that only a third category can express the more important "dynamical relations" (1.567).

The justification for my using the categories to describe these positions is that the relation of the categories provides an answer to special problems in Peirce's realism. The contrast of thirdness and firstness reflects the difference between Peirce's realism and imperfect realism. Even more important, the relation of thirdness and secondness reveals the extent to which his realism is moderate or extreme.[32] We shall take these questions up in order in the following sections.

Firstness and Thirdness

Since secondness is the domain of the actual, we must look for a distinction between firstness and thirdness within the area of the possible. When the problem is set out in these terms, the distinction we seek is not hard to find. We have already seen it in the difference between a may-be and a would-be, which is behind Peirce's pragmatic

---

[32] See my remarks on what makes a realism "moderate": pp. 63 and 84, above.

analysis of "causal" laws and powers.[33] Qualities themselves are "mere *may-be's*" (1.304); and a law "were it but a mere idea unrealized . . . would be a pure first" (1.342). As Peirce says elsewhere: "A quality is how something may or might have been. A law is how an endless future must continue to be" (1.536).

The following passage shows how this distinction between firstness and thirdness applies to Peirce's quarrel with the medieval realist:

> If you ask a mineralogist what hardness is, he will say that it is what one predicates of a body that one cannot scratch with a knife. But a simple person will think of hardness as a simple positive possibility the *realization* of which causes a body to be like flint. . . . Notice the *naïveté* of Firstness [8.329].

What the naïve apparently lack is a fully developed pragmatism. They seem to appreciate that hardness is not simply the hard thing but, rather, what makes the thing hard. Yet they fail to see that what we mean by hardness is a relation of test and response.[34]

But now notice the sophistication of thirdness. If a would-be is now real, the character of certain future actualities is to that extent "destined" or "sure to come about" (4.547n).[35] Peirce's triad of the possible, actual, and destined (1.369, 4.547, 5.459) indicates that the potential in its active sense (as opposed to the "mere possibility" of firstness) implies the reality of the future "insofar as it is predetermined" (7.666), or insofar as it results from active law. Peirce simply draws a metaphysical conclusion from his pragmatism: our meanings refer to the future, so that if a conception is true, the (future) object is real.[36]

---

[33] See pp. 101 ff., above.

[34] In a definition for Baldwin's *Dictionary* Peirce explains that 'quality' is often used to indicate the perfection signified by any predicate (2.374). He goes on to say, however, that "in a more proper sense the term 'quality' will not be applied when the adjective . . . is conceived as signifying a relation" (2.375).

[35] "Fate means merely that which is sure to come true, and can nohow be avoided. It is a superstition to suppose that a certain sort of events are ever fated, and it is another to suppose that the word fate can never be freed from its superstitious taint. We are all fated to die" (5.407n1).

[36] The reader who, like myself, is not particularly taken up with the idea that "the belief that Christopher Columbus discovered America really refers to the future" may likewise not be overimpressed with Peirce's metaphysical analogue. In fact, I find that Peirce's "futurism" tends to detract from his own argument for real possibility, which requires that we hold that there is something real *now* which is not an actuality.

However one feels about the "futurism" involved in Peirce's analysis of meaning, there is still another aspect of his theory of causal laws which cannot be dissociated from the real would-be. Peirce is too much of an Aristotelian to make the actual depend upon the potential in a causal sequence. Consequently, pragmatism's restriction of the actual to the reaction-event, coupled with its insistence that a law be stated in terms of what would be, requires the type of causality in which the future acts upon the present. This is not quite the same as saying that the future event is real now; rather, it implies that, whenever the causal law is real, it operates by final and not efficient causality (5.135, 2.664).[37] But I am getting slightly ahead of my story.

Let us return to the distinction of firstness and thirdness, and ask what differences there are in the types of generality involved. The general scheme of Peirce's answer to the question is the reduction of generality to continuity.[38] The middle term in the argument is the notion of possibility, which allows Peirce to bring into play the distinction between possibility and potentiality that we have just been discussing.

First of all, Peirce criticizes the scholastic notion of generality:

None of the scholastic logics fails to explain that *sol* is a general term; because although there happens to be but one sun yet the term *sol aptum natum est dici de multis*. But that is most inadequately expressed. If *sol* is apt to be predicated of *many*, it is apt to be predicated of any multitude however great, and since there is no maximum multitude, those objects, of which it is fit to be predicated, form an aggregate that exceeds all multitude. Take any two possible objects that might be called *suns* and, however much alike they may be, any multitude whatsoever of intermediate suns are alternatively possible, and therefore as before these intermediate possible suns transcend all multitude. In short, the idea of a general involves the idea of possible variations which no multitude of existent things could exhaust but would leave between any two not merely *many* possibilities, but possibilities beyond all multitude [5.103].[39]

A nonrelative predicate, then, delimits not just a collection of similar actualities but a continuous spectrum of possibilities.

The corresponding continuum in the case of complex predicates—

---

[37] See n. 50, below.
[38] 4.172, 6.190, 6.172, 6.204; see also chap. iii, pp. 76 ff.
[39] See also 2.646, on classification.

that is, in the case of law or thirdness—is a process: "Between the beginning as first, and the end as last, comes the process which leads from first to last" (1.361). The relation of similarity is not adequate to handle the notion of process, even when similarity is treated in terms of a spectrum of possible variations. For the events in a process are related to one another not by being similar but by successively realizing a potency in time.[40] Considering Peirce's treatment of monadic predicates as the limiting case of relative predicates, it seems likely that a qualitative spectrum of possibilities is the limiting case of the continuity of a process.[41]

It seems to me that it is the division of continuity into what I have called spectrum and process that lies behind Peirce's distinction of two sorts of generality: "Generality is either of that negative sort which belongs to the merely potential, as such, and this is peculiar to the category of quality; or it is of that positive kind which belongs to conditional necessity, and this is peculiar to the category of law" (1.427). In either case, ". . . the potential aggregate . . . does not contain individuals at all. It only contains general conditions which *permit* the determination of individuals" (6.185). For Peirce, then, the problem of real generality is transformed into the question: "Are there real continua?" [42] As such, however, it retains a formal resemblance to the inquiries of the scholastic realist. The schoolmen maintained that a nature cannot be identified with any actual individual or collection of actual individuals. Peirce wants to show that the reality of a continuum cannot be reduced to any actuality or collection of actualities.

Peirce criticizes imperfect realism because, even though it recognizes the insufficiency of secondness, it attempts to account for all generality in terms of firstness. On such a view, a process is general because other things could undergo the same process, just as white-

---

[40] As a result, the objectivity of time, as a real modality, becomes quite important for Peirce; see, for example, 6.86.

[41] Admittedly, such a resolution reflects adversely on the status of firstness as an independent category. If Peirce had been aware of this, he might have been led to see that the problem of the generality of similar things has a specific value, which tends to be obscured when it is treated as the limiting case of the problem of continuity. See n. 29.

[42] See p. 67, above.

ness is general because more than one thing can be white. But Peirce wants to say that a process is general because it cannot be reduced to a collection of actual events, that is, it cannot be defined without an implication of real possibility. The generality of whiteness is then formulated in terms of real possibility, and thus treated as a degenerate form of continuity.[43]

Objective Idealism

Having distinguished between perfect and imperfect realism, we are now in a better position to appreciate how the framework of the Scotistic solution to the problem of real generals is transformed in Peirce's presentation. The Common Nature for Scotus had an *esse reale* as a formality. Peirce's analysis of continuity and process makes his law of nature a more complex and perhaps more modern idea; but basically Peirce and Scotus agree that the nature or law must be an intelligibility that is real and objective. Scotus had defined a formality as what can be correctly conceived of an object but is real before the operation of the intellect. Peirce's definition of *reality* seems to me to be nearly a pragmatic reformulation of Scotus' *realitas* or *formalitas:* reality is what *would be* thought in the ultimate opinion of the community.[44]

The most important implication of this is that Peirce's category of thirdness corresponds to Scotus' metaphysical mode: the domain of real intelligibilities. For Scotus, as we saw, the formalities are contracted in the existent thing. But Peirce insists that the pragmatist must deny contraction and thereby give up a moderate realism (8.208).[45] It was pointed out in the last chapter that in restricting the actual to the individual reaction-event, the pragmatist is forced to the doctrine of real possibility. Peirce's theory of the categories provides the same sort of result on a broader scale. Secondness, which is the mode Peirce thinks is proper to the individual, does not really *contain* anything

---

[43] In Peirce's philosophy, continuity is "the keystone of the arch" (8.257). See also 1.62 and 5.415.

[44] Whether the nonpragmatic Scotist would be happy with the reformulation is another question. See Fr. Bastian's reply to Moore's article: *Philosophy and Phenomenological Research*, II, 14 (December 1953), pp. 246–49.

[45] Recall our discussion in chap. ii, pp. 63 ff.

(1.478, 5.107); it is the brute, actual event of reaction. Whatever there is of an intelligible nature falls into the categories of firstness and thirdness. With the individual and the actual thus poverty-stricken, the necessity for maintaining real generality and real possibility can scarcely be avoided. We will take this up again in the next section, where we discuss the relation of thirdness and secondness. At present it is necessary to say something about the status of the law of nature as a third.

Peirce brings out his position in a rather entertaining way in the process of criticizing Pearson's *Grammar of Science*.[46] He supposes that an ignorant sailor has hit upon the idea of the parallelogram of forces, and has been making experiments to see whether the actions of bodies conform to the formula. He has just begun to wonder why inanimate things should conform to a general formula when a disciple of Pearson's lands on the island:

"It is very simple," says the disciple, "you see, you made the formula and then you projected it into the phenomena." *Sailor:* What are the phenomena? *Pearsonist:* The motions of the stones you experimented with. *Sailor:* But I could not tell until afterward whether the stones had acted according to the rule or not. *Pearsonist:* That makes no difference. You made the rule by looking at some stones, and all stones are alike. *Sailor:* But those I used were very unlike, and I want to know what made them all move exactly according to one rule. *Pearsonist:* Well, maybe your mind is not in time, and so you made all the things behave the same way at all times. Mind, I don't say it is so, but it may be. *Sailor:* Is that all you know about it? Why not say the stones are made to move as they do by something *like* my mind? [8.151]

When the disciple gets home, Pearson explains that it is all right to admit that facts are really "concatenated," only there is no rationality about it.[47] The disciple is surprised that events should conform to the formula that a scientist invented, especially since some of these events were predicted. For:

"Then" says the disciple, "it appears to me that there really is in nature something extremely like action in conformity with a highly general principle." "Perhaps so," I suppose Dr. Pearson would say, "but nothing in the least like rationality." "Oh," says the disciple, "I thought rationality was conformity to a widely general principle" [8.152].

[46] K. Pearson, *Grammar of Science* (London: Adams and Charles Black, 1900). See 8.132 ff.

[47] See the passages quoted on pp. 29–30, above.

Consequently, when Peirce says that the world is rational, he does not mean just that we can understand it; he means that things operate or behave in a way in which only things governed by mind can behave. Analogy suggests, he says, that laws of nature are ideas in the mind of a deity (5.107).[48] But he is not really happy with the image. Like any objective idealist, Peirce is interested in dissociating 'idea' and 'thought' from the psychological connotation that someone *has* an idea or that a thought is *in* someone's mind.[49] The thoughtlike character of a real law does not result from someone's thinking it, but from the element of final causation that is involved in its operation. If pragmatism is right in its analysis of the would-be, then lawlike behavior can be specified only in terms of what a thing *tends* to realize.[50]

Peirce carries his analysis one step further by making laws "cosmic habits": tendencies of the cosmos to behave in certain ways.[51] Ultimately, his guess at the "riddle of the sphinx" is that there is in the world a primordial tendency to take habits.[52] At this point, however, there is an unfortunate unclarity in his presentation (that is, beyond the inherent unclarity of the subject matter). Apparently Peirce cannot decide whether there is some *ens necessarium* that acts as *the* final cause, or whether the real laws and tendencies constitute a whole that is trying to realize itself. The issue is reflected in his concern with the status of the ultimate opinion of the community. Early passages, which spoke of the ultimate opinion as something sure to be realized, were edited by Peirce so that they referred only to the hope of such a realization as the motive of the community.[53] Even in the

---

[48] See 6.197 and 6.199; see also n. 8, chap. ii, above.

[49] 1.27, 1.216–19, 4.551, 5.289n1, 8.256.

[50] The "peculiarly psychic activity" which distinguishes panpsychism from materialism (6.277) is, for the most part, based on the inadequacy of mechanistic explanations (1.269, 1.366, 6.71 ff., 6.262, 6.299, 6.553 ff.)—or, in its more abstract form, the inadequacy of explanation by dyadic rather than triadic relations (1.345). The influence of pragmatism on Peirce's doctrines of real final causality can be seen in 2.86, 2.664, 5.135. Compare also the notion of a "natural class" as one which is governed by an active idea: 1.204–24, 1.227, 1.231; see also Wiener, *Values in a Universe of Chance*, p. 300, n. 45.

[51] Peirce is convinced that evolution involves final causes: 1.204, 1.269, 2.86.

[52] 1.409 ff. See also 1.62, 1.175, 6.33, 6.101, 6.262, 6.606, 7.388, 7.513.

[53] E.g., 5.407 (and editors' notes); see also 2.113, 6.610. Cf. Thompson, "The Paradox of Peirce's Realism," *Studies in the Philosophy of Peirce*, pp. 139–42.

later passages it is difficult to tell whether he thinks that the real is something to be attained in the ultimate opinion or something to be constituted by it.[54]

At any rate, his later writings give no evidence that he wanted to retract the objective idealism that he had earlier described as "the one intelligible theory of the universe" (6.25).[55] He admits that his philosophy is somewhat Hegelian in outlook (1.42),[56] and he is ready to praise Josiah Royce's *World and the Individual* as "valid in the main" (5.358n).[57] What we must examine now is Peirce's criticism of other idealists.

As with pragmatism, it is in his criticism of those who are closest to him that Peirce most accurately reveals his own doctrine. Moreover, the critique of idealism is particularly important for an adequate understanding of Peirce's realism; for his most frequent objection to idealists is that they fail to take account of secondness.[58] In setting forth the true relation of thirdness and secondness, Peirce will be giving his view of the relation of laws to events, and thus revealing the extent to which his realism is moderate or extreme.

Thirdness and Secondness

Peirce's objections to idealism are both epistemological and metaphysical; and though our major concern is with the latter, we can best approach it through his remarks about the former. As we have seen, Peirce maintains that the object of knowledge must be like the knowledge of it. Because of his doctrine of immediate perception, he is willing to go one—but just one—step further: "The thought thinking and the immediate thought object are the very same thing regarded from different points of view. Therefore Berkeley was, so far, entirely in the right; although he blundered when from that he inferred his idealism . . ." (6.339).

---

[54] See above, n. 4, intro.

[55] As evidence to the contrary, see 1.216 (1902) and 5.436 (1905).

[56] An analysis of the nature and extent of Hegelian influences in Peirce's thought would be extremely valuable. Peirce himself is not too clear on the subject: contrast 5.436 and 6.31 with 5.37–38, 5.40, 5.90–92, 4.50.

[57] See also 1.343, 8.117, nn. 10 and 12.

[58] 1.368, 1.524, 1.532, 5.436, 8.41.

When Peirce uses 'idealism' in a context like this, he means the doctrine that *to be* is *to be represented;* and that is a doctrine he denies (8.30, 8.129). The reality of the thought object does not consist in someone's thinking it. One of the essential features of perception is the brute insistence of secondness (6.340): the "jab in the ribs" (6.95), which does not consist in my thinking it. The dualism that Peirce says is involved in the doctrine of immediate perception [59] is not that of matter and mind but that of "hard fact" and the mind's becoming aware of it. The unity accomplished in the mind's becoming so aware is not the result of the dependence of the object on the knowing mind, but the result of the mind's conforming to the object: "I find myself in a world of forces which act upon me, and it is they and not the logical transformation of my thought which determine what I shall ultimately believe" (8.45). Hard facts will have their way whether I like it or not, and my "whole motive in reasoning" is to prepare for them (2.173, 5.160).

The neglect of secondness carries over into idealist metaphysics as well. Peirce credits Hegel with emphasizing thirdness, and he agrees that it never will "be possible to find any Secondness or Firstness in the phenomenon that is not accompanied by Thirdness" (5.90). But he strongly objects to the theory that "Firstness and Secondness must somehow be *aufgehoben*" (5.91). Peirce's sympathy for idealism makes his criticism all the more important:

The truth is that pragmaticism is closely allied to the Hegelian absolute idealism, from which, however, it is sundered by its vigorous denial that the third category . . . suffices to make the world, or is even so much as self-sufficient [5.436].

The accuracy of Peirce's interpretation of Hegel (or of Royce) is not in question here. I am interested only in what Peirce says about his own position when he contrasts it with what, as he presents it, is an erroneous doctrine. As a matter of fact, Peirce is not objecting to idealism as such. He says that Royce's work indicates that the idealists may be the ones who can make metaphysics a true science (8.118). Of course, such a result cannot be hoped for if the idealism in ques-

[59] 5.50, 5.86, 5.539, 8.261.

tion disregards the element of secondness; for that would be to disregard the need for experience, without which science is impossible.[60]

It may seem paradoxical, then, for Peirce to object that Hegel restricts his phenomenology to what actually forces itself upon the mind (5.37): this sounds as if Hegel is thereby reducing thirdness to secondness. But Peirce is really accusing Hegel of confusing the brute insistency of secondness with the rational destiny of active law.[61] That is, Hegel holds the present event to be necessary and *therefore* deducible, a position that subsumes the actual event in a process of the *necessary* evolution of Reason.[62] Such a solution conflicts not only with Peirce's cosmology (with the element of real chance), but also with his logic of abduction. It is apparently for this reason that Peirce refers to his own theory as "conditional idealism" (5.494).[63]

In general, then, idealism is justified in the emphasis it puts on the reality of thirdness.[64] What Peirce insists upon, however, is that the distinctiveness and importance of secondness be recognized as well. In a late article on the nature of pragmatism,[65] Peirce summarizes his position and relates it to the cosmological series that he wrote in

[60] "Inquiry must react against experience in order that the ship may be propelled through the ocean of thought" (8.118). See also 8.43.

[61] The paradox involved is somewhat similar to that of the "nominalistic Platonism" which Peirce finds in some philosophers; see above, p. 25. See also 5.537, quoted in part in n. 24, chap. iv.

[62] Cf. 6.218, 6.305. Please recall my earlier warning that I am making no effort to defend or even present the "real" Hegel.

[63] The use of 'conditional' does not imply that Peirce is holding to idealism only until something better comes along. I take it that Peirce wants to contrast his idealism with an "absolute idealism," which would see the process of Reason developing in the world according to a strict and necessary evolution (or emanation).

[64] In discussing the import of an experiment, Peirce says: "While the two chief parts of the event itself are the action and reaction, yet the unity of essence of the experiment lies in its purpose and plan . . ." (5.424). For a more extreme statement: "Now the minor currents and ripples in the history of science no doubt depend upon all sorts of accidental circumstances, chief among which may be reckoned the details of man's cerebral anatomy, and corresponding peculiarities of his mind, but the advance of the deep tide of science cannot fail to be governed chiefly by the essential relations between the laws and classes of the objects of nature"; Widener I C 1b, c, "How Did Science Originate," pp. 5–6.

[65] "What Pragmatism Is," which appeared in the 1905 *Monist*,

1891–93 for the *Monist*.[66] The passage deserves to be quoted at length:

Had a purposed article concerning the principle of continuity, and synthetising the ideas of the other articles of that series . . . ever been written, it would have appeared how, with thorough consistency, that theory involved the recognition that continuity is an indispensable element of reality, and that continuity is simply what generality becomes in the logic of relatives, and thus, like generality, and more than generality, is an affair of thought, and is the essence of thought. Yet even in its truncated condition, an extra-intelligent reader might discern that the theory of those cosmological articles made reality to consist in something more than feeling and action could supply. . . . Now, the motive for alluding to that theory just here is, that in this way one can put in a strong light a position which the pragmaticist holds and must hold, whether that cosmological theory be ultimately sustained or exploded, namely, that the third category—the category of thought, representation, triadic relation, mediation, genuine thirdness, thirdness as such—is an essential ingredient of reality, yet does not by itself constitute reality, since this category (which appears in that cosmology as the element of habit) can have no concrete being without action, as a separate object on which to work its government . . . [5.436].

The need for a concrete embodiment of thirdness, as a distinguishing character of his idealism, is accordingly given a certain prominence.[67] But in terms of his realism, it sounds as if Peirce is defending a theory similar to Scotus' notion of the contraction of formalities in the existent thing—a theory which, as we have already seen, Peirce denies. It remains to determine what he does mean.

We might begin with Peirce's favorite analogy of the court and sheriff. The injunctions laid down by a court require a sheriff to enforce them. Without the sheriff, the rulings of a court are not real, are pure fictions; it is not until the sheriff's hand comes to rest upon my shoulder that I begin to have a sense of the reality of the court's injunction (1.24, 1.212–13). In short, a court with absolutely no enforcement agency attached to it is a pure sham. Of course, this does not mean that the court is subordinated to the sheriff. When we say that the ruler of a country "depends upon" his secretaries, we do not mean that he is "lower" than they are (6.324). As a matter of fact, the sheriff without a court is an even less intelligible situation. The

---

[66] The series is published in the *Collected Papers*, Vol. VI, Book I, chaps. 1, 2, 5, 9, 11.

[67] See 1.218, 1.304, 4.6, 5.48, 5.107.

sheriff retains his fist, but what he does with it is now meaningless (1.213).[68]

The interconnection between court rulings and enforcement should not be allowed to obscure the distinctive activity of each. The law-giver is not a participant in the executioner's blow (6.330), but the legislator is responsible for the death of the criminal in a way that the executioner is not. In general, the court does not *regulate* the sheriff in the same way that the sheriff *controls* the citizens. The sheriff is like a bullet in a gun that the court "aims." Once the trigger is pulled, the bullet goes on its way "blindly," as does any efficient cause; the element of aiming, of direction, is a matter of final causality (1.212–13).

So it is, Peirce says, with any law. Unless it is concretely realized in action, the law is simply not real. But at the same time, the law is neither dependent upon nor identical with actualities. Nor does the reality of a law consist simply in a general description of certain facts; that would not satisfy the causal sense of the would-be which results from his pragmatism.[69] Consequently, to whatever extent there is direction and tendency in the process of activity, to that extent there is the real effect of law (7.532). To be sure, the law does not act by pushing things around, but there is still a real sense in which it is true to say that a law makes things happen.[70]

The prototype of such action Peirce finds in words and ideas. As we saw in Chapter III,[71] Peirce does not identify the word with its inscriptions. The signification of a word—the concept or idea—is a general rule or law that governs the use of the word by an inter-preter. In itself the word is a habit (4.464), which consists in the fact that inscriptions will conform to it (2.292), and that it will be so interpreted (1.542). Analogously, we might say that Peirce treats

---

[68] If the reader is tempted to say that a sheriff's action apart from a court is intelligible in itself, he might consider that classic bit of western dialogue: "Look here, Marshal, you can't set yourself up as judge and jury."

[69] See the discussion in the last chapter, pp. 107 ff.

[70] ". . . let a law of nature—say the law of gravitation—remain a mere uniformity—a mere formula establishing a relation between terms—and what in the world should induce a stone, which is not a term nor a concept but just a plain thing, to act in conformity to the uniformity" (5.48).

[71] In the discussion of "subjective generality," pp. 71 ff.; see also 1.535, 5.105.

Plato and Socrates as "inscriptions" of a law of nature, in this case the rather complicated law we refer to as humanity. As the word or idea is a habit in the community of its users, so *humanity* is a habit of the cosmos.[72]

That the position is extreme and anthropomorphic Peirce readily admits.[73] He argues, however, that the nominalist himself has strengthened the first step to this position by his insistence that a law or general is a word.[74] In concluding that laws are therefore subjective, the nominalist only reveals the inadequacies in his notion of what an idea is. In the first place, he seems to hold that the reality of thirdness can be nothing more than the reality of certain seconds upon which it depends; but we have already seen that Peirce considers this an improper use of 'depends upon.' Besides, Peirce feels that to deny the reality of things whose mode of being consists in the reality of other things is to deny the reality of physical objects which depend on the being of atoms (4.463); it is to say that a whole is nothing but the parts that make it up.[75]

Second, the nominalist balks at Peirce's theory because it turns on the notion that laws make things happen as they do, and that would imply that ideas could produce real physical effects in the world. But

---

[72] Cf. 5.105, quoted above, n. 42, intro.

[73] For Peirce's account of his own anthropomorphism, see 1.316, 5.47, 5.536; and see n. 79, below.

[74] Of Karl Pearson, Peirce says: "Repeatedly, when he has proved the content of an idea to be mental, he seems to think he has proved its object to be of human origin. He goes to no end of trouble to prove in various ways, what his opponent would have granted with the utmost cheerfulness at the outset, that laws of nature are rational; and, having got so far, he seems to think nothing more is requisite than to seize a logical maxim as a leaping pole and lightly skip to the conclusion that the laws of nature are of human provenance. If he had thoroughly accepted the truth that all realities, as well as all figments, are alike of purely mental composition, he would have seen that the question was, not whether natural law is of an intellectual nature or not, but whether it is of the number of those intellectual objects that are destined ultimately to be exploded from the spectacle of our universe, or whether, as far as we can judge, it has the stuff to stand its ground in spite of all attacks" (8.145); see also 1.26.

[75] On the whole "calling forth" its parts, see 1.220; compare the last sentences of 7.666. One imagines, then, that 'consist' is a special term for Peirce: "This mode of being which *consists*, mind my word if you please, *consists* in the fact that future facts of Secondness will take on a determinate general character, I call a Thirdness" (1.26); see also 1.615.

Peirce points to the fact that speeches have started revolutions,[76] and to the even more ordinary account of what it is that makes me open a window in a stuffy room:

So, then, when my window was opened, because of a general truth that stuffy air was malsain, physical effort was brought into existence by the efficacy of a general and non-existent truth. This has a droll sound because it is unfamiliar; but exact analysis is with it and not against it; and it has, besides, the immense advantage of not blinding us to great facts—such as that the ideas "justice" and "truth" are, notwithstanding the iniquity of the world, the mightiest of the forces that move it [5.431].[77]

At this point Professor Goudge interposes the objection that while *"ideas in individual human minds* may have causal efficacy . . . there is no observational warrant for saying that ideas *per se* have any such power."[78] It is, on the face of it, a reasonable enough observation; and in the last analysis it may be a legitimate criticism of the anthropomorphic conception behind Peirce's panpsychism.[79] When directed against the passage just quoted, however, it suggests an oversimplification of Peirce's attitude toward the reality of ideas.

To begin with, Peirce has gone to considerable effort to destroy the position that an idea is dependent upon the mind's having it: it is not my thinking that governs the idea but the idea that governs my thinking.[80] The idea as a psychological fact is an event in my mind, but to describe an idea as something that essentially depends upon my having it is one aspect of what Peirce calls confusing the psychological with the psychical (5.485). In fact, ". . . the soul does for the idea just what cellulose does for the beauty of the rose; that is to say, it affords it opportunity" (1.216).

When Peirce argues for the reality of psychical activity in the world, he does not directly conclude from the fact that someone has a true idea to the presence of that idea, as a psychic entity, in the cosmos. What he argues is that the behavior of the world is like the behavior of a man; the presence of real tendencies in the world—and

---

[76] See the "Patrick Henry" example in 5.105.

[77] See also 1.213, 1.348–49, 2.149, 8.176.

[78] Goudge, *Thought of Peirce*, pp. 257–58.

[79] And behind his pragmatism! See 5.536, and cf. 5.175, 5.412, 5.427, 8.186.

[80] 1.27, 1.216–19, 2.149, 5.105–6, 6.152, 8.151, 8.153, 8.256. See also n. 50, above.

it is pragmatism which requires that the world be described in terms of would-be's—is to be established in much the same way as are habits in man (2.664). And Peirce can argue quite consistently that we proceed not from the existence of a mind in man to the reality of his habits, but from the reality of his habits to the presence of mind.

As a matter of fact, Peirce holds that mind, as it is identified with the consciousness of an individual, is only one kind of thing under the governance of thought.[81] Thought—now dissociated from the psychological activity of thinking—is said to govern the behavior of physical objects just about as it does our thinking, the evidence being the analogous behavior in both instances.[82] The key to this aspect of Peirce's idealism is in the pragmatic realism we discussed in the last chapter: "The true idealism, the pragmatistic idealism, is that reality consists in the *future*" (8.284). The insistent actuality of the present, which distinguishes this world from one of pure possibility, is the essential aspect of secondness, or the area of the individual as such. In its very attempt to incorporate the important element of secondness in its system, pragmatism is compelled to interpret the behavior of the world of fact in terms of tendencies and habits. To the extent that the world is reasonable, it is rational, for to that extent it exhibits the real influence of the future (real final causality). Consequently, Peirce holds to

. . . the extreme position that every general idea has more or less power of working itself into fact; some more so, some less so. Some ideas, the harder and more mechanical ones, actualize themselves first in the macrocosm; and the mind of man receives them by submitting to the teachings of nature. Other ideas, the more spiritual and moral ones, actualize themselves first in the human heart, and pass to the material world through the agency of man [2.149].

The Individual

Although Peirce can be defended against the charge of concluding directly from true ideas to real ideas, there still remains a certain force

---

[81] 7.585 ff.; see also 2.66, 6.489.
[82] See 1.27, 2.664. Remember that a habit is not simply the behavior, but what governs the behavior (2.664–67); and that to be governed is not simply to be describable in general terms (5.538, 6.152).

to Goudge's objection. While it seems plausible that ideas can change the face of the earth so long as there are individuals who can appreciate the ideas and work toward their implementation, it does seem strange that ideas can accomplish anything without the aid of an instrument whose peculiar characteristics are those of a conscious being. Perhaps the objection could be put as a question about Peirce's analogy of the court and sheriff. What in the real world corresponds to the sheriff? If the analogy is to hold true, must not a law work its effect on things that are susceptible to the only kind of causality of which a law is capable?

It must be said that Peirce's answer shows the courage of his convictions: "Particles follow the law simply because, being sprung from the stock of reason, they naturally incline to obey reason" (6.330). Unquestionably, this way of expressing the matter is somewhat disturbing. It may seem a little less gratuitious, however, if we remember the extent to which Peirce expands the range of generality by his "relational" treatment. The very notion of enduring through time, of permanence in any respect, already involves generality (1.427). As a result, when Peirce defines a "thing" as a cluster of forces (1.436, 4.157), he introduces not only the element of reaction, which is typical of secondness, but also the element of habit, which shows the presence of thirdness. On this account, those particles that "obey" the laws of nature are in reality not very different from the laws themselves.

Actually, this position is pretty much what Peirce's logical analysis should have led us to expect. In making the fragment-to-system relation basic, Peirce has prepared the way for a metaphysical interpretation in which Socrates is related to humanity as a part of a process to an entire process. If this implies that the personality of Socrates must be subsumed under the more general process, it does not really disturb Peirce: "To deny the reality of personality is not anti-spiritualistic; it is only anti-nominalistic" (8.82). Apart from the general process of reason, the individual is "a zero" (6.479); he can assert his individuality only in ignorance and error (5.317). A thing (or person) is important only for its contribution to the general process; and it makes this contribution by functioning as a sign in that grand Argument which is the development of reason.[83] In short, Peirce *preaches* against individualism.[84]

Perhaps it is his righteous indignation which accounts for the fact that we never find in Peirce a really clear analysis of individuality.[85] An individual seems to be what rates a proper name (4.354), but this includes—as Peirce's own lists show (4.159, 4.354)—persons and "things" which, just because they are "clusters," are not strictly individual. "Acts," he says, "are the most perfectly individual objects there are" (5.529), but it seems unlikely that, in any ordinary sense, acts should rate a name more than persons do. Besides, individuals have "such a mode of being as to be determinate in reference to every character as wholly possessing it or wholly wanting it" (4.461; see also 3.193). Persons and things cannot fulfill this definition because Peirce holds that in large part they are made up of real potentialities. Acts might fit the definition, but in a rather strange way: as seconds they wholly lack every character. Nor is Peirce's description of individuality as "an inward force of identity" (3.460) much help, for it raises the issue of permanence, which we discussed above as a characteristic of thirdness.

What lies behind the confusion of these various descriptions is the ambivalent role of secondness. On the one hand, secondness is the antigeneral, the brute, blind, and unintelligible—characterizations that are all negative or privative. On the other hand, secondness is the actual, without which laws and types cannot be real. Peirce remarks, quite properly, that the quest for a principle of individuation was a major problem with the scholastics. Scotus, for example, with all his discussion of the reality of the Common Nature, still insists that the individual is the *thing:* the supposit. Haecceity is the ultimate ac-

---

[83] "What is the chief end of man? *Answer:* To actualize ideas of the immortal, ceaselessly prolific kind" (2.763); cf. 5.119, 5.107.

[84] See, for example, 1.176 ff., 1.673, 3.611–13, 4.68, 5.40n2, 5.502–4, 6.605. For an important statement of the way ethics (which includes the ethics of scientific method) grows out of this position, see 1.615. It is in a passage of this sort that Peirce reflects his concern with problems upon which Royce had concentrated: see Feibleman, *Introduction to Peirce's Philosophy*, pp. 472 ff.

[85] See Gallie, "Peirce's Pragmaticism," in *Studies in the Philosophy of Peirce*, p. 69.

tualizing entity, and the individual thus contains the perfection of its attributes.[86]

For Peirce, however, the predominance of continuity tends to eliminate the concept of substance, and the supposit (Socrates, for example) comes to be treated as a process. What we call "things" are not strictly individuals but generals. Socrates is not just a member of a collection, partaking in generality through his similarity to other men; he is a fragment of a system (as in 4.5). A dynamic process himself, the human person is continuous with that system which is humanity and which is, in turn, continuous with the whole evolution of Reason.[87] But the important question still remains: How is the general related to the individual as such—that is, how is thirdness related to secondness? Peirce's answer is that secondness does not contain any thirdness at all (1.478, 5.107). We have seen the same answer in another form: the would-be is never contracted to the *is* (8.208).

Consequently, while it is clear enough that Peirce ultimately subscribes to an extreme form of realism, the precise statement of his position is somewhat complicated. Evidently he holds that generals are real, but one must be careful in giving his answer to the question: Are they really *in* things? First of all, Socrates and Plato are already general themselves; and this does not so much answer the question as change it—as Peirce himself has indicated by expressing the question of realism as: "Are there real continua?" [88] Second, Socrates and Plato are related to humanity as fragments to a system: here again the question changes, for now it depends on whether we want to say that a whole is "in" its parts.[89] But finally, the force of the original question reasserts itself when we ask to what extent a continuum is to be found in its discrete and actual parts. For now we are asking whether the possible (and therefore general) is to be found in the actual and in-

[86] Recall Harris' remark on Scotus and the individual, cited above: n. 65, chap. ii.

[87] Before one concludes simply that this is the fruit of a brilliant mind gone wild (or soft), it might be instructive to reflect on the effects of serving under the "gradgrind" banner that Peirce so detests. Cf. 6.292, 8.117n12.

[88] See n. 1, chap. iii.

[89] For example, is Socrates *in* his hand? Well . . . at least one might say with Plato that it is not so interesting a question as whether a universal is in its instances: see the *Philebus* (14–15).

dividual. Here Peirce rightly describes his answer as an extreme realism, for he denies that the would-be is contracted, or that second-ness contains thirdness.

When Peirce's position is stated in these terms, the ambiguity in his treatment of the individual becomes crucial. However much he insists that the individual is unintelligible apart from the generality of process, Peirce is still committed to the notion that thirdness must be realized in the actuality of secondness. The problem here is simply that while he disagrees with the Scotistic theory that the real general is contracted in the individual (and thus is strenuously opposed to Scotus on the importance of the individual), he substitutes a doctrine which requires that the real general become concrete in a world of actuality. In short, he has replaced the mysterious notion of contraction by an equally mysterious notion of concretion.

The shift in emphasis within the problem of the relation of individual and law suggests to me that Peirce is working with something like the concrete universal of Hegel. Any detailed development of this comparison would probably require another study as complicated as the present one. But what I want to point out here is the difference in the contexts within which Peirce develops his theory of real generality. When he argues against the "nominalists," he talks like a scholastic realist: laws are not supposits, but there is reason to make a distinction within any supposit between, roughly speaking, individuality and nature. In the same context he can describe his position as an extreme realism, for he contends that a nature is not "contracted"—does not exist in the individual supposit under a mode of individuality.

Peirce then goes on, as we would expect, to discuss the status of a (law of) nature and the relation of law and individual. However, when we examine his analysis of these problems, especially that of the relation of law and individual, we become aware of an important, if unclear, shift in terminology and treatment. Where he denied "contraction" he now proposes "concretion." Where we heard before of "individuation" we now hear of "embodiment." And most of all, the force of Peirce's assurance that real generals are not "things" is lost in the light of the categories which lump together laws and "things" as opposed to "bare events."

What accounts for this change, I suggest, is that where Peirce's attack on the nominalist takes place within the context of a "scholastic realism," his positive account of the status of laws and their relation to individuals occurs in the context of idealism. While I think that this shift in context tends to make him gloss over some important difficulties, I should like to emphasize that I do not think it necessarily points to a conflict of realism, pragmatism, and idealism. What my analysis shows, I think, is that, so far as the problem of real generality is concerned, much of what is found in Peirce's idealism can be seen as a development of what is at least implicit in his realism and pragmatism.

Peirce's ultimate answer, so far as I am able to reconstruct it—and this is my guess at the riddle of the (Peircean) Sphynx—is that laws govern but are not *in* the discrete, actual events of secondness. What this requires, of course, is the intermediary action of "sheriffs" who are capable of both appreciating the subtle persuasion of Reason, and exerting an efficient force upon actual events. In the case of human activity the "sheriff" is readily identifiable as the community of interpreters. Whether in the case of nature in general the human community is paralleled by, included in, or inclusive of another community of interpretation, I am not really able to say. If the question can be answered at all, it will only be by a full-scale investigation of Peirce's theory of signs and *its* relation to realism, pragmatism, and idealism.[90]

To gain a broader perspective of the status of real generals in Peirce's philosophy, I have tried to relate the doctrine of the categories to the statement of Peirce's realism. The whole discussion required us to go into an area of Peirce's thought that is generally vague, often metaphorical, and sometimes unintelligible. But it is also an area in which his logical analysis of "systems" and his account of the pragmatic "would-be" attain their full force.

The nominalists are left behind as unable to account for the most important element in our experience: real generality; while scholastic

[90] And the issues of Peirce's phenomenology and normative sciences, which I have been trying to avoid.

realists and Hegelian idealists are criticized for well-intended but inadequate attempts to account for such generality. The "imperfect realism" of the schoolmen is rejected for its static conception of substantial forms. The idealists are criticized for making the process of Reason necessary (deductive rather than abductive), and for failing to take into account the distinctive character of secondness.

What emerges from the discussion is a world of process, characterized by continuity and set in motion by the rule of Reason through final (and not efficient) causality. What we call things and persons are not individuals but generals: fragments—themselves continua—of continuous systems. Precisely how these processes manage to become concrete is not clear, but apparently the agency of a community (or communities) of interpretation is required. For all Peirce's emphasis on the category of secondness, his thoroughgoing anti-individualism leaves the impression that the actuality of discrete individuals is, if I may use a metaphor, only a scar of battles fought at a higher plane, and is unintelligible when considered apart from the general process (or processes) of thirdness.

VI

Peirce and the Problem of Universals

MY PRESENTATION of the structure of Peirce's realism is now completed. I have examined the problem that gives rise to realism in Peirce, his theory of the "logical universal," the influence of pragmatism, and finally the status of the law of nature. Along the way, however, I have had to interject some discussions of technical points in Peirce as well as in Scotus. These discussions, sometimes extended and nearly always distracting, are liable to have distorted the position, relation, and importance of the basic elements of that structure. For that reason I should like to begin this chapter with a résumé of my analysis of Peirce's realism. The reader may find it somewhat repetitious, but it may be helpful to see, in a more schematic form, what I consider to be encompassed by Peirce's realism.

There are, explicitly in Scotus and clearly enough in Peirce, two areas in which the problem of generality arises. The first is that of predicates: terms that can be true of more than one thing. Here again there is a twofold distinction: a predicate is general both because it refers to many things, and because as a symbol (or, as Peirce sometimes says, as a word) it is itself nonindividual. Peirce describes the symbol as a habit, and we also know that it exemplifies thirdness. Although this is referred to as the "subjective generality" of a sign, it is of considerable importance, for Peirce contends that laws, as real generals, are "of the nature of a word or idea."

The objective generality of a predicate is a matter of its reference to many subjects. This becomes critical when the predicate is itself made a subject of further operations. This process, which Peirce calls hypostatic abstraction, can be accomplished in terms of either extension or comprehension. In an extensional treatment we utilize the notion of a collection: something constituted of members all of which have some character, however trifling. In the comprehensional analysis the character itself becomes the subject of discourse. Here Peirce's relational treatment of predicates comes to the fore.

A collection is made up of similar members. But the logic of relatives allows the development of the more interesting notion of a system. In a system the members are not necessarily similar to one another; the mode of connection is something more complex, such as *giver-of-to, cause-of, quotient-of,* and so forth. Any relational character delimits a system whose members are the subjects of the proposition having that predicate. Thus a relative predicate can be general in three ways: (1) as itself a sign; (2) as delimiting a system (or set); and (3) as true of many (sets of) subjects.

Induction is suited only to collections; it infers that the character of a whole class is the same as that of the sample upon which it operates. The character that each member has may be quite complex, of course, but it must be the same in each member. The move from fragment to system—which is pretty much what is ordinarily called seeing connections—is a different mode of inference, namely, abduction. The operation of hypostatic abstraction itself involves abductive inference. To make a predicate a subject is, in the logic of relatives, to treat a relation as a thing; thus it requires, if only trivially, that the relation be recognized as significant to begin with. Peirce points out that the resultant "thing" is a creation of the mind, an *ens rationis.* Some commentators have concluded from this that Peirce is a "moderate realist," holding that a general is real only in the mind. Unfortunately, such a conclusion results from the failure to distinguish the two questions of realism—the two areas in which the question of generality arises. To maintain, as Peirce does, that abstractions are *entia rationis* does not commit him either way on the issue of real generality apart from our concepts.

An abstraction, like a dream, is a fact in someone's mental biography. When the realist contends that some generals are real, however, he is concerned with the reality of that to which such an abstraction refers. Abstractions of second intention refer only to the mind's way of representing objects, and not to the things represented. Real abstractions are also "second order" conceptions, but the objects to which they refer (namely, the thirdness of things) are, or purport to be, real aspects of things, which can be called "realities."

The nominalist contention, according to Peirce, is that wherever generality is found, it is a function of the symbol as symbol—that is, of second intention—and does not reflect a generality independent of the mind. Peirce hails as the nominalist's true contribution the correlation of a general with the activity of a symbol; that is, Peirce argues that the general is of the nature of a word or idea. But for Peirce the important question of whether a general is real still remains unanswered. At this point the issue begins to exceed the limits of logic, for it becomes necessary to distinguish within first intentional abstractions those that are objective and those that are subjective. On Peirce's account, such a distinction cannot be made by the logician, for it turns upon the matter of successful prediction.

The special contribution of Peirce's pragmatism now becomes relevant. The pragmatic formulation makes the rational purport of any conception consist in the truth of a conditional proposition relating to the future. This means that (1) every predicate involves (virtually) a relative character, which brings into prominence the generality of the character itself as a system, in contrast to the more commonly recognized generality of the collection of similar (sets of) subjects; and (2) every predicate becomes a virtual prediction. Of course, pragmatism does not verify predictions; it simply puts our conceptions into a form that will allow for the scientific inquiry which alone can separate law from fiction. The fact of scientific prediction, however, shows that in some cases something more than an accidental succession of events or a simple uniformity is involved. Ultimately, prediction shows there is something real now that accounts for a future actuality; and since the only actuality involved is the future event, the present reality must be a possibility.

It should be clear by now that Peirce's pragmatism involves not only the belief that generals are real, but a special conception of the nature of real generals. This brings us to the last phase of Peirce's realism, where he criticizes the attempt to account for real generality by form alone. The schoolmen, as Peirce sees them, realized the importance of habits or dispositions, but unfortunately they treated them as forms. Lacking the logic of relatives and pragmatism, they were unable to do justice to the relational structure of real generals. The result was a static doctrine of substantial forms that could not account for the important elements of continuity and process.

Scholastic realism was a step beyond nominalism, for it could account for the generality of qualitative possibility, the generality of monadic predicates. But the notion of potentiality, of would-be instead of might-be, could only be grasped in the dynamic conception of law. That is, the unity of a process is found not in the similarity of the events in the process, but in the more complex conception of a system that orders those events. The distinction here is that of firstness and thirdness, which we discussed in the last chapter. Also involved is the idea that a relative is a system that not only delimits a collection of similar (sets of) subjects, but relates the subjects of each set. This activity of relating Peirce calls "mediation," and he considers it definitive of thirdness.

We now come to the true question of the "moderation" of Peirce's realism: the relation of laws to individuals, which he discusses in terms of the relation of thirdness and secondness. His criticism of idealism, particularly what he takes to be the position of Royce and Hegel, almost entirely concerns the idealist's failure to recognize the brute actuality of secondness. Peirce has no quarrel with the pre-eminent position assigned to Reason (or thirdness), and he is willing to call himself an idealist. However, he contends that thirdness manifests itself through actual events—as we saw in studying pragmatism, our knowledge of thirdness is necessarily formulated only in terms of such events—and pragmatism's insistence upon this point, coupled with the narrow definition of the actual event, is what forced the issue of real possibility in the first place. The same argument carries over to the more general question of whether the dimension of thirdness is needed to account for the intelligible character of events in process. That is to say, the argument that a would-be is not the same as any collection of actualities, and that it controls or governs these actualities, is again applied in the broader field of the reality of thirdness. Peirce has so described secondness that nothing is included in it except the bare reaction-event; as a result, he has no difficulty in showing that thirdness is not contained in secondness.

If the individual as such is the bare event, it is difficult to avoid Peirce's conclusion that there must be some real generality in the objective make-up of the world. As to the ordinary notion of a person or "thing" as an individual, Peirce more or less denies it. The person or thing is a "cluster" of potentialities, and therefore a habit or law itself. The important problem of Socrates' relation to humanity is now not so much a question of the relation of an individual to a type, but of a fragment to a system. Such a position, as I have suggested, bears a strong resemblance to the Hegelian concrete universal. Unfortunately, Peirce's theory is not really complete until some account is given of the process of "concretion." Such an account is necessary not only when we formulate the problem as the scholastics did, but even when we formulate it in Peirce's own terms: the reality of continua.

That account is not included in the present monograph simply because I have been unable to find it in Peirce's writings. It could, perhaps, be reconstructed; but this would require an analysis of elements in Peirce's theory which lie beyond the scope of my approach. I do not think, however, that the results of such an inquiry would alter substantially my interpretation of Peirce as an extreme realist. The anti-individualism in Peirce's discussion of realism is no incidental aspect of his thought; it appears in both the "agapism" of his idealist cosmology and the "would-be" of his pragmatism.

Scotistic Elements

Because of the emphasis I have placed upon it, the nature of the Scotistic element in Peirce's realism deserves a separate, if brief, summary. The distinction of two problems of realism is Scotistic, or at least scholastic. And within the logical analysis, Peirce's treatment of abstractions as "second order" conceptions is definitely Scotistic. From this issue the discussion of "real" abstractions arises, and Peirce himself has acknowledged his indebtedness to Scotus for the use of the term "real."

Once the question of logical predicability is handled, Scotus turns his attention to the Common Nature. It is not a supposit, for the evidence indicates that it consists in a less-than-numerical unity. While it is real, the Common Nature is not a separate substance; indeed, the mode of its unity suggests a different mode of being. The Common Nature is to be found, in a certain sense, *in* individual things, but it cannot be identical with the individuality of such things. Ultimately, Scotus decides that the Common Nature is not a *res* but a *realitas:* something essentially conceivable but real before the operation of the intellect. These realities—or formalities, since they are "formally distinct" from one another—are neither physical things nor logical concepts. They are real, but in what has been called a "metaphysical mode."

Scotus' arguments for the real lesser unity are supplemented in Peirce by the arguments from the fact of prediction. Pragmatism and the logic of relatives influence the conception of the structure of these realities: what Scotus held to be formlike nature Peirce conceives of as a law of nature. But Peirce's laws have a different mode of being from individuals and they retain a strong resemblance to Scotus' metaphysical mode—in fact, Peirce also calls them realities.

There are differences in the two theories, of course; in some cases, though, it might be argued that Peirce has not objected to the Scotistic doctrine but only developed it according to modern conceptions. The main difference lies with Peirce's self-acknowledged denial that the nature is contracted in individuals. By making the individual less important, Peirce has more room to develop the idealistic conception of the status of laws. The important point, however, is that in the very fact that Peirce denies the Scotistic doctrine of contraction he reveals the extent of Scotus' influence: the framework of Scotus' solution to the problem of universals, without the notion of contraction, provides the basic points of reference for the structure of Peirce's own theory.

On the Development of Peirce's Thought

Up to this point the organization of my study has been based on what I find to be the structure of Peirce's realism itself, and not on any chronological development in his thought. Apart from Peirce's own self-criticism, I have not made much explicit use of the contrast between early and late writings. Such a procedure is evidently open to objection if it results in a distortion of Peirce's thought. At the same time, I can defend it only against specific arguments. In short, I plead innocent until proven guilty. I do not mean to suggest that Peirce might have reached his idealism through successive stages of realism and pragmatism. To be sure, there is development in his thought, though in the present state of Peirce scholarship it is not always easy to determine to just what extent.[1] In regard to one issue, however, it seems that the notion of a linear development is not applicable; for realist, pragmatist, and idealist elements appear in every major stage of Peirce's writing. The point is important enough in its own right to deserve some comment.

Arthur Burks finds the major watershed of early and late writings in Peirce to be around 1891, when Peirce retired to his farm in Milford, Pennsylvania.[2] This seems substantially correct, but I would like to distinguish as well a very early period, roughly before 1875, and a late period, after about 1903. The first distinction allows us to speak more reasonably of formative years; in 1890 Peirce was fifty years old, and even for him this would be stretching the formative period a bit. The distinction of a late period centers on the Lowell lectures and the Harvard lectures on pragmatism, both delivered in 1903. In delivering these lectures Peirce was provided with a stimulus to attempt an organized synthesis of his thought. But even more important, it seems likely that this first opportunity in a decade to try out his thoughts on others gave rise to a late but important re-evaluation (though not *necessarily* a change). As a matter of fact, we find such an

---

[1] Arthur Burks's chronological bibliography in vol. VIII is a healthy and illuminating antidote to the organizational format of the *Collected Papers*.

[2] Arthur Burks, "Peirce's Theory of Abduction," *Philosophy of Science*, p. 301. See also 1.12.

attitude reflected in the partially completed *Monist* series on the defense of pragmatism.

The prominent position of idealism in the philosophical world during the time of Peirce's early studies obviously had an effect on his own views. We know that he began his serious study of philosophy with Kant and the post-Kantian idealists.[3] It is not surprising, then, that in 1863 Peirce gave high praise to idealism.[4] But we should note that one of his characterizations of the idealist at this time was that he "regards abstractions as having a real existence." [5]

Peirce's studies of Scotus can be placed around 1867–68.[6] In 1871 he shows us the results of this study, rather thinly disguised as a review of Fraser's *Berkeley*. We have already noted the elements of pragmatism, realism, and idealism reflected in this early work.[7]

Peirce tells us that his pragmatism was first formulated in the early 1870's, in discussion at the meetings of the Metaphysical Club,[8] yet pragmatism does not find its way into print until 1871 and is not officially named until even later.[9] But even the early pragmatist articles have their share of realistic and idealistic elements. If anyone thinks that Peirce is growing out of his early idealism, he need only recall that the controversial cosmology series was not written until 1891.[10] It is also important to remember that Peirce's doctrine of the categories, which was originally presented in 1867, does not drop out of his writings at all; on the contrary, it gains increasing prominence.

To the reader who approaches Peirce in order to find out about pragmatism, the period from 1875 to 1903 may seem the most fruitful one. But this does not mean that pragmatism dominates that period. A perusal of Burks's bibliography indicates otherwise, and a reading of the material rather conclusively shows it. If anything

[3] See 1.4, 1.560, 1.563.

[4] "The Place of Our Age in Civilization," Wiener, *Values in a Universe of Chance*, p. 11.

[5] *Ibid.*

[6] Peirce tells us that he began his reading of the scholastics after his study of Kant (1.560).

[7] See pp. 14 ff., above.

[8] See 5.12.

[9] See 5.358n, 5.414.

[10] CP-Bibl. G-1891-1.

dominates the period, it is Peirce's logical studies, of which his pragmatism is only a part, alongside such important issues as the theory of signs, the analysis of abduction and induction, and the whole development of the formal system of existential graphs.

In the 1903 lectures the importance of realism—indeed, the much broader issue of the prominence of thirdness—can hardly be ignored. The proposed *Monist* series of 1905 confirms its significance. It is in these articles, admittedly incomplete and at crucial points vague, that Peirce's latest synthesis of realism, pragmatism, and idealism begins to take shape. Here, as in all Peirce's later (that is, post-1891) attempts at synthesis, the categories occupy a central position.

What this brief chronological survey shows, I think, is that each position—realism, pragmatism, and idealism—is held for its own sake. I do not think Peirce ever had the slightest intention of giving up any of them. Further—and to offset any misunderstanding which the format of my study may have created—let me make it clear that I do not hold that Peirce was driven to idealism, or to pragmatism, or to realism itself for that matter. He did attempt a synthesis of the three, and for this reason I think that any analysis of one of the triad should take some account of the other two. I say "some account" advisedly: for, as I have noted more than once along the way, pragmatism and idealism were discussed here only inasmuch as they affect the structure of Peirce's realism.[11] This is no hidden or disguised claim that realism is the definitive element in Peirce's thought. I have selected it as one of many areas in Peirce's philosophy that could stand a closer analysis.

Toward an Evaluation

In the previous chapters I have made a special effort to keep my own critical remarks to a minimum; but there is room now—perhaps

[11] D. J. Bronstein ("Inquiry and Meaning," in *Studies in The Philosophy of Peirce*, p. 47) suggests that 'conditional idealism,' 'scholastic realism,' and 'pragmaticism' are only different names for Peirce's commitment to real possibility. As valuable as it is to see the interconnectedness of these doctrines, it seems to me a great mistake to neglect the richness of Peirce's thought as it is reflected in the three complementary approaches by viewing them all as somehow the same thing.

even a place—for a brief evaluation of Peirce's realism. Unfortunately, I am not at all sure that a brief evaluation is desirable or even possible. It is not a question of whether Peirce is really a realist or not; I will leave that for whoever is sure he wants to say what a realist really is. The issue is, rather, what is involved in saying that Peirce's theory is either right or wrong.

In the remaining pages I shall be content to point out some of the complexities in Peirce's theory, which any evaluation must take into account. To begin with, I find three issues involved in his realism: (1) the mode of reference and status of predicates; (2) the object of scientific knowledge; and (3) the status of the individual. Doubtless all three are related; but I feel that a good bit of confusion results if each is not given special attention.

To my mind, the significant contribution of Peirce's analysis lies in his bringing out the problem of the scientific object, the problem of what we know when we know what a thing is. I take this to be the pivotal issue in Peirce's realism and I have organized my presentation around it. Whether one ultimately decides for or against Peirce, there is a certain tactical advantage in his having set out the problem as he does. The realist is often enough depicted as the proponent of a cluttered ontology. The nominalist, once he has finished his exposition of the difficulties in the realist position, usually cites the economy of his own system as a major selling point. Peirce is able to shake this privileged position by asking the nominalist to account for the "object" of scientific knowledge. The question may not really clear the air between nominalist and realist, but at least it evens the score.

Discussion of the object of our knowledge of what things are is as old as Plato's theory of Ideas and its Aristotelian criticism. The first problem I mentioned above, that of the behavior of predicates, is not of a much later vintage.[12] I understand it to be largely a logical issue, and I have discussed it in previous chapters as the first question of

[12] Perhaps the confusion of what I have called the two questions of realism began with the early commentators on Aristotle (as in Boethius and Porphyry); for the "problem of universals" took its rise in discussions of the predicables and the categories. Apparently there was an attempt to link Aristotle's logic to a Platonic metaphysics. While not altogether quixotic, such an undertaking is bound to have its difficulties with Aristotle's notion of substance.

realism. Neither Scotus nor Peirce feels that the dispute between nominalism and realism can be settled here. Both find it necessary to go into what I have called the second question of realism: the issue of the object of our knowledge of what things are; and it is this issue which gives the theory of Ideas its resiliency. It is valuable, of course, to show that logic (and language) may give rise to distinctions that do not occur *in rerum natura*. What is more, there are historical reasons for the nominalist's concern with the logical questions involved. But after hearing him out, the realist will likely have a further question to ask. After all, it is not a matter of logic that Peter and Paul are both men—or, for that matter, that Peter is a man.

Individuals and/or Things

My earlier presentation of Peirce's analysis of these first two problems, while not particularly critical in tone, is at least straightforward enough to provide the basis for an evaluation. But in order to explain my mixed reactions to Peirce's realism, it will be necessary to say something about the third problem: the status of the individual. This problem—like the second one, but unlike the first—I find to be a metaphysical one. And its pertinence for realism can be traced, I think, to Aristotle's criticism of the theory of Ideas.

Why is it, after all, that Aristotle treats Peter and Paul as so important in contrast to humanity and whiteness? [13] In the context of the problem of universals, the proper answer seems to me to be that Aristotle considers Peter and Paul to be "things," first substances, or, in scholastic terminology, supposits. As Scotus points out, Aristotle does not argue that perfect exemplars cannot exist; he argues, rather, that if the Ideas exist, they are of no help in solving the problem of different supposits' having "common" attributes.[14] For existing Ideas would themselves be supposits, and as such they could not be made to serve as common attributes without generating contradictions.[15]

However, if Aristotle's solution is taken uncritically to mean that

[13] I realize there is some dispute over the status of the individual versus the form in the interpretation of the Aristotelian *ousia*. My own point is better served if I assume the older reading.

[14] *In Metaph.*, VII, q. 18, n. 3 (XII, 454a).

[15] See p. 49, above.

only "individuals" exist, an unfortunate confusion is introduced into the controversy. For Aristotle's rejection of separate Ideas involves not only the distinction of individual and general, but that of attribute and substance as well. Behind the notion of "first substance" (or supposit), as a whole thing including its attributes, lies a rather extensive metaphysics which it would be improper to view as stemming from the distinction of individual and general. Due perhaps to the impact of Aristotle on the scholastics—an impact reflected in much of our own ordinary usage—the term 'individual' has come to be interchangeable with 'thing' (as a supposit). Moreover, I suspect that many nominalists, who would be scandalized to be called Aristotelians, have more or less unconsciously assumed this part of the Aristotelian metaphysics; and to the extent that their assumption is unconscious, they tend to reject the question of real generality as nothing more than a logical problem.

To some extent Ockham would seem to be a case in point.[16] Scotus' argument for the real Common Nature was that Peter is really like Paul and not really like the ass. He knew well enough the Aristotelian criticism of Plato, and so he insisted that the Common Nature could not itself be a supposit. But he respected the original problem of the objectivity of our knowledge, and so he also maintained that the Common Nature is real. Ockham, of course, had no intention of denying that Peter is more like Paul than like the ass. He merely contended that this is not so because of some further "thing" in addition to the three things involved: Peter is Peter, Paul is Paul, and the ass is the ass, and that is why they are alike or unlike.

Ockham's statement has a ring of common sense about it, but it deserves a closer look. If the realist is being charitable, he may say that Ockham has simply not carried his analysis far enough—although in the heat of battle he will more likely contend that Ockham has missed the point or begged the question. Actually, Ockham's theory of a concept as a natural sign is not so different from Scotus' own position; both hold that the mind makes a representative object and both hold

[16] To present Ockham's position without using the precise terminology of his logic must surely seem an oversimplification. But I am here arguing against what I think is an equally dangerous simplification, which makes of Ockham's position an "obvious" argument against realism.

that this object must refer to real things (in the sense of not being a second intentional concept). The difference, as Peirce correctly puts it, lies in the *fundamentum universalitatis*—in the basis for the generality of the predicate.

I discussed some of the difficulties in Scotus' position in Chapter II. But I would suggest that Ockham's statement is not so clear at it is made out to be. First of all, to say that a single sign may stand for two things indifferently is reasonable enough; but one does want to ask what it is about such things that allows a single sign to be truly representative of them. If sign-making is not purely conventional, there is good reason to ask about the foundation of a sign, particularly in those things that are apt to be signified equally well by one sign.

Second, to say that Peter as Peter is different from Paul as Paul, without the mediation of some third thing, is probably to state one side of the Aristotelian doctrine of supposits accurately enough. But it hardly seems sufficient as an answer to the problem that bothers the realist. And to use 'individual' in this context only compounds the difficulty. As individuals, things would seem to be either all alike or all different.

Ockham does not really expand these points, and in the final analysis it is difficult to avoid Peirce's objection that Ockham makes the mental concept the only ground for generality. It should be pointed out, however, that Ockham was probably not especially interested in this side of the question. His main purpose was to allow the logician and scientist to go about their business without fear of having all their words take ontological root. And on the matter of the logic of predicates Ockham does have some very important things to say.

Objectivity and the Object of Knowledge

Unfortunately, Ockham seems to think that he has ended the controversy when he says that only individuals exist. For my own part, I have no great quarrel with this if Ockham means by it that only supposits exist. But then something remains to be said about the qualities, attributes, characters, or natures of things. Scotus points out that there are facts true of individuals which cannot be accounted for solely in terms of the individuality of things. Here again I am inclined to give a qualified agreement, even though I have no taste for "formalities" either in or out of a metaphysical mode.

To Scotus and Ockham (and doubtless to many others), my attitude must seem to reflect a flagrant case of fence-sitting. I will admit that it gets uncomfortable at times, but I am not really tempted to come down. The issue turns, as I think Peirce has correctly pointed out, on the objectivity of our general conceptions. What I am reluctant to admit is that there is a real, general object existing as, or like, a thing apart from my mind.

I am quite willing to hold that the distinction between the supposit and (even its individuated) nature is not simply a logical one. (It is at this point that Ockham and I probably part company.) And I also think we can recognize that humanity exists in a limited way in Plato and in Socrates. What I consider unnecessary, however, is that the unlimited nature, the nature in itself, has its own existence.[17]

What Scotus, and I think Peirce as well, would object to in this view is that I put an intolerable burden on the process of abstraction. For on the account I have suggested, it is possible to know a nature in a way in which that nature is never found to exist, that is, as non-individuated. And it is probably true that I find a certain "looseness" on both ends of the knowledge relation that would scandalize both Peirce and Scotus. But for what it is worth, I am equally scandalized at the tendency in Scotus, especially as it is reflected in his formalities, to insist that there be in reality something that corresponds to our modes of representing the real world.

My attitude toward Peirce's solution is somewhat more complicated simply because Peirce discards the conception of first substance which Scotus, Ockham, and I still see as a part of the problem. I shall discuss this in a moment. But there is still a sense in which Peirce argues as Scotus does for a real common object.[18] It is true that neither Peirce

---

[17] I am not arguing a point here, but only expressing an opinion—this is not the place to attempt more. As should be obvious, I do not think "the" problem of universals can be solved any more briefly than a proposed solution of it can be evaluated.

[18] According to Peirce, the commonness of qualities, which interested the schoolmen, is but one form—and a degenerate form at that—of real generality.

nor Scotus commits the crude fallacy of concluding directly from a logical concept to a real thing. In failing to see that Peirce and Scotus are working toward the solution to the problem of the object of scientific knowledge—a problem related to, but still different from, that of the logic of predicates—the nominalist may not be able to generate any sympathy at all for their positions. But then Scotus and Peirce are not totally beyond the possibility of backsliding. The Peircean concept of reality, like its Scotistic prototype, formality, strikes me as a relic of the logical Platonism that was the object of Ockham's criticism.

I argued in Chapter IV against the idea that Peirce's pragmatism reduces the meaning of our conceptions to individual actions. But his reformulations come dangerously close to a similar error. He seems to say—and the suspicion grows as one examines the relation of his second and third category—that because our meanings involve a relation of test and response, the structure of reality must itself consist in such relations.[19] In holding to that view, Peirce would be combating a nominalism that makes only individual events real with a sort of extreme logical realism that makes the general relations real. It may be true, for example, that my dog gets quite angry when I step on his tail; and undoubtedly I know something about the dog if I know that he would get angry if I stepped on his tail. While I agree with Peirce that it is not enough to speak of "getting angry events" and "stepping events," I do not see that the dog must consist in "would-be's." A thing that would do such and such in response to a test need not *be* the relation of response to test.

Reasoning of the same sort, I think, lies behind Peirce's futurism: his contention that reality consists in the future. The fact that a charged battery, unlike an uncharged one, would start a motor if I were to connect it requires more than individual events to be real; but surely it does not require that the future actuality be real, but only that the

---

[19] My objection here—which is only a species of the general objection to pragmatism (that it tends to read into the structure of reality our methods of finding things out)—might be countered by a fuller analysis of Peirce's contention that logic is normative. I am not convinced, however, that the results of such an analysis would be kind to Peirce. And so far as Peirce's realism is concerned, I do not see that such a study, however desirable in itself, would change my own view that Peirce's realism is extreme.

present power is real. If the battery is charged now, even if I find this out only by a test a few minutes from now, then the power of the battery is real now.

I have a certain sympathy for Peirce's concern with tendencies, but he does play fast and loose with the notion of potentiality. Partially, it is his restricted conception of the actual that lies behind his excessive emphasis on real possibility. But even beyond this discussion of the actual and the potential, Peirce seems to want to identify our means of finding out about things with the structure of the things themselves. Perhaps Peirce too cheerfully takes upon himself the charge of anthropomorphism.

Realism without Substance

The same attitude, I think, lies behind his unfortunate tendency to treat attributes and supposits as predicates and subjects. The logical subject, as Peirce points out in his logic of relatives, is a blank, an indicator; all intelligible content is to be found in the predicate. But the emptiness of the logical subject carries over into Peirce's metaphysics, where the individual appears as a reaction event, devoid of intelligibility as it is devoid of quality and character.

If my contrast of metaphysical thing and logical subject seems forced, consider the matter of the meaning of proper names. To the logician, proper names are not much more than specialized pronouns; whatever "meaning" is involved must be spelled out in predicates. But in a living context, proper names can be the most meaningful words we have. The name of a friend, for example, is indescribably rich in meaning.

Of course, what I see as a misapplication of logic to metaphysics does not look that way to Peirce.[20] His attitude toward the individual is not grounded only in his logic. As a matter of fact, if one is to appreciate the ultimate significance of Peirce's realism, one must come to grips with his theory of the individual. Let me make the point even broader: if one is to understand any solution to the problem of uni-

[20] Peirce contends that metaphysics must be based on logic and not vice versa. It is certainly an interesting problem and in certain special contexts I would agree with his solution. But when he changes his treatment of conditionals to allow for the "would-be" of his later pragmatism, Peirce seems to be on my side.

versals, he must try to grasp the theory of the individual involved. For some reason, many participants in nominalist-realist controversies, while baffled at the notion of a real general, take quite for granted that everyone should know what a real individual is.[21]

Scotus is particularly interesting just because he is conscious of the problem of the supposit. The rather difficult notion of contraction is a direct acknowledgment of the primacy of the supposit in Scotus' position, as is his insistence that the Common Nature, while real, has only a lesser unity. But I find more courage than prudence in his attempt to solve the problems of subsistence and individuality in one blow (with the theory of the haecceity), especially since he makes the defining characteristic of a supposit its "numerical unity." Whenever Scotus is faced with a distinction or similarity that is not grounded in what is countable, he is forced to establish a formality to account for its objectivity. In a very similar way, Peirce, with his narrow conception of the actual and individual, is able to force the issue of real possibility and generality. Of course, if one accepts this notion of the individual, so far as I can see he is in precisely the difficulty that Peirce attributes to the nominalist.

It is in Peirce's treatment of the individual, however, that he really parts company with the scholastic realists. He is well within his rights in calling his realism scholastic for its emphasis on the problem of knowing what things are. And his treatment of the logical issues like first and second intention—particularly his notion of realities as real intelligibilities—bears a strong enough resemblance to Scotus. But his theory of the individual is no mere modification of Scotus; perhaps it represents more of a change than Peirce himself realized.

To call his theory, as Peirce does, an Aristotelian realism—however extreme—can be misleading. For one of the pillars of the Aristotelian position—and a good half of the problem of universals for the scholastics—is the notion of the supposit or first substance. When

---

[21] I have pointed out before that the scholastics used as their examples "Plato is a man," etc., because they thought that *man* was a specifiable natural class. But it should be noted that, at the same time, they were able to use a good example of a supposit: the human person. A person has a certain unity about him, a certain integrity and, as we say, substance to him that makes it difficult to dismiss him as an instance of a type.

Peirce gives process and continuity the central position in his metaphysics, he places his realism in a new perspective. If one is still thinking, say, of the debate between Scotus and Ockham, it may even be a hindrance to speak of realism at all. I happen to think that Peirce is wrong to disregard the notion of substance; in fact, my major complaint against his categories is that I find in them no place for *things*.[22] But one must understand that this denial of substance brings out both the strength and the weakness of Peirce's realism.

The strength of Peirce's position is simply that he has been able to remove one horn of the dilemma that disturbed the scholastics. If being human is, so to speak, a "part" of Peter, that is, if the nature is a part of the supposit and dependent upon the supposit for its reality, it will always be somewhat paradoxical to speak of Peter as an instance (or "part") of humanity. But Peirce can—and does, by denying within the Scotistic framework the idea of contraction in the individual—deny that the general is ever, in any sense, a "part" of the individual. A "dilemma" with only one horn is no challenge.

In fact, however, Peirce goes even further. The scholastic realist recognized an individuated quality in the various supposits, and sought a ground for the commonness of such qualities. As an example among relations: the relation between Peter and Peter, Jr., is an individual relation and an instance of the general relation of father to son. But Peirce is able to argue that the relation between Peter and Peter, Jr., is itself general; in fact, he holds that whatever displays continuity or potentiality is general. Even Peter is a real general, related to humanity not as an individual to a general, but as one general to another. Consequently, if one admits anything more than actual events to be real, he cannot be a nominalist. In the final analysis it is doubtful that Peirce uses 'common' in the same troublesome sense that oc-

---

[22] My efforts at criticism are plagued throughout both by the fact that I have been dealing in this book with only a part of Peirce's thought, and by a desire to avoid a long-winded presentation of my own position. Consequently, while I acknowledge that Peirce has his reasons for this view, I only want to record here my dissatisfaction at its outcome. Unfortunately, the word 'substance' has different uses and connotations; actually, I am interested most of all in the supposit. That is to say, I am not worried so much about an "it" to ground the process of inquiry as I am about whether Socrates (or any other "thing") can find a place in the categories.

cupied the schoolmen. Peter and Paul, on Peirce's account, turn out to be fragments—parts, not instances—of that law which is humanity.

On the other hand, Peirce's rejection of substance reveals a weakness in his theory. For the theory of substance was a part of scholastic realism (not to speak of its influence on the very structure of our language and our logic). When Peirce abandons the theory, he should rework the entire problem; but this he fails to do.[23] The reason for his oversight, I think, is that when he expresses his extreme realism it sounds very much as if the theory were only an alternative approach to his objective idealism; and Peirce just shifts to the vocabulary of his idealism to carry out his thought.

It is true that extreme realism and objective idealism have many interests in common, just as people who live on both sides of the Franco-German border have interests in common. But while the inhabitants of that border area are often "very close together," they are more often than not standing back to back. What they have "in common" may have quite a different significance for each of them—different reasons, different causes, different goals—depending on how it fits in with the national structure upon whose fringe each one finds himself.

I think that this little bit of philosophical geopolitics escaped Peirce. He began to talk of realism in a context that made it seem quite legitimate to refer to the scholastics. He pointed out that no "great" realist thought of a real general as a "thing"; and one supposes he meant "things" like Peter and Paul. But when he takes up the status of individuals, which he says are nothing apart from the law or type, one again supposes he is talking about Peter and Paul. But eventually he clarifies this, pointing out that a "thing" is not an individual (that is, a second), but a center of forces or habit (that is, a third). All of which would seem to allow Peirce to say that *as individuals*, Peter

---

[23] Peirce's first statement of the categories involved an explicit mention of substance (1.555); the theory of substance is not something he entirely ignores, but something he abandons—or perhaps he would prefer to say, transcends. It *might* help the reader to understand my point of criticism if he recognizes that when Peirce uses 'substance,' he is most often working within a Kantian framework; when I use the term, the context is, roughly, Aristotelian. For an analysis of the disappearance of *substance* from the categories, see Thompson, *Pragmatic Philosophy of Peirce*, pp. 25–33.

and Paul are nothing apart from the intelligibility of the law or type; but *as things,* they have an important status. This last way of stating the issue suggests the need for an analysis that would clarify the relation of individual and thing, which, as I have tried to show, complicates the problem of universals.

The trouble I have with Peirce's position is that, while the interpretation of things as thirds serves to distinguish things and individuals, it becomes difficult to dissociate things from laws and types, which are the paradigms of thirdness; and, of course, "no great realist" wants to hold that laws and types are things. But Peirce has long since ceased to worry about "things." What he sees now as the individual is the bare reaction-event of secondness; and the relation of individual to general he sees as the relation of secondness to thirdness—a problem that he approaches in terms of the concrete realization of thirdness. As I pointed out at the end of the last chapter, Peirce is not really too clear about the process of concretion, although it is possible that a thoroughgoing study of his idealism might shed some light on what he *would* say. What I want to emphasize is that Peirce's extreme realism is not simply his contention that laws are real, but also his attitude toward the relation of individual and thing. When Peirce shifts the context of his discussion to idealism, it is the latter problem that returns to haunt him in the guise of the problem of concretion.

At this point I imagine that an idealist would only suggest that a closer reading of Hegel could have saved Peirce a lot of time and trouble in reaching his conclusion. But the scholastic realist—and the nominalist—will not be so easily satisfied. To be sure, Peirce is concerned with the problem of the object of scientific knowledge; for that reason alone Scotus could see Peirce as a realist, and claim him as kin. Then too, Scotus (and Ockham, and I) can understand something of Peirce's ultimate position by viewing it as an extreme realism. But when it becomes clear—as it is not always clear when Peirce brings up his realism—that "things" are to fall into the category of thirdness, any discussion among the four of us is bound to get quite complex.

Perhaps one can understand now why I want to avoid a "brief evaluation" of Peirce's realism. His theory is not something to which a simple "true" or "false" will suffice. Peirce's realism involves at least three separate but related problems to which three separate *but related* answers must be given. Nor should this be a criticism of Peirce's account. Quite to the contrary, one of the major reasons for studying Peirce is that he is able not only to provide a fresh approach to problems, but to bring a number of problems into significant relationship.

It has become fashionable in many circles today to insist that "system-building" is fruitless. And the implication has been drawn that system-builders have nothing to teach us, other than to provide us with a passel of observations on this problem or that. But a neat and tidy solution to an isolated problem is a *rara avis* indeed. Perhaps it is a matter of one man's fruit being another man's tree—or bird. At any rate, one sometimes wonders where simple consistency leaves off and the troublesome system-building begins. If it is reasonable enough to complain, as many commentators do, that Peirce's thought is fragmentary, is it equally reasonable to object, at the same time, to his attempt to build a system?

My major concern, however, is not to justify Peirce's system-building. I only want to explain why I spent so much effort in the last few sections on problems rather than solutions. It may seem to reflect a negative attitude when I say, as I have already said, that Peirce's contribution lies in having exposed a problem (or network of problems). But after all, one does not have to accept Peirce's system in order to learn from him about being systematic.

Bibliography

Primary Sources

Joannis Duns Scoti Opera Omnia. 26 vols. Paris: Vives, 1891–95.

Secondary Sources

Bettoni, Efram. *Duns Scotus: The Basic Principles of His Philosophy.*
Translated by B. Bonansea. Washington, D.C.: Catholic University of
America Press, 1961.

Day, Sebastian J. *Intuitive Cognition, a Key to the Significance of the Later
Scholastics.* St. Bonaventure, N.Y.: The Franciscan Institute, 1947.

Devlin, Christopher. *The Psychology of Duns Scotus.* Oxford: Blackfriars
Publications, 1950.

Gilson, Etienne. "Avicenne et la point de départ de Duns Scot," *Archives
d'Histoire Doctrinale et Littéraire du Moyen Age,* II (1927), 89–149.

———. *History of Christian Philosophy in the Middle Ages.* New York:
Random House, 1955.

———. *Jean Duns Scot: introduction à ses positions fondamentales.* Paris:
J. Vrin, 1952.

———. *The Spirit of Mediaeval Philosophy.* New York: Charles Scrib-
ner's Sons, 1936.

Grajewski, Maurice. *The Formal Distinction of Duns Scotus.* Washington,
D.C.: Catholic University of America Press, 1944.

Harris, C. R. S. *Duns Scotus.* 2 vols. Oxford: Clarendon Press, 1927.

Heidegger, M. *Die Kategorien- und Bedeutungslehre des Duns Scotus.*
Tübingen, 1916.

Kraus, Johannes. *Die Lehre des Johannes Duns Skotus O. F. M. von der
Natura Communis.* Freiburg: *Studia Friburgensia,* 1927.

Landry, Bernard. *La Philosophie de Duns Scot,* Paris: Librarie Felix Alcan, 1922.

Longpre, Ephraem. "The Psychology of Duns Scotus and its Modernity," *Franciscan Educational Conference,* XIII (1931), 15–77.

Minges, Parthenius. "Der angebliche excessive realismus des Duns Skotus," *Beitraege zur Geschichte der Philosophie des Mittelalters,* VII (Münster, 1908).

Owens, Joseph. The Common Nature, a Study in St. Thomas Aquinas and Duns Scotus. Unpublished Licentiate dissertation, The Pontifical Institute of Medieval Studies, Toronto, 1946.

————. "Common Nature: a Point of Comparison between Thomistic and Scotistic Metaphysics," *Medieval Studies* (Pontifical Institute of Medieval Studies, Toronto), XIX (1957), 1–4.

Swiezawski, Stephan. "Les intentions premières et les intentions secondes chez Jean Duns Scot," *Archives d'Histoire Doctrinale et Littéraire du Moyen Age,* IX (1934), pp. 205–60.

Vier, P. C. *Evidence and its Function according to John Duns Scotus,* St. Bonaventure, N.Y.: The Franciscan Institute, 1951.

Wolter, A. B. *The Transcendentals and their Function in the Metaphysics of Duns Scotus.* St. Bonaventure, N.Y.: The Franciscan Institute, 1946.

CHARLES SANDERS PEIRCE

Primary Sources

Cohen, M. R. (ed.). *Chance, Love and Logic.* New York: Harcourt, Brace and Co., 1923.

Fisch, Max H. (ed.). *Classic American Philosophers.* With an introduction to Chapter I (on Peirce) by Arthur Burks. New York: Appleton-Century-Crofts, Inc., 1951.

Hartshorne, Charles, Paul Weiss, and Arthur Burks (eds.). *Collected Papers of Charles Sanders Peirce.* 8 vols. Cambridge, Mass.: Harvard University Press, 1931–58.

Lieb, Irwin C. (ed.). *Charles S. Peirce's Letters to Lady Welby.* New Haven: Whitlock's, Inc., 1953.

Perry, R. B. (ed.). *The Thought and Character of William James.* 2 vols. Boston: Little, Brown and Co., 1936.

Wiener, Philip (ed.). *Values in a Universe of Chance.* Stanford: Stanford University Press, 1958.

Secondary Sources

Braithwaite, R. B. "Review of *Collected Papers of Charles Sanders Peirce,* Vols. I–IV," *Mind,* XLIII (new series, 1934), pp. 487–511.

Britton, Karl. "Introduction to the Metaphysics and Theology of C. S. Peirce," *Ethics*, XLIX (1938–39), 435–65.

Buchler, Justus. *Charles Peirce's Empiricism*. New York: Harcourt, Brace and Co., 1939.

———. "Peirce's Theory of Logic," *Journal of Philosophy*, XXXVI (1939), 197–215.

———. "The Accidents of Peirce's Theory," *Journal of Philosophy*, XXXVII (1940), 264–69.

Burks, Arthur W. "Dispositional Statements," *Philosophy of Science*, XXII (1955), 175–93.

———. "Icon, Index and Symbol," *Philosophy and Phenomenological Research*, IX (1949), 673–89.

———. "The Logic of Causal Propositions," *Mind*, LX (1951), 363–82.

———. "Peirce's Conception of Logic as a Normative Science," *Philosophical Review*, LII (1943), 187–93.

———. "Peirce's Theory of Abduction," *Philosophy of Science*, XIII (1946), 301–6.

———. "Presupposition Theory of Induction," *Philosophy of Science*, XX (1953), 177–97.

———. The Logical Foundations of the Philosophy of Charles Sanders Peirce, Unpublished Ph.D. dissertation, University of Michigan, 1941.

Dewey, John. "The Pragmatism of Peirce," *Journal of Philosophy*, XIII (1916), 709–15. (Reprinted in *Chance, Love and Logic*, ed. M. R. Cohen.)

———. "Peirce's Theory of Quality," *Journal of Philosophy*, XXXII (1935), 701–8.

Feibleman, James K. *An Introduction to Peirce's Philosophy*. New York: Harper and Bros., 1946.

Freeman, Eugene. *The Categories of Charles Peirce*. LaSalle, Illinois: The Open Court Publishing Co., 1934.

Gallie, W. B. "The Metaphysics of C. S. Peirce," *Proceedings of the Aristotelian Society*, XLVII (new series, 1946–47), 27–62.

———. *Peirce and Pragmatism*. (Pelican Philosophy Series.) Edinburgh: R. and R. Clarke, Ltd., 1952.

Gentry, George. "Peirce's Early and Later Theory of Cognition and Meaning: Some Critical Comments," *Philosophical Review*, LV (1946), 634–50.

Goudge, Thomas A. *The Thought of C. S. Peirce*. Toronto: University of Toronto Press, 1950.

———. "The Views of Charles Peirce on the Given in Experience," *Journal of Philosophy*, XXXII (1935), 533–45.

———. "Further Reflections on Peirce's Doctrine of the Given," *Journal of Philosophy*, XXXIII (1936), 289–95.

———. "Peirce's Treatment of Induction," *Philosophy of Science*, VII (1940), 56–68.

Hartshorne, Charles. "A Critique of Peirce's Idea of God," *Philosophical Review*, L (1941), 516–23.

———. "Charles Sanders Peirce's Metaphysics of Evolution," *New England Quarterly*, XIV (1941), 49–63.

Leonard, Henry S. "The Pragmatism and Scientific Metaphysics of C. S. Peirce," *Philosophy of Science*, IV (1937), 109–21.

Moore, Edward C. *American Pragmatism: Peirce, James and Dewey*. New York: Columbia University Press, 1961.

———. Metaphysics and Pragmatism in the Philosophy of C. S. Peirce. Unpublished Ph.D. dissertation, University of Michigan, 1950.

———. "Positivism and Potentiality," *Journal of Philosophy*, XLVIII (1951), 472–79.

———. "The Scholastic Realism of C. S. Peirce," *Philosophy and Phenomenological Research*, XII (1952), 406–17.

Morris, C. W. "Peirce, Mead and Pragmatism," *Philosophical Review*, XLVII (1928), 460–81.

Murphey, Murray G. *The Development of Peirce's Philosophy*. Cambridge, Mass.: Harvard University Press, 1961.

Nagel, Ernst. "Charles Peirce's Guess at the Riddle," *Journal of Philosophy*, XXX (1933), 365–86.

O'Connell, James. "C. S. Peirce and the Problem of Knowledge," *Philosophical Studies* (St. Patrick's College, Maynouth, Ireland), VII (December 1957), 3–42.

Quine, W. V. "Review of *Collected Papers of Charles Sanders Peirce*, Vol. II," *Isis*, XIX (1933), 220–29.

———. "Review of *Collected Papers of Charles Sanders Peirce*, Vols. III and IV," *Isis*, XXII (1934), 285–97, 551–53.

Schlaretzki, Walter E. The Idea of the Community in Royce, Peirce and Mead. Unpublished Ph.D. dissertation, Cornell University, 1948.

Thompson, Manley. *The Pragmatic Philosophy of C. S. Peirce*. Chicago: University of Chicago Press, 1953.

Townsend, H. S. "The Pragmatism of Peirce and Hegel," *Philosophical Review*, XXXVII (1928), 297–303.

Weiss, Paul. "The Essence of Peirce's System," *Journal of Philosophy*, XXXVII (1940), 253–64.

Wiener, Philip and Frederic H. Young (eds.). *Studies in the Philosophy of Charles Sanders Peirce*. Cambridge, Mass.: Harvard University Press, 1952.

OTHER WORKS

Abbot, F. E. *Scientific Theism*. Boston: Little, Brown and Co., 1885.

Boehner, P. *Medieval Logic*. Chicago: University of Chicago Press, 1952.

———. "Scotus' Teaching According to Ockham," *Franciscan Studies*, VI (1946), 100–7.

Coffey, P. *The Science of Logic*. London: Longmans, Green and Co., 1912.

———. *Ontology, or the Theory of Being*. London: Longmans, Green and Co., 1914.

Copleston, F. *A History of Philosophy*. 5 vols. London: Burns, Cates and Washbourne, Ltd., 1946–59. II: "Augustine to Scotus."

James, William. *Pragmatism: A New Name for Some Old Ways of Thinking*. 2 vols. Boston: Little, Brown and Co., 1943.

Lewis, C. I. *Analysis of Knowledge and Valuation*. LaSalle, Illinois: The Open Court Publishing Co., 1946.

Maritain, J. *An Introduction to Logic*. London: Sheed and Ward, 1937.

———. *An Introduction to Philosophy*. New York: Sheed and Ward, 1937.

William of Ockham, *Philosophical Writings*. Selected and translated by P. Boehner. Edinburgh: Nelson, 1957.

Index

Abbot, F. E., 21, 35, 120
Abduction: theory of, 85–88 *passim*, 108n; and abstraction, 88; and commonness, 89; and pragmatism, 92; as insight, 92, 93; as stimulus to observation, 112n
Abstraction: theory of, 39–41, 52, 79–88, 93, 95, 102; and second intention, 59–63, 80–85; process of, 60–61; second order, 61, 147, 149; hypostatic, 65, 78–81 *passim*, 90, 95, 146. *See also* Intention, second
Aquinas, St. Thomas, 38, 52n, 55–56, 57, 59–60, 64
Aristotle, 48n, 49, 154n, 155, 156
Avicenna's horse, 50–52

Berkeley, G., 131. *See also The Works of George Berkeley*
Bode's law, 27, 84
Buchler, J., 36
Burks, A., 110, 114, 151

Calderoni, M., 7
Categories: discussion of, 21n, 32n, 120–24 *passim*, 153, 163n; listed, 121. *See also* Firstness; Secondness; Thirdness
Causality: and pragmatism, 89n, 90, 108, 109; and nominalism, 110, 119; and potentiality, 125, 126, 135; of ideas, 137–40, 144
Class: use of term, 74–75

Collection: use of term, 74, 75, 76; and simplest form of system, 77; discrete and continuous, 77, 78; as fictitious entity, 79; and abstraction, 82; and induction, 146
Common Nature: use of term, 40–41; and universals, 45, 50, 62; and haecceity, 52–56 *passim*; as formality, 53, 54; and Scotus' physical mode, 57; and the individual, 59, 61, 103, 156, 157; universalization of, by the mind, 59–63 *passim*; and potentiality, 60; when real, 60–61; existence of, apart from mind, 63; as *realitas*, 150; and lesser unity, 161
Commonsensism, 10
Community: of interpretation, 15, 43, 94, 115, 128, 130–31, 143
Comprehension: use of term, 53n, 74, 82–83; in second intention, 82; in abstraction, 146
Connection: real, 88, 89n, 91, 92, 109n, 112n, 113
Consequence: and logic, 70, 71, 120; and pragmatism, 97–100, 107, 110; and causality, 108n
Consequent: in logic, 70; in pragmatism, 97–99, 105–8, 110
Continuity: and generality, 66, 67, 93, 119–20, 126–28, 141, 144, 162; and collection, 77–78; as thirdness, 123, 134; and substance, 141, 162. *See also* Synechism

173

Contraction: of nature, 9, 83, 134; as operation of haecceity, 51, 58; Peirce's objections to, 59, 63–65, 66, 141, 150; and concretion, 134, 142–43, 164

Copula, 70–71, 86n. *See also* Illation

Critical commonsensism. *See* Commonsensism

DeMorgan, A., 27, 73n

Dewey, J., 14n, 17n, 96n

Ding an sich: and nominalistic heresy, 32; two alternatives of, 33; and predicates as mental constructs, 34. *See also* Thing-in-itself

Dualism: Peirce's naturalistic and transcendentalist tendencies, 5; denial of Cartesian, 11

Duns Scotus, J.: Peirce's adoption of, 3, 7, 19, 36, 65, 66; interpretation and authenticity of his works, 37; discussion of, 37–66 *passim;* and other influences on Peirce, 38n; Peirce's criticism of, 63n, 65n; and hypostatic abstraction, 80; and second intention, 81; on law of nature as real and objective, 128; and individual, 140–42, 156, 157, 161; when studied by Peirce, 152; mentioned, 6n, 25, 68. *See also* Realism; Scholastic realism

Essence: as alternative for universal, 40. *See also* Nature

Existence: distinguished from reality, 83n

Explanation: and nominalism, 32, 36, 87n, 91, 107, 108n, 109, 111, 113, 115, 118

Extension: use of term, 53, 74–76; in second intention, 82; in abstraction, 146

Fiction: nominalist view of generals as, 16, 119; and prediction, 26, 27, 65, 107, 147; and abstraction, 40, 52, 79, 83–84

Figment: opposed to real, 3, 23, 30, 31, 83–84, 104, 136n. *See also* Fiction

Firstness: and experience, 121, 122; as positive qualitative possibility, 122; and imperfect realism, 124; and thirdness, 124–28; and secondness, 148

Form: theory of, and imperfect realism, 119; and generality, 119; and relation, 120, 128, 148

Formal distinction: and common nature, 53, 54, 55; as *a parte rei,* 59. *See also* Formality; *Realitas*

Formality, 52, 54, 56, 57, 58, 59, 61, 62n, 63, 128, 150, 159, 161. *See also* Reality

Future: Peirce's emphasis upon, 99, 105, 115, 116, 125, 126, 136n, 138, 147, 159–60

Gallie, W. B., 103n

General: sign, 9; would-be, 17; essential to pragmatism, 17, 96n; object of science, 20; real, 21–22, 25–26, 117, 120, 127, 147–49, 162–63; nominalist theory of, 23; and continuity, 67, 126–27, 134; relations, 103, 139, 162–63. *See also* Generality; Universals

Generality: objective, 23–24, 26, 36, 46, 72, 78, 117, 119, 129, 143, 146; subjective, 23–24, 29, 32, 71–73, 135, 145, 146; relational, 76–78, 93, 103n, 139, 146. *See also* General, Universals

Generalization, subjective and objective, 26–30

Goudge, T. S., 5, 6, 9n, 80, 81n, 137, 139

Habit: belief as, 97; discussion of, 101–2; defined, 102n; and laws of nature, 130, 134; and humanity, 136; as governing behavior, 138n; and words, symbols, 145. *See also* Laws; Power

Haecceity: in Scotistic realism, 51, 58; and common nature, 52–56 *passim;* and formal distinction, 53; difference from other formalities, 58; secondness as, 73, 122; and individual, 140, 141; and supposit, 161. *See also* Individual

Hamilton, Sir W., 10n

Hegel, G. W. F., 17n, 68, 131, 131n, 132, 133, 142, 148. *See also* Universals, concrete

Hypostatic abstraction. *See* Abstraction

Ideas: reality of, 7, 12, 17, 65, 97, 136; efficacy of, 7, 11–12, 17, 137–39; platonic, 26, 55, 62, 154, 155, 156; in the mind of God, 39n, 130. *See also* Word

Idealism: definitions of, 4–16 *passim;* and independent life of laws, ideas, 6; and realism, 7, 8, 16, 163; and pragmatism, 8, 114, 115, 116, 138; distinction between epistemological and metaphysical use of, 11; objective, 11, 56, 57, 128, 129, 130, 131; and common sense, 13n; and definition of reality, 15, 18; and Scotus, 56, 57; general discussion of, 117–44 *passim;* criticisms of, 131, 148; conditional, 133, 153n; and thirdness, 134

Illation, 70, 86n. *See also* Consequence; Copula

Individual: Peirce's treatment of, 25n, 65, 73, 89n, 103, 109, 128–29, 140, 142, 144, 149, 154–57, 160–64; in Scotus, 47n, 49n, 51, 52, 57–59, 64, 103n, 128–29, 140–41, 150, 161; and concretion or contraction, 65, 83, 128–29, 142–43; and idealism, 138–44 *passim.* *See also* Haecceity; Secondness; Supposit

Induction: and nominalism, 112; and collections, 146

Intension: use of term, 74n

Intention: first and second, 43, 45, 93; 161; second, 44, 49, 59–63, 80–85. *See also* Abstraction

James, W., 12, 21, 23n, 79n, 96, 107

Kant, I., 32–33, 35, 71n, 113n, 122n, 152

Kind: use of term, 74

Kraus, J., 57

Laws: reality of, 3, 6, 7, 12, 25; subjective and objective, 23, 26, 27; and subjective generalization, 31; as a predicable, 44, 81; and individuals, 64, 135, 136; and power and habit, 66, 101, 102, 125, 130, 134; and pragmatic realism, 76, 80, 113, 114; and reductionism, 107, 108, 135; and idealism, 116, 143; and thirdness, 123, 129. *See also* Thirdness

Lewis, C. I., 105n, 109n

Logic: medieval, 4, 6, 38, 68, 102, 103, 126; as second intentional, 45; general discussion of, 67–93 *passim;* objective and material, 68; and metaphysics, 68, 160, 161; and relational generality, 76, 77, 78, 93, 103n, 139. *See also* Relatives

Maritain, J., 98

Medieval. *See* Logic; Realism; Scholastic realism

Mental, the, 42n, 43, 55n, 82, 83, 84, 132, 136n

Metaphysics: and logic, 45n, 68, 160, 161; and pragmatism, 125

Mill, J. S., 72n

Minges, P., 57, 59

Moderate realism. *See* Realism

Modes of being: and realism, 25; metaphysical mode, 56, 57, 58, 62, 68, 123, 128, 150; recognized by Scotus, Thomists, 57; physical mode, 64

Moore, E. C., 6n, 33n

Nature: as intelligible structure, 39; as alternative for universal, 40; and individual, 49, 51–53, 102, 103; and abstraction, 60; and "would-be," 102. *See also* Common Nature; Laws

Nominalism: and realism, 6, 20, 89–92 *passim;* and universals, 16, 23, 117, 118, 120, 124, 136, 137, 147; and humanists, 20; and Platonism, 25; and subjective generalization, 29, 30; and prediction, 30, 32, 110, 111; and unknowable thing-in-itself, 32–36 *passim;* and Duns Scotus, 63; and logic of relatives, 67; and abstraction, 80; and uniformity, 87, 89, 90, 112; and power, 90, 91; discussion of Peirce's, 96n, 103–10 *passim*

Object: problem of knowledge of, 11, 24n, 33, 45n, 49n, 57, 62, 132, 155–56, 157–60; scientific, 20–21, 24–26, 48, 49n, 52n, 61n, 154–56, 164

Objective: and subjective, 22–24. *See also* Generality; Idealism; Logic; Possibility

Occult powers, 107–8, 113

Ockham, William of: adopted by humanists, 20; on object of knowledge, 25, 49n, 55n; and subjective generalization, 29, 30; and status of individuals, 156, 157, 158, 159, 162, 164

Owens, J., 40n, 56–57

Panpsychism: and physical laws, 12; and pragmatism, 115; and anthropomorphism, 137

Pearson, K., 129, 136n

Peirce, C. *See specific entries for Peirce's philosophy*

Perry, R. B., 96n

Plato, 49, 62, 141, 154

Platonism, 25, 26, 55n, 61n, 62, 159

Possibility: subjective and objective, 23, 24; real, 65, 77–78, 94–95, 99–100, 105, 110–14, 116, 117, 125, 128, 129, 147–48, 153n, 160, 162; as firstness and thirdness, 77–78, 122, 124–26

Potential: and pragmatism, 99–103, 110–16 *passim*, 117, 160; as opposed to possible, 125–26, 148. *See also* Possibility

Power: as relation, 66, 90, 91–92, 119, 125; and would-be, 66, 101, 102, 105, 123; and reductionism, 107, 108, 109; as explanations, 108, 111, 113, 115. *See also* Habit; Laws

Pragmatic maxim, 5, 5n, 17, 95, 100

Pragmaticism: and pragmatism, 94–97 *passim. See also* Pragmatism

Pragmatism: definition of, 4–15; and realism, 7, 8, 94–116 *passim;* and idealism, 8, 114, 115, 116, 133–34, 138; general and special theory of, 12–13; Harvard Lectures on, 21–22, 100, 110, 151; limited to predicates, 69; and consequence, 71, 98, 99, 105–7; and relations, 74, 106–7; analysis of power and habit, 91, 92, 101–2, 115, 125, 138; as abduction, 92; of W. James, 96; and would-be, 99–103 *passim;* Peirce's re-evaluation of, 103–6; as a reductionism, 106–14; anthropomorphic, 137n, 160. *See also* Pragmatic maxim; Pragmatism

Predicable, 44, 80–81

Predicates: and universals, 44, 62; analysis of, 69, 74; and generality, 71–73, 145, 146; monadic, 73–74, 109; and imperfect realism, 119–20

Prediction: and realism, 21–22, 31, 36, 65, 91, 115, 150; and nominalism, 30, 110–12; and verification, 30–31; and reality of generals, 30, 114, 147, 150; and lesser unity, 150

Prescission, 40, 79, 86. *See also* Abstraction

Process: and individual, 118, 139–40, 144; and similarity, 127, 128, 148

Real: opposed to fiction, 14, 31n, 42–43, 55n, 81n, 83, 84, 93, 132, 147; in Scotus, 15, 42–44, 150; distinguished from reality, 16n; object of knowledge, 22, 34, 55n; modes of the, 25–26, 55n, 57, 61, 111; and pragmatism, 92, 95. *See also* Reality

Realism: extreme, 6, 7, 17, 49, 64, 68, 124, 142, 149, 159, 161, 164; moderate, 6, 38, 49, 52n, 59, 61, 62n, 63, 65, 83, 84, 124, 146, 148, 149; epistemological and metaphysical, 9–19 *passim;* two questions of, 44–66, 48, 61, 63, 65, 83–85, 94, 117, 145–46, 149, 154n; relational and substantial, 103n; imperfect, 118–20, 124, 127. *See also* Scholastic realism

Realitas: in Scotus, 54, 128, 150. *See also* Formality; Reality

Reality: Peirce's conception of, 13–16, 18, 31n, 35, 36, 65, 66, 79n, 92, 94, 95, 97, 115, 136, 147, 161; alternative conception of, 14; and community, 15, 115, 128, 130–31; related to Scotus, 54, 56n, 66, 79n, 128, 147, 161; distinguished from existence, 83n

Relation: technical use of, 32, 73, 90, 109; and form, 102–3, 120, 124, 125n; and prediction, 111; and process, 127; and generality, 139; and collection, 146; and "would-be," 159

Relatives: logic of, 65, 66, 67, 73–76, 78, 81n, 102–3, 146, 148; dyadic and monadic, 73–74

Rhema, 69, 79, 90, 107

Royce, J., 10, 38n, 131, 140, 148

Schiller, F. C. S., 12n, 96, 101n
Scholastic realism: role of, in Peirce's philosophy, 5–6; and science, 20, 31n; Peirce's characterizations of, 30, 36, 87n, 94, 96, 97; and individual, 39, 47, 50, 51, 59, 161–64; early theories of, 39n, 41, 42; terminology of, 40–41; and real commonness, 46, 103, 127; *operari sequitur esse*, 102; as imperfect realism, 119, 148. *See also* Realism
Scotus. *See* Duns Scotus, J.
Secondness: as an haecceity, 122; and reaction, 122, 164; and nominalism, 124; and imperfect realism, 124; and the individual, 128–29, 140–41; and thirdness, 131–38 *passim*, 141; and pragmatism, 138; and habit, 139; and laws, 143; and firstness, 148. *See also* Individual
Subjective, the: and the objective, 22–24. *See also* Generality; Generalization; Possibility
Subjective parts, 47
Substance: and realism, 103n, 141, 163–64. *See also* Supposit
Supposit: and scholastics, 39–40, 57, 58, 161n; highest form of unity, 47; and nature, 49; and physical mode, 57; and contraction, 64, 161; and process, 141; and problem of universals, 155–57; 162–64. *See also* Individual
Synechism, 17, 113. *See also* Continuity
System: defined, 76–78, 146; as a general, 89n, 91, 93, 103, 141, 143, 147, 149

Thing-in-itself: unknowable, 32, 48; two alternatives of, 33; and objective correlates, 33–34. *See also* Ding an sich
Thirdness: and pragmatism, 21n, 66, 97; and secondness, 69n, 72n, 131–38, 141; and firstness, 74n, 124–28, 131–43 *passim*; described, 123–31; and metaphysical mode, 128–29; and idealism, 133–34; and nominalism, 136; and process, 148–49; and concretion, 164. *See also* Laws

Thomists: controversy with Scotists, 41n, 55–57, 64n; on abstraction, 59–60. *See also* Aquinas, St. Thomas
Thompson, M., 4, 5n, 65n, 68n, 109n
Turner, W., 7n, 38n

Unity: lesser, 46–50 *passim*, 63, 65, 66, 117, 150; numerical, 47, 48, 50, 161
Uniformity: kinds of, 22, 31; objective and subjective, 26, 29, 30; of nature, 87–88; and real connection, 87n, 91, 112, 135n, 147; chance, 89, 91, 112, 119, 129
Universals: problem of, 7, 10, 19, 38, 39, 41, 43, 51, 53n, 78n, 93, 158n, 161, 164; thoughtlike, 16, 68; and scholastics, 19, 40; *ante rem, in re, post rem*, 39n; in Aristotelian terms, 40; alternate terms for, 40; as such, 41; as predicates, 42, 44; Scotus' use of term, 44–46, 50, 62–63, 65; logical, 45; and commonness, 46, 52; concrete, 55n, 78n, 142, 149, 164; and contraction, 63–65, 150; as *entia rationis*, 83; fourth type of, 120. *See also* General; Generality; Word

Whewell, W., 86n
Whitehead, A. N., 5n
Williams, D. C., 89n
Woods, F. A., 104
The Works of George Berkeley: reviewed by Peirce, 14, 21n, 38n, 92, 152. *See also* Berkeley, G.
Word: universal as, 16, 17, 71, 72, 114, 135, 136, 145, 147. *See also* Generality, subjective; Ideas; Universals
Would-be: in pragmaticism, 13, 17, 94n, 96, 98–100, 104–7, 110–12, 143, 149; as habit or power, 66, 91–92, 101–2, 123, 125, 130, 138, 159; and consequence, 98; and cause, 126, 135; in definition of reality, 128; and contraction, 141–42, 148, 159